For the sin they do by *two and two*
they must pay for *one by one.*

- Rudyard Kipling

Even so every good tree brings forth good fruit;
but a corrupt tree brings forth evil fruit.
A good tree cannot bring forth evil fruit,
neither *can* a corrupt tree bring forth good fruit.
Every tree that brings not forth good fruit is hewn down,
and cast into the fire.
Wherefore by their fruits ye shall know them.

-      Matthew 7:17-20

The

Obama

Error

By Stephen Pidgeon

Forward

I begin this discourse with a heavy heart, because ultimately, it is not appropriate to discuss the life of another human being with negative references to the sins of his past, particularly for the purpose of destroying his legacy before the general public. This book is needed, however, for the purposes of historical understanding – that those in future societies might make a review of the current times and more accurately assess those factors that resulted in the collapse of what a mere ten years earlier was the sole superpower on earth. The character of our subject here is most definitely a factor, and ultimately, *the* factor in the end of the constitutional republic of the United States of America. In the words of the immortal Yeshua HaMeshiach: *It is finished!*

Before proceeding further, then, it is necessary to address this human being known to us Barack Hussein Obama in peace (shalom) and in the spirit of the living God to call this fellow into the covenant. Let us consider a couple of things.

Obama has given a confession in Arabic that "there is no god but Allah." This declaration makes him a Muslim, whether he agrees with the theology or not. The Quran that Obama so dearly loves to quote says the following:

"We know best who deserve to be burnt in (the Fire). There is not one among you who will not reach it. Your lord has made this incumbent on Himself. We shall deliver those who took heed for themselves, and leave the evil-doers kneeling there." Al Quran 19:70-72.

All Muslims are judged in hell. This will include Mr. Obama, given his confession. The question he must ask himself is whether his good deeds outweigh his bad deeds, because they will be weighed. He may seek to do an inventory now and compare in his own mind, because should the balance tip in favor of evil, he will be left kneeling in the fire.

Mohammed created a religion inspired by the words of Satan, as he readily admits in the Quran. The most notorious contradiction in the Quran is as follows:

Sura an-Najm (Star) 53:19-22

Now tell me about Al-Lat, Al-Uzza, and Manat,
The third one, another goddess.
What! For you the males and for him the females!
That indeed is an unfair division.

أَفَرَأَيْتُمُ اللَّاتَ وَالْعُزَّى
وَمَنَاةَ الثَّالِثَةَ الْأُخْرَى
أَلَكُمُ الذَّكَرُ وَلَهُ الْأُنثَى
تِلْكَ إِذًا قِسْمَةٌ ضِيزَى. سورة النجم ـ سورة ٥٣ : ١٩ـ٢٢

Al-uzza is another name for Ishtar (pronounced Eash'-ter) (also known as Astarte, Ashterah or Ashtoreth, Isis, Diana, Artemis, Rus Khancy, etc. – a Babylonian fertility goddess). This admission was homage to the pantheon of pagan gods revered by Mohammed's rivals in Mecca, which of course, was sufficient to entirely destroy the central premise of his theological claim – that there was no god other than the moon god his family worshipped, namely, Allah. This moon god was worshipped by the son of Nebuchadnezzar in ancient Babylon, but his name at that time was *Sin*.

When Mohammed realized that he had greatly erred, he claimed that the verses were given to him by Satan:

"We have sent no messenger or apostle before you with whose recitations Satan did not tamper." Al Quran 22:52.

This recitation is sufficient to disestablish the teachings of all the prophets which preceded him (that is, all of the writers of the Tanakh, and the New Testament prophets). It is this very verse which immunizes the Muslim from accepting the truth of the divinity of Yeshua, because all scripture "is tampered" and has been therefore altered by Satan, leaving the believer in these words subject to forces other than the Word – namely the sword of Jihad, wielded by the followers of Mohammed. Yet it was Mohammed who set out the words of Satan in his own discourse, denying the deity of Christ, denying the existence of the Holy Spirit, and denying the truth of the Holy Scriptures. It is no surprise that Mohammed, as expressed in the last Surah of the Quran, should "seek refuge" "from among the jinns (demons) and men."

This religion of Islam is the religion Obama seeks to bring to this country – a country he does not understand as a constitutional republic, but one he chooses to define in his own mind as a *Caliphate* (hopelessly overloaded with infidels) and one of the great *Islamic* countries of the world (his own confession) over which he rules as *Caliph*, notwithstanding those stupid infidel masses that "cling to guns or religion or antipathy to people who aren't like them (like non-American Muslims) or anti-immigrant sentiment (including illegal immigrants) or anti-trade sentiment as a way to explain their frustrations." These are Obama's words, not mine.

Before we enter into this book, I am going to give my non-binding opinion, given what I have gleaned from the existing facts, and maybe we can sort out this thing a bit. The remainder of this book is primarily about the *crimes* of Obama, based on hard evidence. The fact that he took office without an objection from a single elector, a single Senator, or a single dissenting federal judge means that the constitutional republic of the United States died on January 21, 2009. All of those in government have no legitimate right to govern and are simply there because no one has prevented them from occupying their offices. They have no lawful right to these offices, because these offices were created by a constitution that no longer is of any force and effect. If they do not hold their office by means of the constitution, but what authority do they claim their office?

As for Obama, there is much to say. I do not believe Obama is his birth name. The birth certificate he recently released is a bald forgery; a ninth grader could have produced a more convincing document. The ten layers of add-ons over the Nordyke pro forma weren't even covered up, as everyone who downloaded the form using Adobe illustrator was able to discover the layers. Obama is empowered when he lies and nothing is done to remove him from office. Like an evil demon in a science fiction movie, his power grows from his ability to lie without repercussion. The newly forged "birth certificate" is just another example.

What follows in this forward are my opinions, because obtaining the actual data is conveniently completely blocked by operation of law. Nonetheless, here are my views:

I don't believe Obama was born in Hawaii, or for that matter, in Kenya. Obama was most likely born in Harborview Hospital in Seattle, Washington.

I don't believe Obama was born on August 4, 1961, but was actually born around July 1, 1961, which I will explain as soon as we discuss his biological father.

I don't believe the name on his original birth certificate was Barack, or Barry, or anything of the sort, as I believe this name was given to him a month later by his grandmother who was busy creating a new identity for him immediately following his birth.

Stanley Ann Dunham, Obama's mother, was the daughter of two members of the Communist party, and there is reason to believe that her father had betrayed the US during WWII by selling B-29 plans to the Germans. The family hated the US, but lived here for the prosperity of it all. Both parents were operatives, and Madelyn went on to become a fairly well-placed banking operative for the international banking cartel we now call the New World Order (NOW). Stanley Ann would follow in her mother's footsteps in this regard.

As a teen, Stanley Ann was a progressive Marxist, who preferred men of color and men who were most certainly Muslim. I don't believe she ever married Barack Hussein Obama – for that matter, I don't believe they ever met, yet the family was able to secure divorce papers from a local magistrate in Hawaii, based on the sworn statement of Stanley Ann that there was in fact a marriage previously, and the signature of Barack Hussein Obama making no contest to the divorce (that included no child support and no visitation).

Stanley Ann was also promiscuous. She posed nude for some publisher of cheap pornography around 1959 (at the age of 16) and these photos have survived to this day. The photos are not relevant; the fact that she was willing to pose gives you some idea of her mindset at that time. When you marry her promiscuity to her love for Muslim men of color, and her true belief in communism, you have the fertile ground for belief in my next claim.

Stanley Ann's parents left Mercer Island in April, 1960 to permanently move to Hawaii, but they left her behind to finish high school. She was expecting to enter collage at the University of Hawaii that fall, and classes began the first week in September. She didn't arrive in Hawaii until September 26, 1960. Why?

For the communist movement in the United States, a very important event was set to occur in New York City, beginning on September 16, 1960 and continuing to September 26. Communist dictator Fidel Castro was going to appear at the United Nations and speak. This speech did occur, and it happened before JFK was elected, before JFK attempted the assassination of Castro and before the slaughter at the Bay of Pigs. Stanley Ann left Mercer Island and attended this event. Born on November 27, 1942, she was still 17 when she made this trip. She arrived in New York as a promiscuous, naïve, communist groupie, and a true believer in helping the cause.

Who, you might ask, coordinated this event in New York? It was none other than the leader of the Nation of Islam, a fellow whose birth name was Malcolm Little, but who had adopted the name Malcolm X, before accepting his Islamic name al Malik al Shabbazz. Malcolm X was already distanced from his wife at this point, who would go on to announce her longtime affair later in 1963. Fidelity to marriage was not an issue for either of them in 1960. Giving birth to a child, however, was a different problem altogether.

Let us take a moment to consider this name Malik. Malik is a well-known Arabic name that means *king*. Why? Because it is derived from the well-known Hebrew term meaning *king*. The word is מֶלֶךְ melek *meh'-lek – mem (M) lamed (L) chaf (K)*. The Hebrew letters mem, lamed and chaf are expressed in our alphabet as M, L, K. Don't those letters sound familiar? One wonders if the parents of Dr. Martin Luther King knew of this Hebrew *tadusha*.

The name Malcolm is of a different origin. There is also a biblical origin for this name:

> For Solomon שְׁלֹמֹה went יֵלַךְ after אַחַר Ashtoreth עַשְׁתֹּרֶת the goddess אֱלֹהִים of the Zidonians צִידֹנִי, and after אַחַר Milcom מַלְכָּם the abomination קוּץְשׁ of the Ammonites עַמּוֹן.
>
> 1 Kings 11:5

Now Milcom (מַלְכָּם) is somewhat similar to our name for king (MLK) but here appearing as MLKM (omitting discussion about final Kaf and final Mem), also expressed as Malcolm, and described as "the abomination of the Ammonites." Infants were sacrificed in the fire before Milcom. There is something in the name.

Under the laws of the state of Washington, if a mother is unmarried at the time of the birth, and there is no establishment of paternity or consent of the biological father, the mother may not place a name in the father slot of the birth certificate. This must remain blank, or make specification that the father is unknown. However, the mother may give the child any surname she so desires.

Because *we still do not have* an original birth certificate, we don't know the choices made by Stanley Ann Dunham as she sat recovering from a relatively easy birth in the maternity ward of Harborview Hospital that morning in July in Seattle. We can, however, venture a guess.

If Stanley Ann made it to New York by September 16, 1960, in time to greet Fidel, it would still have taken several days before Malcolm X came to determine that she was "available." My guess is that the conception occurred on the weekend of September 23-24, 1960. If that was the case, then she would have given birth on July 1, 1961, not August 4, 1961.

For those of you seeking to research this issue further, here are the roadblocks we have met. First, all birth records in Washington are made available only as certificates. Second, only qualified individuals can obtain these birth records, which necessarily excludes those of us who lack "standing" (which is to say, we are mere citizens and tax-payers, not "important" people to the judges we elect and whose salaries we pay). Third, hospital records are protected by both state and federal privacy laws. Finally, the Seattle Post-Intelligencer, which was the paper of record in Seattle at that time, has shut down and is only available as a blog webzine.

Stanley Ann – who may not have yet spoken to Malcolm X about the baby, made a decision to name the child on the birth certificate. Did she name him after Malcolm? Maybe she did. Did she give him the father's actual birth name of Little? I doubt it. More likely, she gave the child her family's last name to keep congruity between her and the child. So a birth record for Malcolm Stanley Dunham, or something of that sort somewhere in the vital records of the state of Washington is likely.

Stanley Ann was seen on Mercer Island by eye witness Susan Blake at a time so close to the birth of the baby that she was still struggling to change diapers. Any parent can tell you that learning to change a diaper is about a 24 hour process. After the first dozen, you acquire the skill. This young mother did not return to Hawaii until January of 1963, only when she was certain that this fellow Barack Hussein Obama had left town.

What events followed? Stanley Ann, being unable to contain herself, contacted Malcolm X and told him he had a son. She also called her mother, and explained that the child would have Negroid (Hemetic) coloration. Malcolm X immediately ruled out ever coming to Seattle, where jurisdiction could attach, and began to make plans to "cover" the birth of this child. Madelyn began to take steps to cover the illegitimacy of the birth. Malcolm contacted his communist friend in Hawaii, Frank Marshall Davis, who was also a friend of the Dunhams via their mutual communist ties, and arrangements to redocument the birth were made.

Frank Marshall Davis contacted the Kenyan operative brought to Hawaii to study communist agitation in Kenya as paid for by the Ford Foundation, and offered a cash stipend should he agree to give documentation to this child born in Seattle. This operative is Barack Hussein Obama Onyango, and he apparently agreed – not only to allow his name to be used, but to take such further steps as may be necessary from time to time to cover this fraud, all for the sake of the worldwide communist revolution. All of this took roughly a month to accomplish, so the date of the birth had to be moved forward. Even then, they couldn't get all the documentation together as planned, as so they ended up with two different dates: August 4, 1961 as the supposed date of birth, and August 8, 1961 as the supposed date of the announcements. The only thing on file in Hawaii is the affidavit of Madelyn Dunham attesting to the facts of this birth. There is nothing else. Adobe Illustrator did not exist in the 1960s, and neither did Obama's BC.

Little Malcolm never knew his birth name. His grandmother took that name away from him and covered for the leader of the Nation of Islam. Did cash change hands? In the case of the Dunhams, it is doubtful, because they had a reason to engage in this cover-up: they sought a means to establish this baby as legitimate.

15

Obama Onyango almost certainly took money for the favor, maybe even more than once, given the divorce documents.

Notwithstanding the pleadings to the contrary, Stanley Ann was likely married for the first time to Lolo Soetoro, and Indonesian Muslim. She packed up the family and moved to troubled Indonesia, where she gave birth to a daughter, and where Obama was adopted by his step-father along at the same time as his other step-sister Lia (now deceased). Something happened during this time in Indonesia that caused Stanley Ann to drop her son like a hot potato back in the lap of the woman who changed his name, Obama's grandmother Madelyn. This decision was made shortly after the separation between her and Lolo, but Stanley Ann continued to work in Muslim Indonesia, and then in Muslim Pakistan for Peter Geithner and NWO. Barry was given over to his grandmother to rear without further ado. Madelyn insisted on the tax write-off for Obama as a dependent, because Anna wasn't taking it anyway, living in Indonesia.

The knowledge of Barry's actual lineage, however, was not lost on the far left. There were people in Chicago who knew he was the son of X – the son of royalty in the minds of the Komsomol – an heir by blood to the hard left leadership of the communist revolution in the US.

Something again happened that caused his mother to spend time with her son. He was suddenly useful with his Muslim name and his Muslim heritage, and his Indonesian passport, and in 1981, this loose cannon of pop-culture slop began to move through a metamorphosis to emerge as Barack Hussein Obama. Did he try another name first? There is a document that appears above where someone named Barak Mounir Ubayd made a name change to Barack Hussein Obama in British Columbia in 1982.

16

The document shows a registration of the name change candidate in British Columbia in 1973, around the time Barry was 12. Did the Dunham family seek a backdoor to change Barry's name from Barry Soetoro to a name of Barry's choosing? Who knows? At any rate, the name Barack Hussein Obama appears to be legally obtained under Canadian law by a fellow who presented himself as Barak Mounir Ubayd.

To make matters worse, Obama was also adopted by the Crow Tribe of the Apsaalooke Nation in Montana, and was given the Crow name Awe Koota Bilxpaak Kooxshiiwiash. This may be the most lawful name he has.

In Obama we have a curious mix. His mother was trained by the Jesuits, yet she spent her whole life in Islamic countries. She tried to train Obama in Jesuit schools, but he elected to follow Islam. He still does:

In Obama's book Audacity (the one he actually wrote) he said "In the wake of 9/11, my meetings with Arab and Pakistani Americans ... have a more urgent quality, for the stories of detentions and FBI questioning and hard stares from neighbors have shaken their sense of security and belonging," he laments. "I will stand with them should the political winds shift in an ugly direction."

He still on occasion pays homage to his mother's direction, showing up in a Black Liberation Theology church for "Easter," one of two times he has attended a so-labeled Christian church since taking office. He pretends he is Christian, while he lives the life of a Muslim.

Let us then return to the names of his birth: MLKM, not MLK. One is an abomination (or as Jerome Corsi would say, an *Obamanation*), the other a king. Obama wrestles with the two identities, neither of which includes

17

the views of a fundamentalist Christian, pro-constitutional-republic, American.

So, before I document the crimes of this fellow since he has entered the public eye, allow me to direct this discourse to Barry himself.

Salvation remains an option for you even now, notwithstanding the demands of those who surround you. You have prayed at the Kotel for the protection over your wife and family, yet your actions bring a curse for seven generations. Your claim to Islam will find you kneeling in hell, where the Muslim god of your choice will weigh your decisions to bomb civilians in Pakistan by means of unmanned drones, to kill the son of Qaddafi when his nation had not lifted a finger against us in decades, your promotion of infanticide through not only funding late term abortions in our country and other nations, but including your willingness to insist that babies who survived abortions should be left to die, against your good deeds, which are? You will not escape the tortures of the lake of fire by means of your own confession.

Your friends will ridicule my statements to you here, but I will say them anyway. It is still possible to confess He who shed his blood for your sins – all of your sins, which you know are many and egregious. It is possible for you to be made perfect in the sight of Y'hovah through the blood of the risen one, Yeshua HaMeshiach. You may reject this, but let it not be said that the option wasn't placed before you. Believe on Yeshua, his sacrifice and atonement, the propitiation for your sins, and be saved. Renounce your other gods, and confess the true *I am*.

Table of Contents

Dossier

Name: Legal name: Barry Soetoro (Soebarkah)
Assumed name: Barack Hussein Obama
Birth name: Unknown
Claimed name: Barack Hussein Obama II

Aliases: Barry Obama, Barack Obama, Barack Hussein Obama, Barack Hussein Obama II

Citizenship: Primary: Indonesian
Secondary: Citizen of the Commonwealth (British)

Heritage: Legal Father: Lolo Soetoro (through adoption in Indonesia)
Legal Mother: Stanley Ann Dunham/ Obama/Soetoro
Claimed Father: Barack Hussein Obama (Kenyan / Bedouin (Palestinian))
Claimed Mother: Stanley Ann Dunham/ Obama/Soetoro (American)
Suspected Biological Father: Malcolm Little (Malcolm X) American
Suspected Biological Mother: Stanley Ann Dunham/Obama/Soetoro (American)

Religion: Islam
Mother's background: Catholic, married twice to Muslim men
Fathers' background: Islam (Soetoro, Obama and X)

Occupation: Communist organizer / professional politician

Politics: Stealth Jihad/Marxist Communism/Union Socialism/Black Liberation Theology

Crimes: Mispersonation / Identity theft
Fraud to obtain a federal position
Birth certificate fraud; Social Security fraud; Draft registration fraud; Election fraud
Violation of the Logan Act
Violation of the Foreign Corrupt Practices Act
Bribery
Treason
Federal Conspiracy
RICO

Special Notation:

This individual is engaged in a broad conspiracy and is joined by hundreds of others who appear to be exploiting him for their own agenda in the destruction and overthrow of the United States, and is therefore difficult to arrest and prosecute. Many of his co-conspirators are members of unions and large, well-funded NGOs, members of the media and corrupted judges throughout the country. Most of his documented history has already been destroyed.

Preface

This book is about a man we call Barack Obama. This book is difficult to write, because the criminal activity of the suspect continues on a daily basis, and the criminal activity is so extraordinary that it cannot be ignored. The good news is that with each and every criminal act, the underlying theory concerning the character, history and agenda of Obama becomes more and more evident, even to the brainwashed, drug addicted, passed-out-cold Americans who spend their days staring at their accumulation of Chinese-built collectables instead of paying attention to the critical world events that unfold around them.

The efficacy of the decision to place Obama at the seat of ultimate power in the United States in January of 2009 is now bearing ripe fruit – and it is a fruit rotten to the core.

For those of us who desire to retain cognitive skills, the largest point of interest this year was the disclosure by the White House of Obama's long form birth certificate. The release of this document is a long series of crimes which I will have the unfortunate pleasure of documenting along with the other crimes set forth herein. I was interviewed by a statewide newspaper here in Washington when it was released who sought my statement, to which I said, the document is prima facie evidence that Obama is constitutionally ineligible to hold the office.

As I was filming two broadcasts for World Ministries International, it was announced that the long firm birth certificate had been released. Dr. Jonathan Hansen asked me my opinion. I am not a betting man, but I waged fifty cents (fittycent) that the BC would be determined to be a forgery within 48 hours. I was wrong.

It was determined to be a fraud within four hours. There are so many reports on its construction as a layered document created on Adobe Illustrator, that I will not belabor it with source quotes. Look it up. I will not dignify this fraudulent document with a critical analysis. It is exactly what I would expect from Obama. The failure of any governmental agency to seek the veracity of this document is prima facie evidence that the constitutional republic is dead. R.I.P.

This birth certificate completely contradicts Hawaiian Governor Abercrombie's disclosure that no long-form birth certificate for Obama existed in Hawaii – only a notation. What kind of notation? It was a notation that an affidavit of Madelyn Dunham was the foundation document to establish Obama's birth in Hawaii and nothing more. Abercrombie holds political values consistent with abortion infanticidalists and race-based infanticidalists, consistent with those who promote the sexual exploitation of children and the homosexualization of the American culture, consistent with enemies of America who promote the destruction of the doctrines upon which the United States Constitution was established in favor of a global governing class and worldwide socialism, and consistent with a person who respiratorily-ingested Hawaiian products that originate primarily in the area of Puna on the big island. In short, Abercrombie is a loyal Democrat.

Abercrombie decided he should take on the issue of Obama's birth certificate and end the controversy once and for all by disclosing it, to ensure that the issue did not play a factor in the 2012 "election."[1] Former Governor Lingle

---

[1] Ben Johnson, *Hawaiian Governor: I'll Stop the Birthers*, Floydreports.com
http://www.exposeobama.com/2010/12/27/hawaiian-governor-ill-stop-the-birthers/

should have warned him *before* he shot off his pie hole, that he would find the same thing she found: nothing, but that if he opened his mouth, he would make her out to be a liar. So Abercrombie makes the disclosure and tells national commentator Mike Evans that not only did he not find a long-form birth certificate in the state files, he couldn't find a record of him over at the two hospitals in Honolulu where all the babies were born at that time.[2]   Obama then made both of them out to be liars, kicking Abercrombie under the bus with all of the other friends of Obama.

Mike Evans went on to tell the known world this information before the White House got to him to tell him to shut up, and then, like a good perjurer, he – like so many others before him – reversed himself.[3]   Evans, unlike Lou Dobbs and Michael Savage, may have escaped being politically assassinated by the operatives at the White House by means of his recanting.

The lack of a long form birth certificate has been verified by two democrats: Tim Adams, a Hawaiian elections clerk who had access to vital records in Hawaii, and the liberal Democrat Governor of the State of Hawaii, Neil Abercrombie. Both of these gentlemen made credible

---

[2] Redbaiter, *Mike Evans Repeated Abercrombie Conversation Claims on Two Other Stations*, Jan. 28, 2011, TrueblueNZ, http://www.nydailynews.com/news/politics/2011/01/27/2011-01-27_journalist_i_never_spoke_with_hawaiis_gov_about_obamas_birth_certificate.html

[3] *Mike Evans Back Tracks on Birth Certificate Story* www.youtube.com/watch?v=hvrb7YqdvxE

statements (Adams has given a sworn affidavit)[4] that there is no long form birth certificate giving evidence of the birth of Obama in Hawaii – the place Obama claims as his birthplace. Remember (for those of you who have not yet manifested a desire to regain your ability to think), it is by the testimony of two or more witnesses that the truth is established.

For those of you in the anti-Birther movement – *and darling, you know who you are* – the failure to establish an American birth *site* by Obama is the failure to establish an American birth *right* under the 14th Amendment. If you are one who is going to hold up the forged Birth Certificate, allow me to remind you that you are joining serious federal crimes as you will see.

Those covering up the information about Obama's birth are co-conspirators with Obama to commit serious crimes.

As I write this preface, I am already moving on conceptually to a post-Obama North America in my follow-up books Behold! A Red Horse! (a book about World War III, now underway) and Behold! A Black Horse! (a book concerning the failure of the food supply and fiat currencies worldwide, and its predicted consequences)). I make the reference "post-Obama North America" because the United States of America in its form of a constitutional republic has not survived Obama.

---

[4] Citizen Wells, *Tim Adams affidavit, No Obama birth certificate in Hawaii, No medical records Queens Medical Center Kapi'olani Medical Center,* Jan. 25, 2011
http://citizenwells.wordpress.com/2011/01/25/tim-adams-affidavit-no-obama-birth-certificate-in-hawaii-no-medical-records-queens-medical-center-kapiolani-medical-center/

The global revolution now underway that will ultimately lead to a worldwide thermo-nuclear war began on the ground in January, 2011, although its impetus was put in place beginning January 22, 2009, at Obama's illegal inauguration. Here is the timeline in 2011 so far:

- January 1, 2001 – **Sunni Pakistan experiences riots**, protestors going violent over the attempt to end the death penalty for blasphemy against Islam.
- January 12, 2011 – **Sunni Lebanon falls** with the resignation of the Hezbollah faction within the government. This was driven by Hillary Clinton's demand to indict members of Hezbollah for the assassination of the former prime minister. Hillary pushed, Hezbollah flexed, the government fell, and Hezbollah – the "army of Allah" and a military wing of Iran, now controls Lebanon.
- January 15, 2011 – **Sunni Tunisia falls** when President Zine El Abidine Ben Ali flees to Saudi Arabia following 30 days of riots driven by high unemployment, food shortages and price inflation, government corruption, freedom of speech and poor living conditions. "Freedom of speech" is state media code for the ability of the Muslim Brotherhood to operate with impunity in their drive to overthrow the established government of the country.
- January 16 – **Sunni Sudan** sets itself to either divide or continue in civil war.
- January 17 – **Sunni Libya experiences riots** on food, and blames the riots on overspill from Tunisia.
- January 18 – **Sunni Morocco experiences riots** on food and corruption following Tunisia.
- January 21 – **Sunni Syria experiences riots** from Kurdish nationals who are also rioting in Iran.

29

- January 23 - **Saudi Arabia and China** ink a deal on energy cooperation. Four other agreements were also signed by representatives from the two sides, including one on economic, trade and technical cooperation, and another on avoiding dual taxation.
- January 24 – **Russian airport** is bombed by Muslim militants from the North Caucasus region of Russia, killing 37 and injuring 200.[5]
- January 25 – **Sunni Egypt enters** into insurgency and riots. Egyptian press calculates Mubarak's net worth at $70 billion.
- January 25 – **Sunni Jordan experiences riots**, Jordanian protestors demanding regime change because of rising prices and unemployment
- January 26 – **Sunni Saudi Arabia** entered into a secret agreement where Pakistan, a nuclear power, to share its nuclear technology with Saudi Arabia. It is also reported that a Pakistani transport plane was seen loading North Korean missiles at a North Korean airport last year.
- January 26, 2011 – the uprising against the Assad regime begins in Syria.
- January 27 – **Sunni Yemen experiences riots**, protestors demanding regime change.
- January 28 – **Sunni Algeria reshuffles** its cabinet following food riots.
- January 30 – **Saudi Arabian** leadership is warned to flee. Saudi Prince Turki bin Abdul Aziz Al Saud has warned the country's royal family to step down and flee

---

5 BBC, *Moscow bombing; Carnage at Russia's Domodedovo Airport,* January 24, 2011, BBC News Europe, http://www.bbc.co.uk/news/world-europe-12268662

before a military coup or a popular uprising overthrows the kingdom.[6]

- February 11 – **Russian leadership** yields to the implementation in Chechnya's of Muslim dress requirements. Chechnya formerly asserted Sharia over Russian law in 2010, and its police officers and others are authorized to shoot women with paint guns who appear in public without the hijab.[7]

- February 15 – **Libyan protests** begin, and Qaddafi reacts with force, pushing the nation into open civil war. As of March 5, 2011, the revolution may have failed, given the call by Louis Farrakhan, the titular leader of the Nation of Islam in the United States, to Barack Obama to remind him that Qaddafi was an ally.

- March 1 – **Turkey offers to invade Libya** if the EU will agree to admit Turkey as a member.[8],[9],[10] Obama

---

[6] *Fears of Uprising in Saudi Arabia, Prince Warns Royals to Flee,* Pakalert, January 30, 2011
http://www.pakalertpress.com/2011/01/30/fears-of-uprising-in-saudi-arabia-prince-warns-royals-to-flee/

[7] Reuters, *TIMELINE-Islamic-style orders in Russia's Chechnya,* AlertNet, February 11, 2011
http://www.trust.org/alertnet/news/timeline-islamic-style-orders-in-russias-chechnya/

[8] http://www.menewsline.com/article-22151-Turkey-Offers-To-Invade-Libya.aspx

[9] http://www.network54.com/Forum/248068/thread/1299146272/last-1299165313/Turkey+Offers+To+Invade+Libya+(menewsline)

[10] http://www.shocbat.com/blog/archives/799

backed the plan.[11] French President Sarkozy expressed his opposition in unprintable language.[12]

- March 4 – **Pakistan suffers its second assassination** of a high level official by Muslim extremists because he favored abolishing the death penalty for blasphemy against Islam.[13]
- March 11 – **Day of Rage** started in Saudi Arabia, which was designed to accomplish the overthrow of the royal family in Saudi Arabia. The Saudis have planned a Libyan reception, and ultimately, the day of rage was "shot down."
- March 19 – **US bombs** Libya with 110 Tomahawk Cruise Missiles.
- March 25 – **Sunni Syria** cracks down on massive protests against the regime, and begins using troops against civilians

---

[11] http://csea-1.newsvine.com/_news/2011/03/02/6169604-obama-said-to-back-turkey-offer-to-invade-libya

[12] Barack Obama supported the Turkish proposal, believed to have also been endorsed by Saudi Arabia. Obama, regarded as *a close ally* of Erdogan, said Ankara deserves membership in the EU. But Brussels appeared cold to the Turkish plan. French President Nicolas Sarkozy opposed the Erdogan proposal despite U.S. pressure. "What Sarkozy said is unprintable, but basically that the United States is not a member of the EU and cannot dictate who should be a member," the diplomat said.
Intelligence Briefing, *Obama said to back Turkey offer to invade Libya,* WorldTribune.com, March 1, 2011
http://www.worldtribune.com/worldtribune/WTARC/2011/me_turkey0214_03_01.asp

[13] http://articles.latimes.com/2011/mar/03/world/la-fg-pakistan-christian-assassinated20110304

- March 28 – **Sunni Pakistan** abandons the US as its arms partner and enters into a strategic military alliance with China.[14]
- April 12 - **Saudi Arabia** announced its plan to sign a nuclear cooperation agreement with China.
- April 16 – **Sunni Pakistani** Prime Minister Yousuf Raza Gilani told Afghan President Hamid Karzai that the Americans had failed them both, and said. "Mr. Karzai should forget about allowing a long-term U.S. military presence in his country."
- April 27 – **Sunni Obama** confers with Turkey Prime Minister Erdogan enacting a new Axis Alliance.[15]
- April 30 – **NATO strikes** a home in Tripoli, Libya, with three missiles, killing Qaddafi's 29 year old civilian son and three of his grandchildren.

The enactment of an agenda is underway, and this book will close the links concerning the role in all of this by he who calls himself Obama. While this strategy has

---

[14] IANS, *Pakistan drops US, embraces China as new arms partner: Report*, Times of India, March 28, 2011
http://articles.timesofindia.indiatimes.com/2011-03-28/pakistan/29354063_1_nuclear-capable-jf-17s-pakistan

[15] A new Axis-alliance have been formed. Rome and Berlin have been replaced by Washington and Ankara. But the agenda is the same. *"World dominion"*. Only when there is abundance of chaos, there will be a desperate call for *"peace"* and proper Global rule. The message is the same as in the chaotic times that took the Nazis to the Governmental offices in Berlin. Ivar Fjeld, *Obama and Erdogan: The new Axis powers arise,* March 27, 2010
http://ivarfjeld.wordpress.com/2011/04/27/obama-and-erdogan-the-new-axis-powers-arise/

been contemplated by the shadow government for well over a century, the person placed with the responsibility of bringing forth the reality of the emergence of the neo Ottoman empire is Obama – the *Zero*, in a series of actions that constitute serious acts of egregious treason, ethnic genocide, international war crimes, and crimes against the constitution of the United States.

"The Third World War must be fomented by taking advantage of the differences caused by the 'agentur' of the 'Illuminati' between the political Zionists and the leaders of Islamic World," Masonic Grand Commander Albert Pike wrote in 1871.[16] The question within the ranks of the so-

---

[16] The Three World Wars described by Alpert Pike as a result of a Satanic vision which he described in a letter that he wrote to Mazzini, dated August 15, 1871 have been orchestrated on the same terms for many generations.

"**The First World War** must be brought about in order to permit the Illuminati to overthrow the power of the Czars in Russia and of making that country a fortress of atheistic Communism. The divergences caused by the "agentur" (agents) of the Illuminati between the British and Germanic Empires will be used to foment this war. At the end of the war, Communism will be built and used in order to destroy the other governments and in order to weaken the religions."

"**The Second World War** must be fomented by taking advantage of the differences between the Fascists and the political Zionists. This war must be brought about so that Nazism is destroyed and that the political Zionism be strong enough to institute a sovereign state of Israel in Palestine. During the Second World War, International Communism must become strong enough in order to balance Christendom, which would be then restrained and held in check until the time when we would need it for the final social cataclysm."

Nazism and Zionism were both *invented* by Pike's associates, that he called Illuminati. In addition, Communism as an ideology, and as a coined phrase, originated in France during the Revolution. In 1785, Restif coined the phrase four years before revolution broke out. Restif and Babeuf, in turn, were influenced by Rousseau - as was the most famous conspirator of them all, Adam Weishaupt.

called Illuminati have hoisted their leader to give method to the rise of the Islamic World - an otherwise incompetent group of under-educated third-worlders whose religious philosophy is so self-contradictory that they have as a group destroyed themselves via the logical consequences of their own agenda and continue to fight amongst themselves until they have rested in powerless microcosms of sufficiently reduced scale for the remainder of the world to reduce their impetus to jihad to manageable means. In short, the Caliphate could not rise without the systematic betrayal of the West within. Enter the Ikhwan, Barack Hussein Obama – stealth jihadist, Muslim Brother, Sunni agentur, and betrayer of the free world. He *is* the lawless one.

"**The Third World War** must be fomented by taking advantage of the differences caused by the "agentur" of the "Illuminati" between the political Zionists and the leaders of Islamic World. The war must be conducted in such a way that Islam and political Zionism mutually destroy each other. Meanwhile the other nations, once more divided on this issue will be constrained to fight to the point of complete physical, moral, spiritual and economical exhaustion...We shall unleash the Nihilistsand the atheists, and we shall provoke a formidable social cataclysm which in all its horror will show clearly to the nations the effect of absolute atheism, origin of savagery and of the most bloody turmoil. Then everywhere, the citizens, obliged to defend themselves against the world minority of revolutionaries, will exterminate those destroyers of civilization, and the multitude, disillusioned with Christianity, whose deistic spirits will from that moment be without compass or direction, anxious for an ideal, but without knowing where to render its adoration, will receive the true light through the universal manifestation of the pure doctrine of Lucifer, brought finally out in the public view. This manifestation will result from the general reactionary movement which will follow the destruction of Christianity and atheism, both conquered and exterminated at the same time."

On November 6, 2010, Barack Obama left the United States to make the most expensive trip in Presidential history. The trip took him to India, to Indonesia and to South Korea, and included an entourage of about 3,000 people. The entourage was the biggest ever in terms of logistics and manpower for any US president.[17] This trip overlapped Veterans' Day in 2010, November 11. Obama delivered a few remarks at the U.S. Army Garrison in Yongsan in Seoul, South Korea, and participated in a wreath-laying ceremony there.[18]

Although he was not available to participate in the honoring of US Veterans on American soil, he was able to be present in Jakarta, Indonesia for the Indonesian "Heroes Day" where Obama was able to praise those Indonesians "who have sacrificed on behalf of this great country. [Indonesia]." Obama went on to discuss his personal history with the "great country" of Indonesia, saying "When my stepfather was a boy, he watched his own father and older brother leave home to fight and die in the struggle for Indonesian independence."[19] He then went on to lecture Americans to stop mistrusting Islam, to condemn our allies in Israel for continuing to build necessary

---

[17]http://www.dailymail.co.uk/news/worldnews/article-1325075/Obama-India-visit-Biggest-US-President-40-planes-6-armoured-cars.html#ixzz15CWgZijR

[18] Washington Post staff, *Veterans Day plans for the Obama administration*, Wednesday, November 10, 2010; washingtonpost.com

[19] Hurt, Charles, *Bam AWOL on Vets Day,* New York Post, November 11, 2010,
http://www.nypost.com/p/news/national/bam_awol_on_vets_day_IxEo yioHbtjAsNjGmbZoIP#ixzz15CbztJGa

housing in the capitol city of Jerusalem,[20] and visiting Indonesia's largest mosque,[21] the Istiqlal Mosque, the largest mosque in Southeast Asia. He did not disclose whether he entered the country on an Indonesian passport.

Sultan Knish[22] has pointed out that Obama was conspicuously silent about the international crimes committed by the "great country" of Indonesia. "While Obama found time to blast Israel for building housing in Jerusalem, he made no mention of the Indonesian genocide in East Timor. No word about the Indonesian mass murder of between 100,000 to 200,000 people in a country whose population totaled little more than half a million. No mention by Obama of the meat hooks where Indonesian-backed militias hung their victims, before mutilating and killing them, or the fields of the dead where the corpses of men, women and children were piled into mass graves. You won't hear of the machete squads who hacked people to death in full public view and on video. You certainly won't hear about the ethnic cleansing, the mass deportations, the gang rapes or even the murder of Western reporters. And there's a simple reason for all that. Indonesia is a Muslim country. Their victims in East Timor were Christians."[23]

---

[20] Fiery Spirited Zionist, *Obama Condemns Israel In Indonesia,* November 11, 2010.
http://fieryspiritedzionist.blogspot.com/2010/11/obama-condemns-israel-in-indonesia.html

[21] Earth Times, *Obama visit's Indonesia's Largest Mosque,* November 10, 2010
http://www.earthtimes.org/articles/news/352796,visits-indonesias-largest-mosque.html

[22] A blog by Daniel Greenfield

[23] Sultan Kish, *A Smiling Obama Returns to Bloody Jakarta,* November 11, 2010.

Blowing off US Veterans in favor of the jihadist Muslims in Indonesia and their "Heroes Day" is not the first time *Mr. Hawaii* ("O") ditched his responsibilities to honor those who have fought and died on behalf of this nation, even those who have fought and died under his command. Obama skipped out on laying a wreath at Arlington National Cemetery this last May as well. Apparently, he sought to avoid Section 60, where the war dead from Iraq and Afghanistan are buried, including those who have died under his command.[24]

To add further intrigue to the question of the authenticity of Obama, it is also reported that Obama opened his remarks with a traditional Muslim greeting and used Indonesian phrases to speak about his childhood in Indonesia, saying that "While my stepfather, like most Indonesians, was raised a Muslim, he firmly believed that all religions were worthy of respect," Obama said. "In this way, he reflected the spirit of religious tolerance that is enshrined in Indonesia's Constitution, and that remains one of this country's defining and inspiring characteristics."[25] One might remember that the slaughter of 200,000 Christians in East Timor is one of Indonesia's "defining" characteristics practiced in the spirit of religious tolerance,

---

http://sultanknish.blogspot.com/2010/11/smiling-obama-returns-to-bloody-jakarta.html?utm_source=feedburner&utm_medium=email&utm_campaign=Feed%3A+FromNyToIsraelSultanRevealsTheStoriesBehindTheNews+%28from+NY+to+Israel+Sultan+Reveals+The+Stories+Behind+the+News%29&utm_content=Yahoo!+Mail

[24] Kornblut, Anne; O'Keefe, Ed; *President Obama will skip Memorial Day visit to Arlington National Cemetery,* Washington Post, May 28,2010
[25] Parsons, Christi, *In Indonesia, Obama speaks of unity among faiths,* Los Angeles Times, November 10, 2010

and if Obama is paying respect to the Indonesian constitution, it would be the first one he has honored so far.

Obama's stepfather was not the only one raised a Muslim. Obama not only attended a Muslim school in Jakarta, and, according to his school principal Tine Hahiyary, Obama studied "Mangaji" (or "Mengagi"), which involved learning to recite the Quran *in the Arabic language,* and not the student's native tongue. Mangaji classes were not for non-Muslims or moderate Muslims. One of Obama's classmates, Rony Amiris, describes Obama as having been a very devout Muslim. Amiris was quoted as saying that "Barry ("O") was previously quite religious in Islam."[26]

As you can see, Indonesian is not the only language with which this fellow is familiar. In an interview with Nicholas D. Kristof of the New York Times, taken on March 6, 2007, called "Obama: Man of the World," Obama talked about being a street kid in Jakarta, and about going to a Muslim elementary school. During this interview (and yes, a recording of this interview exists), Obama recited from memory the Muslim call to prayer in Arabic, chanting the opening lines of the *Adhan*, with what Kristof said was a "first class accent." Obama then went on to call the Muslim call to prayer "one of the prettiest sounds on earth at sunset." The opening of the *Adhan* recites the Shahada (Shahadatan), which is the Muslim confession of faith. In Islam, once it is said, whether voluntarily or by force, the person making the recitation is Muslim. Obama gave this in perfect Arabic without accent.[27]

---

[26] http://www.theobamafile.com/ObamaEducation.htm

[27] Conservative Thinker, *Obama recited the Muslim call to prayer in Arabic on February 27, 2007 (caught on tape),* September 28, 2010

Let's now contemplate your right hand. Using your fingers, count how many people you know – no, how many people you have ever known – who can give the Muslim *Shahadatan* in perfect Arabic. If you were able to count to one or more, count how many of them were born American.

Our constitution – the document that creates the office of the President – speaks directly to issues of this nature in Article II, Section 1 provides as follows:

> *No person except a natural born Citizen, or a Citizen of the United States, at the time of the Adoption of this Constitution, shall be eligible to the Office of President; neither shall any Person be eligible to that Office who shall not have attained to the Age of thirty-five Years, and been fourteen Years a Resident within the United States.*

As John Marshall wrote in 1803 case *Marbury v. Madison*:[28] "*It cannot be presumed that any clause in the Constitution is intended to be without effect.*" Selah. Let us contemplate this for just a second. Most countries in the world are not nations of laws, but rather, feudal nations, where power and the machinations of the state are executed on the basis of fealty, and where a person's status is dependent upon the degree of his or her sub-infeudation. We, in the nation of the people, by the people, and for the people, have clung to a different ethos: an ethos that looks with awe on the rule of law.

The nation has been captured, however, by a foreign mindset; a mindset of cronyism, backroom politics, and loyalties outside the oaths declared, where public servants

---

[28] *Marbury v. Madison*, 5 U.S. 1 Cranch 137, 174 (1803)

give one oath publicly to support the hallowed Constitution of the United States, and then work privately to overthrow every last letter of it in favor of an international order that will result in transitory profits for the multinational corporation which installed them in office to begin with.

This ineffectualization of one or more clauses in the Constitution is a concept that has surfaced now with a vengeance, as Barack Hussein Obama continues to usurp the power of the state in violation of Article II, Section 1 of the United States Constitution. His ongoing violation of the Constitution has become destructive to the entire national polity, and now brings with it an indigenous corruption sufficient to destroy the economies of the entire world. How long will we continue to remain silent?

Since August of 2008, the country has suffered a sustained economic downturn that continues to devalue our property, our gross domestic product, our gross receipts, and now our currency. The responsibility of the continuation of this economic difficulty lies primarily with the leadership of Barack Obama and his co-conspirators in Congress and secondarily with his co-conspirators who continue to give him cover.

This would-be messiah has done what he was trained to do: engage in a communist overthrow of the United States. Unfortunately, this in not all he is up to. Obama strikes me as shameless, arrogant, unaccountable, disdainful, ignorant, underskilled, malevolent, misguided, and pushy. He has also led me to conclude that he is pro-partial-birth-abortion,[29] a radical infanticidalist,[30] a pro-

---

[29] http://www.lifenews.com/2008/04/27/nat-3896/

[30] http://www.wnd.com/index.php?pageId=45553

eugenics genocidalist,[31] and a homosexualist.[32] He has given credence to the notion that he is an occultist who seeks out spiritual forces that are anathema to the one true God, and, like Adolf before him, a proponent of a civilian military force in the model of Hitler Youth, the nationalization of critical industries including the automobile industry (not yet the "peoples" car), the promotion of eco-fascism, and the denunciation of a class of citizens he describes as his personal enemies.

Why stop here? Obama has demonstrated a propensity to favor idolatry, witchcraft and sorcery, ethnic hatred, variant sexual expression, the expression of wrath against his enemies (like you and me), the raising up of sedition against the constitutional republic, the speaking heresies against the one true God, the promotion of envy, the promotion of the murder of the unborn (and the born who survive abortion), the enabling of the murder of the deformed, the enabling of the murder of the disabled and the murder of seniors, who has been asked by his doctor to roll back his excessive drinking and partying, while he continues to chain smoke before and after his lectures on health care.

It would be simpler to call him "a crook" in the model of Richard Nixon. His friends in Chicago are an interesting group. His wife had a political plum job that paid in excess of $300,000 until she lost her law license.

---

[31] http://www.newsmax.com/Headline/obama-death-panels-medicare/2010/12/26/id/381043

[32] Ron Paul Condemns Obama's Decision to Abandon DOMA, February 24, 2011, http://theiowarepublican.com/home/2011/02/24/ron-paul-condemns-obama%E2%80%99s-decision-to-abandon-doma/

Her job was to defer African Americans from accessing the emergency room at Valerie Jarrett's hospital. The Obamas acquired a house from a now convicted felon Tony Rezko. Rezko was convicted on several counts of fraud and bribery in 2008. Rezko, after becoming a major contributor to Rod Blagojevich's successful gubernatorial election, was indicted on federal charges in October 2006 for using connections to state boards to demand kickbacks from businesses that wanted to do business with the state. Rezko was found guilty of 16 of the 24 charges filed against him. Rezko's lawyer holds the title to Obama's house in Chicago. Rezko's sister did a boundary line adjustment on the vacant lot next door to ensure that the Obama's would always have a vacant lot as a back yard.

Speaking of Rod Blagojevich – Rod has something to say about the participation of Obama in the sale of Obama's Senate seat. So far, the co-conspirators within the judiciary have worked hard to make sure that this evidence – like the evidence of all of the other crimes of Obama – does not surface. Obama spent his time in Chicago with Rod Blagojevich, (now convicted), Tony Rezko (now convicted), Rahm Emanuel (sudden millionaire out of Fannie Mae), Bill Ayres (unindicted domestic terrorist), Rev. Jeremiah Wright (communist agitator disguised as a teacher of Black Liberation Theology), and Rashid Khalidi (funding agent for the PLO). Obama has denied knowing Blagojevich, gagged Rezko, ditched Emanuel, distanced himself from Ayres, kicked Rev. Wright under the bus, and suppressed the videos concerning his relationship with Khalidi. Obama makes Nixon look like a saint.

We haven't mentioned the crimes Obama has committed since taking office, but we will if we can keep up with them. The usurper has trashed the constitution and almost all of the United States Code; yet, the people who have a responsibility to preserve the nation within the law enforcement agencies are engaged in criminal acts such as conspiracy, misprision, and RICO violations to cover for Obama. The nation cannot -- is not -- withstanding this conduct, and we will not remain a nation much longer. In fact, the Western financial world cannot withstand this abuse. Obama and his criminal cronies have caused the Federal Reserve to inflate the volume of our currency to unprecedented heights. This was done intentionally to crash the value of the currency against other world currencies in order to "adjust" our debt to other nations. The immediate effect of this currency manipulation, by the way, is starvation in the Third World. The secondary effect is food riots. Can we hear Bernanke's confession on this?

Let me remind those of you who hold the responsibility of preserving our laws in this nation of what John Marshall said back in 1803:

That the people have an original right to establish for their future government such principles as, in their opinion, shall most conduce to their own happiness is the basis on which the whole American fabric has been erected. The exercise of this original right is a very great exertion; nor can it nor ought it to be frequently repeated.

The Government of the United States is of the latter description. The powers of the Legislature are defined and limited; and that those limits may not be mistaken or forgotten, the Constitution is written. To what purpose are powers limited, and to what purpose is that limitation committed to writing, if these limits may at any time be passed by those intended to be restrained? The distinction between a government with limited and unlimited powers is abolished if those limits do not confine the persons on whom they are imposed, and if acts prohibited and acts allowed are of equal obligation.[33]

The Washington Times, on July 22, 2010 stated boldly that Obama "has engaged in numerous high crimes and misdemeanors," going on to conclude the "Mr. Obama should be impeached."[34] Unfortunately, the Times made only conclusory remarks without the necessary substantiation, but the remarks are nevertheless vainglorious. Times' writer Jeffrey Kuhner claims Obama is slowly "erecting a socialist dictatorship;" that he is "subverting democratic procedures and the rule of law; presiding over a corrupt, gangster regime; and assaulting the very pillars of traditional capitalism."[35] Even his mentor has lost use for him. On November 16, George Soros told financiers of the Democratic party that Obama must go, saying "if this president can't do what we need, it is time to start looking somewhere else."[36]

The rancor is continuing. When Obama sided with the Republicans to extend the Bush tax cuts, Democrats are turning on him as well. "This is a lack of leadership on the part of Obama," fumed Moran (D-Va.) "I don't know where the f*** Obama is on this or anything else. They're

---

[33] *Marbury v. Madison,* 5 U.S. 1 Cranch 137, 176-177 (1803)

[34]Kuhner, Jeffrey T., *KUHNER: President's socialist takeover must be stopped*, Washington Times, July 22, 2010
http://www.washingtontimes.com/news/2010/jul/22/the-case-for-impeachment-142967590/

[35] *Id.*

[36] Lerma, Xavier, *George Soros says Obama must go,* Pravda, November 22, 2010

45

AWOL."[37] The frustration with Obama on the tax cut compromise caused one of his fellow Democrat lawmakers to mutter "f— the president" while the president negotiated with Republicans.[38] Now the democrats know how the members of our military feel.

In the meantime, even Obama insiders are talking about getting rid of him by means of paragraph 4 of the Twenty-fifth Amendment, to wit:

4. Whenever the Vice President and a majority of either the principal officers of the executive departments or of such other body as Congress may by law provide, transmit to the President pro tempore of the Senate and the Speaker of the House of Representatives their written declaration that the President is unable to discharge the powers and duties of his office, the Vice President shall immediately assume the powers and duties of the office as Acting President.

Thereafter, when the President transmits to the President pro tempore of the Senate and the Speaker of the House of Representatives his written declaration that no inability exists, he shall resume the powers and duties of his office unless the Vice President and a majority of either the principal officers of the executive department or of such other body as Congress may by law provide, transmit within four days to the President pro tempore of the Senate and the Speaker of the House of Representatives their written declaration that the President is unable to discharge the powers and duties of his office. Thereupon

---

[37] Crabtree, Susan, *Dems show signs of abandoning Obama elsewhere after frustration with tax deal*, The Hill, December 9, 2010

[38] Palmer, Anna, Profanity, *Anger Spill Over in House Democratic Caucus Meeting*, Roll Call, December 9, 2010

Congress shall decide the issue, assembling within forty eight hours for that purpose if not in session. If the Congress, within twenty one days after receipt of the latter written declaration, or, if Congress is not in session, within twenty one days after Congress is required to assemble, determines by two thirds vote of both Houses that the President is unable to discharge the powers and duties of his office, the Vice President shall continue to discharge the same as Acting President; otherwise, the President shall resume the powers and duties of his office.

Enter the Ulsterman. A White House insider has been called the modern day "deep throat" as he exposes the inside information on what is actually happening in the White House. Here is what was reported by Ulsterman on October 26, 2010:

Go back to Chicago. That is the key. There is other crap around the White House, other things that could trip them up, but Chicago is where the real heavy deal is that could bring the administration down. Go back and review Blagojevich. Go back and review Rezko, Barton, Stern, Giordano, Carothers, Jarret. It's one and the same. It's all connected, and it's big. And people know. The White House is -expletive- itself over this stuff. Pelosi has it. Clintons have it – more of it than they had in 2008.

The information – the story. At least some of it, enough of it. It's all a chess match you know. A series of moves. Right now the White House is scrambling, and they don't know enemies from friends anymore. The party is attempting to localize the damage so it doesn't spread. Make it just about Chicago, and worst case, Obama – but not the party. And so you look back to Chicago, you look at the Justice Department, connect the dots. One investigation will potentially reveal the other. And it's all setting up to happen now if the November elections go down with a Republican landslide. Obama will be left without protection. His inner circle is scared to death. I mean truly frightened by the prospects of what could be coming at them in the coming months. They have enemies both in the Republican Party and the Democratic Party. President Obama is lost. Absolutely lost.[39]

Of course, this Washington insider is true believer in the Democratic machine, and can only see one side of the equation. Here is his ultimate conclusion:

The word is out there – President Obama is in real trouble. They may not have the specifics, but the story of a big scandal coming is circulating now within the party – both parties. So why put your own political career on the line supporting a president who is facing such a fiasco? Simple – they won't. And so you are seeing the separation happening. The party itself is starting to separate itself from the president. You ever watch those nature programs where the herd doesn't hang out with the sick one? You got that poor sick antelope or whatever standing all by itself and when it tries to join back with the herd they run away from it? They'll even attack it themselves if they have to. That's what happens in politics. If you are in real trouble, the others separate from you. That is what is happening to the president right now.

And the lions are starting to gather...[40]

Conservatives want to rid themselves of this born-again Mussolini; Soros wants to ditch the ineffective

[39] Ulsterman, *White House Insider: "President Obama is lost. Absolutely lost."* October 26, 2010, US Politics
http://newsflavor.com/politics/us-politics/white-house-insider-president-obama-is-lost-absolutely-lost/#ixzz168ypiJrk

[40] *Supra.*

flunky; and Democrats want to distance themselves from this Pariah. Who then seeks the rule of law in this country?

The hour to preserve the nation has passed. We have failed to act before the election of 2008, and we stood by idly to allow *Zero* ("O") to rise. We have remained silent and inactive even through the last election, choosing to place the collective head in the sand and allowing Schwarz, Henry Kissinger, David Rockefeller, Zbigniew Brzezinski, and the coven of Skull and Bones led by George H.W. Bush to push us into the cataclysm predicted by Albert Pike. Now it is time to reap what has been sown.

Impeach or don't impeach: whatever. I favor the rule of law – and not just any law – but "the law of nature and of nature's God" - the cornerstone of the creation of this republic. We must act to restore the rule of law, and we must do so by lawful means, for the law cannot be restored through lawlessness. The end cannot justify the means, because the means are the end.

You cannot restore the law unless you hold your leadership accountable to it. Allowing the Ikhwan ("O") to hold office above the law is to accept *dhimmitude* – a subjection to second class status. Learn the law; assert the law; and demand the law, for the Law will come out of Sion and the Word of the Lord from Jerusalem.

Chapter One

The unlawful birth of Barack Obama

The story of Stanley Ann Dunham, the mother of Barack Obama, is an interesting one. She was born on November 27, 1942 in Leavenworth, Kansas.[41] Her parents had eloped from the senior prom, and although Stanley Ann started kindergarten in Wichita, the family moved and she started first grade in Oklahoma.[42] At this point, the family disappears off the map in the United States. There is a family photo that shows her in her elementary school uniform taken around 1952 which features the initials NDJ.[43] There are those who believe these initials are the initials of an elementary school called *Notre Dame de Jamhour*, a private Jesuit school.[44] This school, however, was not in Kansas, but in Beirut, Lebanon. School records are now very difficult to obtain, because the area is controlled by Hezbollah. When Stanley Ann returned to Seattle, she started middle school fluent in French. There were virtually no schools in the United States teaching the French language to elementary school students in the 1950s

---

[41] http://public.ourfamilylegacies.info/individual.php?pid+I2153&ged=US_presidents.ged

[42]http://knol.google.com/k/president-obama-s-mother-and-grandparents-lived-in-ponca-city-oklahoma-in-early#

[43]puzo1.blogspot.com/2010/07/some-of-**stanley-ann-dunham-**obama.html

[44] http://www.ndj.edu.lb/old/jesuites/presprov.htm

and there were no Jesuit or Catholic schools in Kansas, Oklahoma or Texas with the initials NDJ at that time.

You might ask yourself the question why such a simple middle class family from Kansas would go to Beirut for seven years, and the answer may be more than you wish to know. There are those who say espionage was a family affair even going back as far as WWII, with the sale of certain Boeing blueprints to the Nazis from a location in Kansas. Seven years allowed the statute of limitations to run. In the meantime, Stanley Ann gains a penchant for Middle Eastern ethnicity and an intrinsic love and understanding for Islam.

After her father secured a job selling furniture in the Seattle area, the family moved to Mercer Island so Stanley Ann could attend a very progressive, i.e., Marxist, public high school. She excelled at her studies in the politics of the far left and had a propensity toward multi-racial dating – a propensity highly disregarded during this period of American history, but something quite average for people whose world view was primarily Lebanese. No one can say if she was promiscuous at that time; however, she did pose nude for an emerging pornographer in the late 1950s or early 1960s, given that she sported a Toni-type perm for the poodle cut, which was only in style in 1957-1958. This means she was posing nude at age 16.

In her senior year, her parents packed up and moved to the island of Oahu, Hawaii, and actually left her behind to finish the school year. She graduated high school on Mercer Island in the spring of 1960 and finally entered the University of Hawaii on September 26, 1960, at 17 years of age. If the birth date of "O" was actually August 4, 1961, Stanley Ann would have conceived with "O" the morning of Halloween.

The question is: is Barack Hussein Obama the natural father or just the fall guy?

There was a claim made that she married Barack Hussein Obama (Sr.) in February, 1961 at some civil ceremony on the Island of Maui, and gave birth to Barack Jr. on August 4, 1961, however, no marriage license or marriage certificate has ever been produced, and there is no witness anywhere on earth that can attest to, or that has attested to, such a ceremony. For purposes of this discussion, let us assume that it did in fact occur. Is it possible that Anna was already pregnant before she met BHO senior? If so, how did it happen, and the more important question to Obama is: Who's your daddy?

Consider that in September 1960, communist hero Fidel Castro arrived in New York to attend the meeting of the United Nations General Assembly. He arrived in New York on September 16, 1960, and he and his entourage stayed at the Hotel Theresa in Harlem. The father of Black Liberation Theology and one of the most respected Black Nationalists / Anti-American revolutionaries of the 1960s - Malcolm X - was a prominent member of a Harlem-based welcoming committee made up of community leaders who met with Castro. Castro was so impressed by Malcolm X that he requested a private meeting with him. At the end of their two-hour meeting, Castro invited Malcolm X to visit him in Cuba.

During the General Assembly meeting, Malcolm X was also invited to many official embassy functions sponsored by African nations, where he met heads of state and other leaders, including Gamal Abdel Nasser of Egypt, Ahmed Sékou Touré of Guinea, and Kenneth Kaunda of the Zambian African National Congress. It is noteworthy that in 1964, Malcolm X called Patrice Lamumba – the murdered leader of the Congo "the greatest black man who ever walked the African continent." The Soviet Union went on to honor Lumumba by naming its Moscow-based communist agitation training school after him.

Is it possible that Anna – being at home alone in the fall of 1960, caught a bus out to New York for the Castro visit, only to become a groupie to emerging leadership of Malcolm X? Malcolm X at that time was already critical of the leadership of the Nation of Islam for adulterous activity, and an affair with a 17-year-old might have been deleterious to his rising career. On the other hand, he may have cared less, and even more likely, had no knowledge that his mid-afternoon tryst resulted in a pregnancy. Nonetheless, it is medically possible that she became pregnant in New York during this visit, assuming there was such a visit.

This means Anna would be showing about the time of the second semester in Hawaii. If she was pregnant with the child of X, knowledge of such a pregnancy could have moved back through the insider circles via Frank Marshall Davis – a communist party member living in Hawaii and a personal acquaintance of Anna's mother and father, who could have conveyed the message to X, only to find a pay-off being arranged for a Ford Foundation operative currently attending the University of Hawaii named Barack Hussein Obama to take the heat for X.

Under such circumstances, where did Anna go to have the baby, and what was his name on the birth certificate? For that matter, exactly when was he born? Let's look at the evidence that is currently before us.

> "The University of Hawaii at Manoa is only able to provide the following information for Stanley Ann Dunham:

Dates of attendance:
Fall 1960 (First day of instruction 9/26/1960)
Spring 1963 - Summer 1966
Fall 1972 - Fall 1974
Summer 1976
Spring 1978
Fall 1984 - Summer 1992

Degrees awarded:
BA - Mathematics, Summer 1967 (August 6, 1967)
MA - Anthropology, Fall 1983 (December 18, 1983)
PhD - Anthropology, Summer 1992 (August 9, 1992)

Sincerely,
Stuart Lau"

****

Stuart Lau
University Registrar
Office of Admissions and Records
University of Hawaii at Manoa
Ph: (808) 956-8010
****

And this:

Ms. Stanley Ann Dunham was enrolled at the
University of Washington for:
Autumn 1961
Winter 1962
Spring 1962
The records responsive to your request from the
University of Washington are above as provided by
the Public Disclosure Laws of Washington State.

This concludes the University's response to your Public Records request. Please feel free to contact our office if you have any questions or concerns.

Madolyne Lawson
Office of Public Records
206-543-9180

If the marriage of Stanley Ann Dunham and Barack Hussein Obama actually occurred, it was lawless in every respect. First, to be lawfully married in Hawaii, both parties needed to be residents of Hawaii for two years before getting married. Stanley Ann Dunham had only been a resident for five months. She must have lied to get the wedding license if such a license was ever obtained.

Barack Hussein Obama (the elder, or "Barack senior"), in the meantime, was committing bigamy, which was a crime in Hawaii at that time. Of course, who could prove it, since his first wife (and first child) was back in the British Colony of Kenya. Barack senior left Mombasa, Kenya for Hawaii on a Ford Foundation grant to obtain training in methods to overthrow an existing government to create a Marxist government, or to influence policy that would eventually lead to a communist government. Barack senior's policies were such that he favored a 100% income tax.[45]

Barack senior returned home in the summer. He attended the fall semester at the University of Hawaii in 1958, and the spring semester in 1959. Then he went home for the summer. We know this, because he fathered a child that summer. He returned to Hawaii for the fall of 1959

[45] *Obama's father supported a 100 percent income tax rate*, April 6, 2010
http://www.hyscience.com/archives/2010/04/obamas_father_s.php

and the spring of 1960, and returned home for the birth of his son, one of Barack's half-brothers. This was his wife Kezia's second child, by the way.

When he returned to Hawaii for the fall of 1960, he may have met the 17-year-old Stanley Ann in Russian class, the language of international communism at that time. He started the semester on time; she was late arriving, starting on Monday, September 26 – the day Castro spoke at the UN. Before the end of the semester, Stanley Ann was noticeably pregnant. Stanley Ann dropped out of college before she began to be noticed as pregnant. According to the back-filled record, Stanley Ann and BHO were married in February, 1961. There is no record, no witnesses, and no one recalls the two of them ever living together, or for that matter, BHO ever mentioning her to anyone. Although the records indicate that BHO was able to finish the spring semester of 1961, there is every reason to believe that he returned to Kenya for the summer, as he had the previous two years. Did Stanley Ann, his new wife, go with him in order to have the baby out of the country? Or, was she never really his wife, and was back in Washington preparing to have a baby?

In Kenya, polygamy was legal or tolerated, but only if you were a practicing Muslim. Barack senior's father was a convert to Islam the generation before, and Barack senior had obtained an Arabic name by the will of his converted father. Barack is short for Mubarak, and has as its origin the celebration of al Buraq, the white horse that allegedly carried Mohammed to heaven. The middle name, Hussein, is part of the Islamic tradition where children who are in line to possibly qualify as the Twelfth Imam – the Mahdi – are required to carry the name Hussein or Hassan, as these were the names of the two sons of Fatima, the daughter of Mohammed. This is why Sadam took the last name Hussein.

Barack Hussein Obama the elder then returned the favor granted to him by his father, by converting from Islam to atheism as a Marxist communist. By the time he would have married 17-year-old Stanley Ann Dunham, he had already repudiated his status as a Muslim because of his atheism, therefore losing his tolerated privilege to engage in polygamy in Kenya. (He was never forthcoming on this issue, as he married two more times while retaining his marriage to his first wife Kezia, never bothering to inform Kenyan authorities that he was no longer a Muslim). Barack senior's marriage to Stanley Ann Dunham – if it occurred at all - was therefore unlawful in both Hawaii and Kenya.

Nonetheless, given the recently disclosed "birth certificate," Barack Hussein Obama the elder is claimed to be the documented father of the Zero by his own fabricated admission (and this documentation is ludicrous at best, fraudulent otherwise), in which case his citizenship based on the documentation provided by Obama, automatically passes to the child.

There is absolutely no bona fide documentation of parentage in the public domain, including the dummied birth certificate. Besides this ridiculous exercise in Adobe Illustrator called the Obama long form birth certificate, there are at least two forged certifications of live birth purportedly from the state of Hawaii, and an inference from Stanley Ann – Barack senior divorce decree (which does not mention the son by name) that testify to the parentage of Obama. All of the documentation is false, so other than the admission against interest made by Obama, there really is nothing upon which a finder of fact could establish the father.

It is a fact of history that citizenship in the Western World until the twentieth century passed through the father only. This had been the case since William the Conqueror entered England in 1066, and before then, a person was known by his membership in a tribe, not a nation. Citizenship in the United States did not pass through the mother at all until the immigration act of 1934. Citizenship through the mother became more obtainable with each modification of the immigration laws in this country, the most relaxed version being enacted in 1986. The question is: what was the citizenship of Barack Obama junior at birth? Kenya was a colony of Great Britain in the year 1961. Residents of Kenya were therefore citizens of the crown at birth.

Under the British Nationality Act of 1948, Barack Hussein Obama II was a British Citizen at birth, no matter where he was born, assuming that parentage could be established. The parentage of Barack Hussein Obama II, as a matter of law, has never been established. However, Obama has admitted that Barack senior is his father, and has admitted that he was a Kenyan. Although we cannot establish with substantial evidence that Barack Hussein Obama is the father of Obama, we have the admission against interest by Obama, and circumstantial evidence. However, there is no documentary evidence of anyone else. There is, however, convincing photographic evidence of the lineage between Obama and Malcolm X. [46], [47], [48], [49]

---

[46] http://gawker.com/5071373/bombshell-obama-malcom-x-love-child

[47] http://www.oilforimmigration.org/facts/?page_id=284

[48] http://israelinsider.net/profiles/blogs/is-obama-the-secret-son-of

[49] http://www.youtube.com/watch?v=GBgmpuubX1k

Something could have happened between Barack senior and Stanley Ann over the summer of 1961. Supposedly, the couple had rented a little mother-in-law in Honolulu. However, the address identified in the "newspaper announcements" of the birth in Hawaii was that of the Dunham family. Sara Obama, the paternal grandmother of BHO, tells a different story, recalling how she was in the delivery room at the birth. If Stanley Ann, having dropped out of college because of the pregnancy, left Hawaii with her new husband when he returned home during the summer, she would have found that her new husband was already married, and had two children, one of whom was only a year old. In addition, she would have found herself in a Muslim community where women have less status than animals, and she would have found herself in the position of wife number two, married to a notorious wife beater, as Barack senior's fourth wife later testified. It is also possible that Obama senior never considered her his wife.

Maybe she would have left Kenya earlier, but couldn't because of the advancing pregnancy. However, as soon as she gave birth, she would have returned to the states, but this time, back to Mercer Island, not Oahu. She was seen so early after the birth that she did not yet know how to change diapers, a skill mastered in but a few days. She would stay in the Seattle area until she was certain that Barack senior had left Hawaii for Harvard. He was required to remain in Hawaii for one semester beyond the standard four year matriculation, finally graduating following the completion of the fall semester of 1962.

Let's go back and revisit those enrollment histories above. The University of Washington confirmed that "Ms. Stanley Ann Dunham" was enrolled in the autumn of 1961, not Ms. Anna Obama, although she was supposedly married in February earlier that very year. Well now, something's fishy there! Now, take a look at the divorce decree. That decree looks like 1) either a forgery placed later in the file, or 2) a divorce put together to give credence to a marriage that never took place, by a magistrate outside of the regular court system. Either way, we have no documentation of the marriage, and an anomaly in the divorce decree.

Ms. "Stanley Ann Dunham" returned to Hawaii in January, 1963, and returned to the University of Hawaii as Stanley Ann Dunham, not Anna Obama. Barack senior had left town the month before. She waited a year, and established divorce documents in 1964, which Barack senior did not defend, although his signature acknowledges service.[50] The court approved the divorce in March, 1964. Unfortunately, there was a two year residency requirement before you could file for divorce in Hawaii, and Anna had only one. Someone must have lied, or looked the other way. In either event, the divorce itself was not lawful as a result.

This, of course, would make her subsequent marriage to Lolo Soetoro in 1967 also an unlawful marriage. It was during this marriage that the family packed up and moved to Indonesia. Once in Indonesia, Soetoro, an Indonesian native, established his step-son as his adopted son, so that he might enter school. But Obama was *not the only child* adopted at that time by Lolo Soetoro. Obama also had a step sister name Holiyah who was also adopted by both Lolo Soetoro and Stanley Ann Soetoro, and with whom Obama shared a room back then.[51]

---

[50] See divorce decree.

[51] Story Reports, *Previously Unknown Obama Stepsister Dies,* StoryReports.com, August 16, 2010

However, Holiyah Soetoro, who was called Lia, died "suddenly" and "unexpectedly" just before Obama visited Indonesia in 2010. According to the Indonesian obituaries, Barry Soetoro ("O") and Lia Soetoro were always together as children, playing together, traveling on family vacation together and even bathing. Yet Obama fails to mention her at any level. She certainly doesn't appear in *Dreams of my father*. Obama was in Indonesia from age 6 to age 10.[52]

At one point, Obama registered at the Franciscan School as Barry Soetoro, a Muslim student and an Indonesian citizen. Once his citizenship was secured in Indonesia, his American citizenship (if any) was terminated, and Obama's citizenship was lawful only in Indonesia. Some have argued that he continued to have a Fourteenth Amendment right to claim American citizenship[53] through the birthright of his mother. However, this birthright is only retained if he was born in the United States, which he has not established, and apparently cannot establish notwithstanding the Adobe BC. If he was born offshore, he could not claim citizenship in America, because his mother was too young to pass citizenship under the Immigration Act in place at that time.[54] If he was born onshore, he would nonetheless still be required to take an oath of naturalization to regain

---

[52] Corsi, Jerome R., *Previously Unknown Obama Stepsister Dies,* WorldNetDaily, August 11, 2010

[53] Fourteenth Amendment, All persons born or naturalized in the United States, and subject to the jurisdiction thereof, are citizens of the United States and of the State wherein they reside.

[54] See below.

citizenship following his eighteenth birthday.[55] This also never occurred.[56] One thing is certain, if you have to take an oath of naturalization to secure American citizenship, you are not a Natural Born Citizen.

In the event that Obama was born outside of the fifty United States, and when only one parent is American and the other a foreign national, the law governing his citizenship was established by the Nationality Act of 1940, Section 201, 54 Stat. 1137, [57] and the Immigration and

---

[55] *ELG v. Perkins,* 307 U.S. 325, 59 S.Ct. 884, 83 L.Ed. 1320 (1939).

[56] This may have changed, however, when he was sworn in to the office of the President. The oath he took during the inauguration may be sufficient to be construed as an oath of naturalization; however, given his failure to register for the draft before his 26th birthday puts even an oath of naturalization out of reach.

[57] "Section 201. The following shall be nationals and citizens of the United States at birth:

"(g) A person born outside the United States and its outlying possessions of parents one of whom is a citizen of the United States who, prior to the birth of such person, has had *ten years' residence in the United States or one of its outlying possessions, at least five of which were after attaining the age of sixteen years*, [emphasis added] the other being an alien: <u>Provided</u>, That in order to retain such citizenship, the child must reside in the United States or its outlying possessions for a period or periods totaling five years between the ages of thirteen and twenty-one years: <u>Provided further</u>, That, if the child has not taken up a residence in the United States or its outlying possessions by the time he reaches the age of sixteen years, or if he resides abroad for such a time that it becomes impossible for him to complete the five years' residence in the United States or its outlying possessions before reaching the age of twenty-one years, his American citizenship shall thereupon cease.

(h) The foregoing provisions of subsection (g) concerning retention of citizenship shall apply to a child born abroad subsequent to May 24, 1934."

Nationality Act of 1952.[58] Section 301(a)(7) of the Immigration and Nationality Act of June 27, 1952, 66 Stat. 163, 235, 8 U.S.C. §1401(b), Matter of S-F-and G-, 2 I & N Dec. 182 (B.I.A.) approved (Att'y Gen. 1944), required that

---

[58] The Immigration and Nationality Act of June 27, 1952, 66 Stat. 163, 235, 8 U.S. Code Section 1401 (b). (Section 301 of the Act).

"Section 301. (a) The following shall be nationals and citizens of the United States at birth:

"(1) a person born in the United States, and subject to the jurisdiction thereof;

"(7) a person born outside the geographical limits of the United States and its outlying possessions of parents one of whom is an alien, and the other a citizen of the United States, who prior to the birth of such person, was physically present in the United States or its outlying possessions for a period or periods totaling not less than ten years, at least five of which were after attaining the age of fourteen years.

(b) Any person who is a national and citizen of the United States at birth under paragraph (7) of subsection (a), shall lose his nationality and citizenship unless he shall come to the United States prior to attaining the age of twenty-three years and shall immediately following any such coming be continuously physically present in the United State(s) for at least five years: Provided, That such physical presence follows the attainment of the age of fourteen years and precedes the age of twenty-eight years.
(c) Subsection (b) shall apply to a person born abroad subsequent to May 24, 1934: Provided, however, That nothing contained in this subsection shall be construed to alter or affect the citizenship of any person born abroad subsequent to May 24, 1934, who, prior to the effective date of this Act, has taken up a residence in the United States before attaining the age of sixteen years, and thereafter, whether before or after the effective date of this Act, complies or shall comply with the residence requirements for retention of citizenship specified in subsections (g) and (h) of section 201 of the Nationality Act of 1940, as amended."

when a child is born abroad and one parent is a U.S. citizen, that parent would have had to live ten (10) years in the United States, five (5) of which were after the age of fourteen. At the time of Obama's birth, his mother was only eighteen years old, and therefore did not and could not meet the residency requirements to pass to her son U.S. Citizenship. The Act of November 6, 1966 (80 Stat. 1322), amended Section 301 (a) (7) of the Immigration and Nationality Act of 1952 to read as follows:

"Section 301 (a) (7) a person born outside the geographical limits of the United States and its outlying possessions of parents one of whom is an alien, and the other a citizen of the United States who, prior to the birth of such person, was physically present in the United States or its outlying possessions for a period or periods totaling not less than ten years, at least five of which were after attaining the age of fourteen years."

The immigration laws in effect at the time of and as amended five years after Obama's birth simply did not allow for citizenship at birth for children born abroad to a U.S. citizen parent and a non-citizen parent if the citizen parent was under the age of nineteen.

Obama has failed to demonstrate that he was born in Hawaii, and he has spent around $2 million to prevent people from accessing any of his records in Hawaii – and that doesn't count the bribes. He was born out of wedlock to an underage mother and a bigamist father who then promptly abandoned him and his mother.

By the mid 1960s, Obama's change in citizenship and name change were fixed as a matter of law. Barry Soetoro ("O") was no longer a citizen of Great Britain or Kenya, or the United States (if he was at all at that time). Barry Soetoro was, as a matter of law, an Indonesian Muslim. As a matter of law, this is his status this very day.

When Barry Soetoro returned to Hawaii to live with his grandmother, he unlawfully readopted portions of his birth name, calling himself Barry Obama ("O"), because he didn't care for his stepfather, and his mother wasn't there to tell him no. He then went on to attempt to abandon his Indonesian citizenship and to cover his Muslim faith while schooling in Hawaii.

Obama also attempted to ignore his adoption to Lolo Soetoro, and to move on as he needed to – at least until it came time to finance college. Around his twentieth birthday, the UK modified its citizenship rules, and new regulations applied for people who were formerly citizens of the Commonwealth. Although technically Obama was required to opt for his Kenyan citizenship before his 21st birthday (1982), the law provided for a grace period of two years. Because Kenyan citizenship was available to him through 1983, he obtained Commonwealth Citizenship in 1983 by default, assuming no adoption.

To summarize: by 1983, was either an Indonesian citizen, or a Commonwealth citizen. One thing is certain: nothing on the record establishes him as an American citizen.

Barack Obama is the name Barry Soetoro took when he ran for president, but Barack Hussein Obama is the name he took to assume office, although his birth name is allegedly Barack Hussein Obama II and his legal name is Barry Soetoro.

The president is without any lawful citizenship, without a lawful birth, without a lawful ancestry, without a lawful faith, and is holding the office of President under an assumed name. He is truly the lawless one.

Chapter Two

The childhood years

For everyone that does evil hates the light,
neither comes to the light,
lest his deeds should be exposed. John 3:20.

It appears that Barry Soetoro ("O"), whose birth name was allegedly Barack Hussein Obama II ("O"), is an illegal alien to the United States, an Ikhwan[59] Muslim jihadist, operating under a false name, illegally funded by Saudi Arabia, an aspirant to the Muslim Brotherhood, with an agenda to overthrow the United States by means of economic jihad and to establish a new international Islamic Caliphate, who is in the employ of Giorgi Schwartz, aka George Soros, on behalf of the international banking cartel to loot the nation in their favor, so these banksters might be able to secure enough gold during the transfer to maintain their positions in the New International Caliphate they are helping to establish.

One gets the impression that Barry Soetoro ("O") is a narcissistic, megalomaniacal, pathological lying, Masonic Illuminist, paying homage to the Marxist-communist agenda of his alleged father (a man who did not acknowledge him as a child) by continuing to push Senior's policies of Kenyan anti-colonialism against the British Empire (ignoring that the British left Kenya 46 years ago, and that the US is not the UK), and carrying the tainted

---

[59] An Ikhwan is a "brother" of the Muslim Brotherhood (Al-Ikhwan Al-Muslimun); http://www.thewahhabimyth.com/ikhwan.htm

water of his Marxist/Islamist mother to solve the problems in Pakistan.

Given just this portion of his agenda and the steps he has taken so far to achieve these goals, one question that arises is whether he should be *impeached.* Impeachment – the written accusation by the US House of Representatives of either treason, bribery, or high crimes and misdemeanors, and the subsequent trial by the Senate, and including a determination that he should be removed from office, and his subsequent removal from office is not the final disposition of the matter, as after he is removed from office, he can be tried for the very same high crimes and misdemeanors that led to his impeachment.

Before we get to the crimes of treason, bribery, and other high crimes and misdemeanors,[60] let us at least consider preliminarily the allegations made above.

His legal name is Barry Soetoro. Not quite as exotic as Barack Obama, the name he used as a candidate for the presidency, or as worldly as Barack Hussein Obama, a name he decided to use when he took the oath of office for the presidency, or even Barack Hussein Obama II, the name purportedly given to him by his mother at birth.

The law in the United States is actually pretty clear on the subject of a legal name. You have one legal name, and this is the name you must use to obtain your social security stipend. You have one legal social security

---

[60] Article II, Section 4 of the United States Constitution provides that the "President, Vice President and all civil Officers of the United States, shall be removed from Office on Impeachment for, and Conviction of, Treason, Bribery, or other high Crimes and Misdemeanors.

number, which is mandatory for the non-exempt and is now issued at birth. Your legal name is the name you must use to register in school, and to later register for the draft (at least if you are male) following your 18th birthday and before your 26th birthday. If you want to go by a different name, you can change it in a court of law, usually by a simple motion for a name change. This procedure allows the bureaucracies governing vital statistics to keep an accurate record of exactly who you are, when and where you were born, when you got married, who you married, who you divorced, and when you died. The IRS also has a critical interest in this.

Barry Soetoro ("O"), whose name was legally changed from Barack Hussein Obama II, his alleged birth name, when he was adopted in Indonesia by his step-father Lolo Soetoro, never legally restored his birth name; rather, he just *assumed* it. In the legal profession, we call that an *assumed name*, or an *alias*.

We can establish with some degree of certainty that Stanley Ann Dunham was his mother, and we assume that Barack Hussein Obama was his father, although this cannot be determined to a *legal* certainty, given the documentation that is not on the table. He has admitted that Barack Hussein Obama was his father, and the book written on his behalf *Dreams of my father* is apparently about Barack Hussein Obama, but there is only the practice of calling him his father over the decades that warrants the conclusion that Barack Hussein Obama – the Kenyan – is in fact the father. Verification of parentage by sight points to a different sire.

For those who claim that Obama has produced a birth certificate, you are simply wrong. The White House has produced a hopelessly staged "birth certificate" that is so blatantly fraudulent, the entire world is calling it a forgery. That won't stop one hundred percent (100%) of federal law enforcement from completely ignoring the issue. Well done, good and faithful servant!

Before this, all we had were the previous forgeries that the Obama on the internet that they called a Certification of Live Birth. An actual Certification has never been produced to any qualified body. Neither has the Adobe BC been produced to a finder of fact. Claiming that the short form Certification of Live Birth – particularly the internet image that is altered to black out the certificate number – is a Birth Certificate is the act of an abject moron. Even a brain dead junkie could tell the difference, especially now that he has released the long form (that was simply no longer available). The news "reporters" and "journalists" at FOX, CNN and MSNBC are so brainwashed they can't tell Peanut Butter from Jelly. One wonders where HR at these organizations found these double-digit IQs.

FactCheck.org also did not produce a Certificate of Live Birth. Instead, the organization produced inconclusive photographs of a document that purported to be a Certification of Live Birth and the testimony of the two Obots who work there that the document, in their hopelessly unqualified opinion, appeared genuine. To be clear: no birth certificate, and no certification of live birth or any document that purports to establish the birth site and birth information of Obama has ever been "produced" to an authorized finder of fact (unless you count the Kenyan birth certificate that was provided and entered pursuant to a sworn affidavit in the *Keyes* case).

The discrepancy is so large that the issue requires a trial to make a finding of facts. Such a trial should now be held in the Senate of the United States under Articles of Impeachment. His acknowledged father was a British citizen at the time of his birth, a fact he readily admits, and he (Senior) later became a Kenyan national when Kenya achieved its independence. Obama was therefore a British subject at birth, and obtained a right to affirm a Kenyan citizenship through to August 4, 1984. However, Obama obtained a full Commonwealth Citizenship (and consequently, an EU citizenship) in 1983, pursuant to the British Nationality Act of 1981. Given the divorce documentation between Stanley Ann Obama and Barack Hussein Obama in March of 1964, Obama senior's parentage was established as a matter of law – whether or not it was factually true, and because it was done so without the objection of Senior, even if Obama had different parentage, BHO Senior is the lawful father, because of his failure to object within two years of marriage and assigned parentage.

Therefore, Obama's citizenship passed to the younger (sometimes referred to as "Zero") by means of his parentage, even if Obama senior was not lawfully married to Dunham at the time. Whether Junior obtained "native born" citizenship by means of the Fourteenth Amendment to the US Constitution[61] is a more complicated question, since it depends on whether he was born on US territory, whether he was subject to the jurisdiction thereof at the time of birth, whether he took an oath of naturalization after his 18th birthday, whether he served in the military of a foreign country, and whether he was present in the United States between his 18th and 26th birthdays and successfully registered with the Selective Service System.

---

[61] The Fourteenth Amendment to the United States Constitution provides in its opening sentence as follows: "All person born or naturalized in the United States, and subject to the jurisdiction thereof, are citizens of the United States and of the State wherein they reside."

Importantly: if he was not born on US territory, he has no legal right to call himself an American except through a process of naturalization, and no process of naturalization has ever occurred.

His citizenship is further complicated by his adoption in Indonesia by his stepfather Lolo Soetoro, an Indonesian national who apparently adopted by Barry ("O") and his stepsister Lia at the same time, which made him an Indonesian citizen during his childhood. The restoration of any American citizenship (assuming the possibility existed *ab initia*) would also require a process of naturalization.

There is no evidence to demonstrate a Hawaiian birth for Zero. Timothy Adams, a senior records clerk in Honolulu during the 2008 campaign, having had access to complete government databases, found no record of Zero being born in Hawaii. He even checked with both the Honolulu hospitals named by Zero and Zero's sister as the birth site, neither of which had any documentation of birth.[62] "There is no birth certificate," said Tim Adams. "It's like an open secret. There isn't one. Everyone in the government there knows this."[63]

Even assuming *arguendo* that he was born on US soil – which at this point is almost impossible to conclude - once he was adopted by his father Lolo Soetoro, he became an Indonesian citizen. While in Indonesia for four formative years, Barry ("O") first attended a Catholic

---

[62] Kovacs, Joe, *Hawaii elections clerk: Obama not born here; Official who oversaw ballots in 2008 race says hospital birth certificate non-existent,* June 10, 2010, WorldNetDaily. http://www.wnd.com/?pageId=165041

[63] *Id.*

private school, and then moved over to the Muslim Menteng One School in Jakarta, where he studied the Quran in Arabic, attended classes on Islam, and volunteered for Muslim prayer.[64] From age 6 to age 10, the boy now known as Barry Soetoro was a young Muslim, and an Indonesian citizen who *preferred* Islam even over the reticence of his mother.

In order to enter the schools at all under the brutal Suharto regime in Indonesia, he needed to be an Indonesian citizen, and to be an Indonesian citizen, his adoption was necessary. When a child is adopted, the child's birth name is changed typically to the chosen name of the family, and it is possible to change not just the last name, but the first name as well. It is also possible to hyphenate names, add or delete middles names, change spellings, and even reduce the name to just one name. The Indonesian records in the case of Barack Hussein Obama II indicate just such changes:

Fig. 1

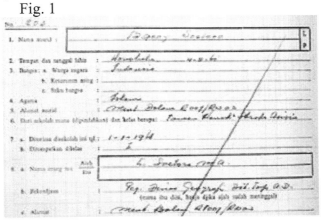

---

[64] Barrowclough, Ann, *Barack Obama joined Muslim prayers at school, teacher says,* The Australian, November 8, 2010, http://www.theaustralian.com.au/news/world/barack-obama-joined-muslim-prayers-at-school-teacher-says/story-e6frg6so-1225949239614

Here is the registration for a certain Barry Soetoro. In English, it illustrates that the father is Lolo Soetoro, the son's name is Barry Soetoro, his citizenship is Indonesian, and his religion is Islam. Someone (probably his mother) also made the claim that he was born in Honolulu, Hawaii to go along with the story they were already telling.

Fig. 2

REGISTRATION OF GRADEBOOK

NO. 203.

1. the name of the pupil: barry soetoro

2. The place and date of birth: honolulu [illegible]

3. The nation
   a. of Citizenship: Indonesia
   b. The foreign descendants:
   c. The ethnic group:

4. the religion: Islam

5. address of the pupil: [illegible]

6. from which school (moved from) and what class: ???

7. a. date accepted: 1-1-1968 (January 1, 1968)
   b. Grade: 1 (First grade)

8. a. the name of the parents Mr./Ms.: L. Soetoro [illegible] (Lolo Soetoro)
   b. Occupation/Job: (???? Geography ????)
   (name of the mother will only be used if father is deceased)
   c. Address: [illegible]

9. The name of the guardian:
   (??? was filled up, ??? parents of the pupil were not available, already ???? ????
   because another thing)
   b. Occupation/Job:
   c. The address: [illegible]

10. Left this school:
   a. ?? was finished, outside from the class: the date:
   b. ?? [illegible] ?? the date: no.
   c. ?? the school to:

11. Other information:

Obama's adopted stepfather, Lolo Soetoro, was a reserve Indonesian army officer called back into service in the army in 1965 to support Suharto in a coup to depose Sukarno. Like Hussein Onyango before him, Soetoro had been trained by the CIA at the East-West Center at the University of Hawaii. The CIA had Suharto to both lead Indonesia and to destroy the PKI – the Indonesian Communist Party. Suharto eventually killed between 500,000 and 1 million members of the (PKI) in the 1965 coup. Soetoro was one of the thousands of Indonesian soldiers that were trained in the United States between 1958 and 1965. The CIA deployed these assets in the long-planned overthrow of Sukarno.

Stanley Ann, now Anna Soetoro, took a position in Indonesia in 1967, whose responsibilities included making surveys of the political inclinations among the population of Java on behalf of the CIA and the operatives of the international banking cabal. Those that she identified as Sukarno supporters were targeted by the CIA, which provided the lists to Suharto and his foot soldiers including Lolo Soetoro.[65]

At that time, ethnographic and cultural intelligence was used in a classified U.S. intelligence program created in 1964, called Project CAMELOT. The use of anthropologists was supported through grants laundered by the Ford, Rockefeller, and Carnegie Foundations. Most of Stanley Ann's activities under USAID in Java were funded by the Ford Foundation.[66]

Once the young Obama became an Indonesian citizen, the hurdle to his obtaining American citizenship was not insurmountable, however, as he could restore himself to his American citizenship following his 18th birthday by the giving of an oath of naturalization before a magistrate in any jurisdiction, if he was in fact born in Hawaii. This never happened prior to his assuming the Presidency. In addition, because he failed to properly register for the draft before age 26, he is permanently

---

[65] Wayne Madsen, *Obama's Mother Worked For CIA*, April 18, 2011, PakAlertPress

http://www.pakalertpress.com/2011/04/18/obamas-mother-worked-for-cia/?utm_source=feedburner&utm_medium=feed&utm_campaign=Feed%3A+pakalert+%28Pak+Alert+Press%29

[66] *Id.*

disqualified from making a naturalization decision. As a consequence, whether or not he was born in the US, he is an alien to the United States.

However, an oath of naturalization is out of reach for this man because of his inability to manifest the necessary intent to become an American, and his inability to give a legitimate oath. His allegiance is elsewhere – fundamentally elsewhere - and at some level, the inability to tell the truth and the lack of intent to embrace things American, rules out citizenship for him at every level.

At the age of 10, Obama's mother sent Barry back to Honolulu to stay with her parents while she pursued her international dreams. Obama's grandparents moved Barry into the private Punahou School from 1971-1979. This school is racially diverse with whites in a distinct minority. The final day of school is known as "Kill Haole Day" ("Kill Whitey Day").[67] The last two years of Obama's high school years were marked with drug use, partying, and bad grades. Obama told the world in his autobiography that "Pot had helped, and booze; maybe a little blow when you could afford it. Not smack, though."[68]

It was in Hawaii that the second layer of the Obama education began. He took on Frank Marshall Davis as his father figure and mentor. Davis was a member of the Communist Party of the USA, poet, propagandist, "bitter opponent of capitalism," and radical, racist agitator. In 1948, Davis had fled Chicago after the FBI and the House

---

[67] Associated Press, *Obama had multiethnic existence in Hawaii; Sections of potential 2008 candidate's life drawing greater scrutiny*, Feb. 6, 2007.   http://www.msnbc.msn.com/id/17003563/

[68] Tapper, Jake, *Clinton Co-Chair Resigns Over Obama Drug Remark*, ABC News, December 13, 2007

Un-American Activities Committee investigated his subversive anti-American activities.[69] Obama himself has documented this relationship. This is the place where he began his studies in communism, socialism, and a form of racism now called Black Liberation Theology.

Although he has claimed to be a "Christian" in word, he is a Muslim jihadist in deed. Better stated, his is an *Ikhwan* in deed – a latent and undisclosed member of the Muslim Brotherhood whose identity has been concealed (although he revealed it in Cairo, in the Arabic language).[70] Muslims in furtherance of *jihad* may use *taqiya* – lying to infidels – to further *jihad* and the promotion of Islam, and Obama has done nothing but lie to the American people since well before entering the Presidency. While all politicians stretch the truth, Obama's lying is at pathological levels. He apparently believes he is empowered every time he lies, since no one can do anything about it. In his mind, the bigger the lie, the greater the power. While we may be offended by such bald-faced lying, the tactic is an approved tactic of Muslim Brotherhood in the furtherance of *jihad* and the Muslim conquest of America.

Obama's biological father was a Muslim, his birth father was a Muslim; his adoptive father was a Muslim; his mother married two Muslim men and spent her life working in Muslim Indonesia, and Muslim Pakistan. She worked at Bank Rakyat of Indonesia, a part of an "Islamic banking cooperative" in Indonesia from the mid-seventies, and moved on to a job with the Ford Foundation and the Women's World Bank which took her to Lahore, Pakistan,

---

[69] Harnden, Toby, *Frank Marshall Davis, alleged Communist, was early influence on Barack Obama*, The Telegraph, August 22, 2008

[70] http://www.youtube.com/watch?v=tCAffMSWSzY

beginning in 1984-1985. She stayed there until 1991, when she came down with sickness which would eventually lead to her death in 1995. Although Barry did not continue in a Muslim school after he returned to Hawaii when he was ten-years-old, as soon as he left Hawaii for college, his friends, his roommates, and his traveling buddies were all Muslims. He left the Muslim Punahou School and went on to "stoning it" at Occidental College in California in 1979 and 1980. Things became intensely more Islamic thereafter.

Chapter Three

The college years

In 1981, Barry Soetoro, operating under the assumed named Barry Obama, transferred from Occidental to Columbia. In between, he traveled to Pakistan with two wealthy Pakistanis - Mohammed Hasan Chandoo and Wahid Hamid. According to Dr. Orly Taitz, Obama spent over a year in Pakistan on this trip, returning in September, 1982.[71] Obama traveled with Hamid and stayed in Karachi with Chandoo's family; this according to Bill Burton, Obama's press secretary.[72] Chandoo is now a self-employed financial consultant, living in Armonk, N.Y., and was a major bundler for the Obama campaign, raising $100,000. His brother, Mohammed Askari Chandoo, is a self-employed finance wonk in Karachi, Pakistan, who has lived in Pakistan, Greece, the United Arab Emirates, England, and the U.S. He has been active in politics for several years, doing things like organizing voter registration drives at masjids and helping to raise money for Barack Obama's (D-IL) successful senatorial campaign.

Wahid Hamid, a fellow student who was an immigrant from Pakistan and traveled with Obama, is now

---

[71] http://obamareleaseyourrecords.blogspot.com/2011/03/fac-filed-in-lawsuit-about-obamas-bogus.html

[72] Francesa, Mike, *In 1981 Barack Obama visited Pakistan stayed with Mohammed Hasan Chandoo, who are the Chandoo Brothers?* War69.com
http://www.mikefrancesa.com/wordpress/?p=1190

a vice president at Pepsico in New York, and according to public records, has donated the maximum $2,300 to the Obama campaign and is listed as a fund-raiser for it.[73] The other fellow with whom he traveled was from India, a fellow named Vinai Thummalapally. Vinai owns a DVD/CD company in Colorado Springs, Colorado, and originally hails from the town in India that Obama visited on the same trip.

Obama claims he was gone just three weeks, but the lack of data in the US indicates it was more like two years. The only person who can vouch for a different timeframe is Obama's roommate, an illegal alien from Pakistan named Sadik. Obama claims, in his book "Dreams of my father" that he spent his "first night in Manhattan curled up in an alleyway" before shortly thereafter sharing a place with Sadik. There are no alleys in Manhattan, however. Obama described Sadik as "a short, well-built Pakistani" who smoked marijuana and snorted cocaine, and the Associated Press eventually tracked him down. His real name is Sahole Saddiqi. Obama met him when the two attended Occidental and Obama roomed with him and a group of Pakistani students . . . at Occidental, not Columbia. "We were both very lost," Siddiqi told the AP. "We were both alienated, although he might not put it that way. He arrived disheveled and without a place to stay."

When Obama made his trip to Pakistan, he went from being disheveled and without a place to stay, to visiting one of the richest families in Pakistan, and went on to meet with the future leadership of the nation. In fact, his host during this trip was Mian Muhammadian Soomro, the

---

[73] *In 1981 Barack Obama visited Pakistan stayed with Mohammed Hasan Chandoo, who are the Chandoo Brothers? Op. cit.*

caretaker Prime Minister of Pakistan.[74] This was a remarkable transformation for a dead-broke stoner in the US on an F-1 visa. Just how was this arranged?

Are we to believe that Obama was in Pakistan on a simple college trip with friends, given that Pakistan was in turmoil in 1981 and ruled under martial law? Millions of Afghan refugees were living in Pakistan, while the Afghan Mujahedeen operated from bases inside Pakistan in their war with the Soviets. One of the Mujahedeen leaders that based his operation in Quetta, Pakistan was Usama Bin Laden. Pakistan was on the banned travel list for US Citizens at the time and all non-Muslim visitors were not welcome unless sponsored by their embassy for official business. The broke Obama went from sleeping in a non-existent alley in Manhattan to travelling the world with wealthy Pakistanis to visit the caretaker Prime Minister when Pakistan was under martial law. Does anyone see an issue here? Which embassy vouched for Obama as being there on official business? If there was no voucher, then necessarily Obama made the trip as a self-identified *Muslim* visitor and the national of some nation other than the United States.

At that time, Pakistan was under the control of General Muhammad Zia-ul-Haq. Ul-Haq was the President of Pakistan from July 1977 to his assassination in August 1988. He overthrew ruling Prime Minister Zulfikar Ali Bhutto in a bloodless coup d'état on July 5, 1977 and imposed martial law. As a fundamentalist Sunni dictator, he pushed for the Islamization of Pakistan, and worked to subsidize the Mujahadeen during the Soviet invasion of Afghanistan. Ul-Haq died along with several of his top generals and the US Ambassador to Pakistan Arnold Lewis

---

[74] Slim guy, *Obama's Paki Connections,* Atlas Shrugs, September 28, 2008.

Raphel in a suspicious aircraft crash near Bahawalpur (Punjab) on August 17, 1988.

Coincidentally, in the very same year as Obama's visit to Pakistan, his mother was hired by the Ford Foundation at the Regional Southeast Asia Office in Jakarta, Indonesia as the program office for Women and Employment. Part of her duties took her in and out of Pakistan, and eventually she was hired away from the Bank Rakyat of Indonesia to work for the Asian Development Bank in Lahore, Pakistan. Bank Rakyat is 70% owned by the Indonesian government and has been since the war of independence in 1945. It is also part of the "Islamic banking cooperative." In 1986, she and her daughter Maya traveled the Silk Road in China from her base in Pakistan. She stayed in the Hilton International Hotel (now Avari Hotel), Lahore, and travelled daily from Lahore to Gujranwalla. When Barack Obama visited Pakistan during this period, he would stay in the same hotel. These trips are not mentioned in *Dreams*.

Obama claims that he attended Columbia University during this period, yet nobody-but-nobody there recalls him being there, and he can give virtually no account, other than sleeping in a non-existent alley in Manhattan for one night. He refuses to talk about his years at Columbia to the New York Times, refuses to release his Columbia transcript, refuses to identify even a single fellow student, co-worker, roommate or friend from those years other than some drug dealer that supposedly roomed with him for a couple of months. Fox News contacted 400 of his classmates and no one remembered him. He was supposedly a Political Science major, yet no one in that class, including Michael Baron and George Stephanopoulos could find a single soul who saw him on campus. Not even the members of the Black Student Organization and the anti-apartheid groups

81

Barry identified as carrying his membership can remember him.

Obama claims that he wrote a thesis in his senior year on the evolution of the arms reduction negotiations between the Soviet Union and the United States. This thesis has never been released. One thesis identified in the worldwide press that was actually written by a fellow named Obama was something crafted at Patrice Lamumba University in Moscow, Russia several years later on a topic that was a bit more Marxist. You will recall that Malcolm X – potentially the biological father of Obama – considered Patrice Lamumba to be the greatest Black African to ever live on the continent.

We hear so much about the implementation of the "Cloward-Piven" strategy – a "strategy that is nothing more than a watered down Marxist diatribe by a couple of burned out ex-hippies passing the flower power gas at Columbia during "the day;" yet if Obama never attended Columbia, how did he pick up on this indoctrination? One can only conclude that if Obama never attended Columbia, then his diploma was most likely *purchased* from Columbia University, using a loophole that converted "life experience" into credits under programs created by Columbia University apparatchiks. The program appears to have been funded by Palestinian interests, who were funneling Saudi money into American academia in order, in part, to cultivate the illegitimate heir apparent of the true leftist *and Islamic* nobility found in Malcolm X, an anointed demi-Caliph during the heyday of the civil rights movement. The Saudi money targeted a particular Marxist-Islamic activist who was cultivated from birth to bring about the overthrow of "the man" and to do so as a compromised insider, consistent with the Muslim Brotherhood agenda. The facts suggest that Obama never

82

attended Columbia University – he just *received a degree* there, arriving at Columbia just long enough to accept the award in 1983. Before and after his graduation, Barack Obama simply disappeared from a matriculated American scene until he reemerged at Harvard in 1990.

Where he was from 1981 to 1990 is shrouded in incompletes and international travel on passports that were not American into regions where al Qaeda would later bloom. There is reason to believe he spent some of this time in Lahore, Pakistan, working in and out of Afghanistan in support of the Mujahedeen at war with Soviet occupying forces. Was Obama involved in the assassination of Ul-Haq and the overthrow of his regime? Who knows? Obama was apparently recruited for his ability to make greetings and speak in Arabic and to iterate the Shahadatan in Arabic without accent. The Mujahedeen with whom he may have had affiliation included the wealthy Saudi operative Usama bin Laden (also known as CIA operative Tim Osman), future members of al Qaeda, and future Taliban, all of whom frequented the villages of Pakistan; which is to say, other *Ikhwan* of the Muslim Brotherhood.

There is also a reason to believe he may have spent some of this time, 1988 into 1989, at the famous Patrice Lamumba School[75] in Moscow, Russia – a boarding school for recruits being trained in the techniques of communist overthrow.[76] This is what Barry could call following the

---

[75] Associated Press - Moscow, *Soviet Union's Demise Leaves Lumumba Students in a Bind,* Watertown Daily Times.

[76] The Patrice Lumumba school is also known as *The Peoples' Friendship University of Russia* (Российский университет дружбы народов, РУДН). It holds itself out as an educational and research institution located in Moscow. It was founded in 1960, and its stated objective at the time was to help nations of the Third World, mainly in

"dreams of my father," - one father (the one whose name keeps appearing on the forged COLBs) whose promotion of communism became so acute, he was forced out of office within the Kenyan government, and died as an unemployed, wife beating, mean alcoholic on metal legs, and a biological father who worshipped at the throne of Marx, Lamumba and Mohammed.

This is an important bit of information. The preponderance of the evidence indicates that Obama never *attended* Columbia, yet there are those who continually rant and rave about him practicing Saul Alinsky's *Rules for Radicals* and following the Cloward-Piven strategy. The Cloward-Piven strategy was the strategy of the two Columbia professors Cloward and Piven. However, Obama never took class one at Columbia. So exactly where did Obama learn these advanced techniques in communist overthrow that he has been using since taking office? Say what you will about the Zero ("O") – there are few on earth who have executed a communist overthrow with greater efficiency. Could it have been Patrice Lamumba in Moscow? He appears to have been an "A" student.

There is some indication that this was the case, however, the young Obama's schooling in communist agitation ran into problems when Soviet money ran out in 1989. You might recall that the collapse of the Soviet Union happened during these years, and the poor Patrice Lamumba students were left in the same condition as

---

Asia, Africa and South America, at the height of the Cold War by providing higher education and professional training. On February 22, 1961, it was renamed in honor of Patrice Lumumba, the leader of what later became the Democratic Republic of the Congo, who had been overthrown and murdered in a coup only days earlier.

everyone else in Russia – in the cold, in the dark, and with little food. Here's a news clipping on the struggle:

Now Lumumba's dorms are crumbling. The Russian government and the university have little money. Once a Soviet showpiece, the university and its students are a burden.

The entrance to all dormitories at Lumumba are guarded by police who demand to see the passports of all visitors.

In Obama's building, the lights do not work in the elevators. The garbage chute is clogged and heating is a problem.

Named for a Congolese revolutionary, Lumumba was considered in the West to be an ideological training ground for future cadres in Soviet-backed regimes such as Ethiopia, Nicaragua and Vietnam.

As the collapse of communism became more apparent, Obama revised his thesis to address the problems of cooperation between the International Monetary Fund and Africa. He hopes to work in private practice or for his country's government.

Did you read what I just read? Let's take a look at that thesis subject again:

As the collapse of communism became more apparent, Obama revised his thesis to address the problems of cooperation between the International Monetary Fund and Africa. He hopes to work in private practice or for his country's government.

Obama claims that he wrote a thesis in his senior year on the evolution of the arms reduction negotiations between the Soviet Union and the United States. The thesis written by Obama at Patrice Lamumba concentrates on the redistribution of wealth from the IMF to Africa. Obama has continued to work on this same scheme of redistribution today. (Don't argue with the newspaper clipping, ye who would point to newspaper clippings in the Honolulu newspaper as dispositive proof of a Hawaiian birth).

Once Barry ("O") returned to the US, he took advantage of his status as the son of a Harvard graduate (*alum*) and as an international Muslim student with a degree from Columbia (and a revised thesis from Moscow), with tuition paid by an undisclosed patron in a grant from a source in Saudi Arabia, to enter Harvard Law School. He had inherited his mother's glibness (now made obvious *ad nauseam*), and was able to pole-vault himself into being the president of the law review (not editor) although he never published a single thing. He claims he paid for this education by means of student loans; however Khalid Al-Mansour, an advisor to Saudi prince Al-Walid bin Talah, told Manhattan Borough president, Percy Sutton, that he was raising money for Obama's Harvard tuition, and in fact negotiated a $20 million grant to Harvard at the same time from the same funding agent that paid for Obama's Columbia degree.

Khalid Al-Mansour is a Muslim lawyer and a black nationalist, and before becoming a Muslim, al-Mansour in the 1960s was named Don Warden. According to David Horowitz, he was deeply involved in San Francisco Bay Area racial politics as founder of a group called the African American Association and a close personal adviser to Huey Newton and Bobby Seale, notorious Black Panthers. Apparently Al-Mansour helped to establish the Black Panther Party but later broke with them when they entered coalitions with white radical groups.[77] This bit of information is important, because Al-Mansour would have first-hand knowledge of Malcolm X and the status of Malcolm X within the Black Marxist movement in America.

Al-Mansour is an outspoken hater of the United States, Israel, and white people generally. In recent years he

[77] David Horowitz's FrontPageMag.com/DiscoverTheNetworks.org: Profile: Khalid Abdullah Tariq al-Mansour

has accused the U.S. of plotting a "genocide" designed "to remove 15 million black people, considered disposable, of no relevance, value or benefit to the American society." He has told fellow blacks that "whatever you do to [white people], they deserve it, God wants you to do it and that's when you cut out the nose, cut out the ears, take flesh out of their body, don't worry because God wants you to do it." – A peculiarly Islamic notion. Alleging further that Palestinians in Israel "are being brutalized like savages," he accuses the Jews of "stealing the land the same way the Christians stole the land from the Indians in America."[78]

Al-Mansour's contact Prince Talal, on the other hand, is the largest donor to CAIR, a Muslim Brotherhood group declared by the U.S. Government in 2007 to be an unindicted co-conspirator in a terrorist financing trial. CAIR has since been found by a federal court to have been involved in "a conspiracy to support Hamas" – a designated terrorist group that has murdered at least 17 Americans and injured more than 100.[79] Hamas was founded by the Muslim Brotherhood, and so we have come full circle – from the Muslim Brotherhood, through the Muslim Brotherhood, for the Muslim Brotherhood.

Once Obama left the law school, he did what he was trained to do: he engaged in social activism as the first step of his long march to promote a communist overthrow of the United States. He did so as a "community organizer." The operative word here is "community." You

---

[78] *Id.*

[79] *Federal judge confirms CAIR is Hamas; Unsealed ruling reveals 'ample evidence' tying group to terror,* WorldNetDaily, November 23, 2010
http://www.wnd.com/index.php?fa=PAGE.view&pageId=232181

could call him a "communityist" but it is easier to say "communist." He is now currently engaged in organizing communities in Egypt, Tunisia, Yemen, Libya, Syria, Lebanon, Algeria, Morocco, Sudan, Pakistan (Pok' ee ston), and now Saudi Arabia. The leaders of these nations do not realize they have been kicked under the bus by the Mahdi, but the deal to rebuild the Caliphate allows for the leadership to emerge from Turkey. See *Behold! A White Horse!* for the details on this arrangement, when it was made, and its parameters, etc.

Community organizing was not his only skill. He also spent a great deal of time working on non-profit boards and foundations in order to direct money to al Fatah and the Palestine Liberation Organization. He has been and continues to be a significant funding agent (that is, an "aggregator" or "agentur") for Hamas and the PLO. As time wears on, his true roots emerge:

Barack Hussein Obama II, the biological son of the first American martyr for the Nation of Islam, the birth son of a Muslim Kenyan communist, the adopted son of a Muslim Indonesian intelligence asset, and the grandson of a Muslim itinerate worker and his Palestinian/Assyrian wife, is the foremost agent in the world for the bringing of Islam to the nations.

Obama sits at the head of a beast that is now coming up out of the earth with two horns like a lamb, yet one is larger than the other – the Shiite horn of Iran (the little horn) and the Sunni horn of the Neo-Ottoman Empire (the big horn), yet Obama speaks like the Chinese dragon. He exercises all of the power of the joint Islamic Empire (of the two horns), and will soon cause the earth and everyone who dwells on the earth to worship Islam and the New Caliphate – an entity that suffered a deadly head wound following WWI and the collapse of the Ottoman Empire, but which is now miraculously healed.

He will soon use weapons that will appear as fire coming down from heaven on the earth and everyone in the world will see the use of these weapons over global television. At that point, people will begin to believe that Obama has a power that is supernatural. He will require that the nations develop an international currency that carries the mark of the new Caliphate on its face (*not* the New World Order), and by this means, the new Caliphate will be empowered to speak its control over the peoples of the earth, requiring fealty of everyone on earth, with death being the penalty for a failure to yield.

The new currency will be transacted by digital means, and people will either accept the subcutaneous digital identification system, or they will be unable to buy and to sell. The new empire can be identified by its symbol, expressed in Greek as χξς (chi xi stigma *khee xee stig'-ma*) a marking of war meaning *in the name of Allah.*

This, by the way, is coming very soon, as the Federal Reserve in the United States under Obama has spent more money than every other American administration combined since the beginning of the nation. He has more than doubled the nation's deficit in just 2 years, and has increased the national debt to GDP – the next debt increase renders the nation insolvent.

In the meantime, the White House pushes the International Monetary Fund – an organization whose world headquarters is just a couple of blocks from the White House – to promote a commodities-back one-world currency. This stuff is not accidental. It is economic jihad against the United States, and now the whole world. The overthrow is on, and Zero is the center of the maelstrom.

Chapter Four

The pre-election years

Barry ("O") carried with him one other conviction, however, greater than his allegiance to Marx: his allegiance to Islam. There is a reason why he said the Muslim call to prayer is the "prettiest sound in the world."[80] Once you begin to follow his activism in the 1990s, you will see that he spent most of his time working to obtain non-profit funding for the Palestine Liberation Organization (the PLO) and al Fatah, Yasser Arafat's jihadist organization in Israel. He has always worked on behalf of Muslim jihad, when he wasn't working for the Socialist Worker's Party, the unions, or the *Weathermen* (an aging hippie domestic American terrorist group from the 1970s, whose leadership celebrated the Charles Manson/Sharon Tate murders and who advocated the slaughter of up to 25 million Americans in furtherance of their dreams to create a US communist utopia).[81]

After taking the oath of office in 2009, Barry ("O") did something in public that had never been seen before: he bowed to the king of Saudi Arabia. This demonstration of fealty had an underlying reason – in fact, hundreds of millions of reasons. The funding of the 2008 presidential campaign has never been completely documented or fully reported, because it included over $300 million in funding that came in from offshore in incremental amounts too

---

[80] 2009 Speech in Cairo.

[81] Bugliosi, Vincent; Gentry, Curt; *Helter Skelter*, 1974, Amazon.com

small to report.[82]   Many of these funds were derived from off the shores of the Mediterranean and Red Seas. Because co-conspirators in the Justice Department are covering for him, we will hear nothing about these violations of federal disclosure laws. Yes, there was also Obama fund raising going on in the Gaza Strip, a place that identifies itself as 80% in support of Hamas as its leadership.[83] Hamas is a Designated Terrorist Organization, as is al Qaeda, Hezbollah, the Palestinian Liberation Front, and the Palestinian Islamic Jihad, and all of these groups are officially enemies of the United States and the children of the Muslim Brotherhood. Within the Muslim Brotherhood, the funds that go to one group, allow that group to move the funds to another, laundering the direct funding of terror from people like Obama.[84] Aiding and abetting Hamas or any other of these groups is an act of treason to the United States.

As an *Ikhwan*, Obama is promoting the emergence of a new international caliphate – distinctly not the new

---

[82] Timmerman, Kenneth R. Tuesday, *Secret, Foreign Money Floods Into Obama Campaign*, September 29, 2008
http://thesteadydrip.blogspot.com/2008/09/moneyobama-secret-foreign-money-floods.html. "A Newsmax analysis of the 1.4 million individual contributions in the latest master file for the Obama campaign discovered 1,000 separate entries for Mr. Good Will, most of them for $25."

[83] *OBAMA TAKES HAMAS MONEY . . . oops. That's illegal,* August 6, 2008. "According to Federal Election Commission filings, Barack Obama has received illegal donations from Palestinians living in Gaza, a hotbed of Hamas terrorists."
http://gollygeeez.blogspot.com/2008/08/obama-takes-hamas-moneyoops-that.html

[84]Foreign Terrorist Organizations,
http://www.state.gov/s/ct/rls/other/des/123085.htm

world order the Europeans desire – as he seeks to rebuild the Ottoman Empire as a Sunni Caliphate whose capitol will be Jerusalem, and whose jurisdiction will be worldwide. This is the city where he would like to establish himself as the world's sole governing authority – the first dictator to control the entire world. His first and foremost objective is to wrest Jerusalem out of the hands of Israel, which is why the very first phone call he made as President was to Abbas, the head of the Palestinian Authority.[85] Did he promise Jerusalem?

However, it fits his plan to work also (notwithstanding any conflict) on behalf of that son of Aaron, Giorgi Schwartz, aka George Soros, a Hungarian of Jewish descent whose father changed the family name that allowed George to go on to work with the Nazis to imprison Jews during WWII, an era he refers to as the best time of his life, 1944 being the best of the best.

Although it can be said, "once a Nazi, always a Nazi," Soros is now a multi-billionaire who has been accused a playing a pivotal role in 1997-1998 market collapse in Southeast Asia which created a financial tsunami so large, it drove the collapse of US markets in the spring of 2000. For those who can't remember: On January 14, 2000, the Dow peaked at 11,722.98, and lost 58% of its value in the ensuing crash. On March 10, 2000, the NASDAQ peaked at 5,132.52, and collapsed to a low of 1,108 by October of 2002. The Stock Market Crash of

[85] Knowles, David, *Obama's First Call Abroad Goes to Palestinian President,* Politics Daily, January 21, 2009
http://www.politicsdaily.com/2009/01/21/obamas-first-call-abroad-goes-to-palestinian-president/

2000-2002 caused the loss of $5 trillion in the market value of companies from March 2000 to October 2002.[86]

Soros was also thrown out of Russia, Belarus and other Eastern European countries for meddling,[87] and was convicted in France for buying and selling Société Générale shares in 1988 after receiving information about a planned corporate raid on the bank.[88] He appears to be currently engaged in overthrowing the constitutional republic of the United States and destroying its currency by means of misprision of mispersonation, misprision of treason, currency manipulation, and conspiracy to overthrow the government of the United States of America (among other criminal acts) in order to enact his personal agenda, an agenda that is worth a short review:

The Soros Agenda:[89]

- INFANTICIDE: promoting taxpayer-funded abortion-on-demand;
- AIDING AND ABETTING TERRORISM AFTER THE FACT: defending the civil rights and liberties

---

[86] Goldfarb, Brent D., Kirsch, David and Miller, David A., *"Was There Too Little Entry During the Dot Com Era?"* (April 24, 2006).

[87] Thompson, Scott; Hoefle, John; Steinber, Michele; George Soros, Britain's Imperial Torpedo, EIR, Sept. 12, 2008
http://www.larouchepub.com/eiw/public/2008/2008_30-39/2008_30-39/2008-37/pdf/09-10_3536.pdf

[88] Insider trading conviction of Soros is upheld - Business - International Herald Tribune
http://www.nytimes.com/2006/06/14/business/worldbusiness/14iht-soros.1974397.html

[89] Horowitz, David; Poe, Richard; *The Shadow Party: How George Soros, Hillary Clinton, and Sixties Radicals Seized Control of the Democratic Party,* Amazon.com

of suspected anti-American terrorists and their co-conspirators;

- SUBVERTING ULTIMATE JUSTICE FOR MURDERERS: opposing the death penalty in all circumstances;
- WEALTH DISTRIBUTION TO ILLEGALS: promoting social welfare benefits and amnesty for illegal aliens;
- DESTRUCTION OF AMERICAN NATIONALISM: promoting open borders, mass immigration, and a watering down of current immigration laws;
- DISARMAMENT: advocating stricter gun-control measures;
- PROMOTING ACCEPTANCE OF A DRUG CULTURE: advocating the legalization of marijuana;
- DESTROYING NATIONAL PRIDE: promoting the view that America is institutionally an oppressive nation;
- ADVANCING MARXISM/COMMUNISM: promoting the election of leftist political candidates throughout the United States;
- **TREASON:** DESTROYING AMERICA'S DEFENSES: opposing virtually all post-9/11 national security measures enacted by U.S. government, particularly the Patriot Act;
- **TREASON:** DEFAMING THE AMERICAN MILITARY: depicting American military actions as unjust, unwarranted, and immoral;
- SEDITION: financing the recruitment and training of future activist leaders of the political Left;

- SEDITION: advocating America's unilateral disarmament and/or a steep reduction in its military spending;
- ADVANCING SOCIALISM: promoting socialized medicine in the United States;
- ADVANCING GLOBAL TOTALITARIANISM: promoting the tenets of radical environmentalism, whose ultimate goal, as writer Michael Berliner has explained, is "not clean air and clean water, [but] rather ... the demolition of technological/industrial civilization";
- ADVANCING GLOBAL TOTALITARIANISM: bringing American foreign policy under the control of the United Nations;
- ADVANCING ETHNICISM AND RACISM: promoting racial and ethnic preferences in academia and the business world alike.

Schwartz has no ethic other than the self-confessed ethic of obtaining ever-more money. As such, Schwartz is a poor representative of the *Bildeberger* group[90] and its underlying world bankers, as he does not care enough to protect their interests. Obama is ultimately working against them as well, which they will only come to understand when they are forced onto a prayer rug five times a day. Nonetheless, the other hundreds of millions that funded the Obama campaign for president originated with Soros, and Soros continues to spend money even now to promote his

---

[90] The *Bilderbergers* are a group of operatives working in the trilateral world that includes members of Central Banks, European nobility, propaganda ministries, and highly placed personnel within the governments of Europe, North America and Eastern Asia. They received their name from their meeting place in the Bilderberg Hotel in Arnhem, Netherlands.

policy of "managed decline" of the currency within the US, and ultimately, the "managed decline" of the United States itself.

Glenn Beck made the following statement about Soros: "George Soros is collapsing our dollar and that he is subverting the Constitution and planning for a collapse of [the American constitution]. He is collapsing us. I'm not asking you to believe me; I'm going to show you everything he has in place. And then I'm going to show you history – what he has done before. And it's clear. He does it the same way every time. First thing he does is buy the media. Then, he surrounds himself with revolutionaries. If you think President [Obama] has surrounded himself with dangerous men wait until you see the henchmen around George Soros."[91]

Although Soros may be the funder in chief, Obama's agenda is that of the Muslim Brotherhood: *Allah is our objective; The Prophet is our leader; Qur'an is our law; Jihad is our way; and Dying in the way of Allah is our highest hope.* Their goal, as stated by Brotherhood founder Hassan al-Banna, is to reclaim Islam's manifest destiny, an empire, stretching from Spain to Indonesia.[92] Obama's goal is bigger than this. Obama's desire for the United States can be expressed as the Brotherhood has aptly put it:

> *The process of settlement [of Islam in the United States] is a "Civilization-Jihadist" process*

---

[91] Brooks, Joe, *Preview: Glenn Beck exposes George Soros' "plan to collapse America,"* November 9, 2010, 9:10 p.m., http://wireupdate.com/wires/12164/preview-glenn-beck-exposes-george-soros-plan-to-collapse-america/

[92] Davidson, Lawrence (1998) *Islamic Fundamentalism* Greenwood Press, Westport, Conn.

with all the word means. The Ikhwan must understand that all their work in America is a kind of grand Jihad in eliminating and destroying the Western civilization from within and "sabotaging" their miserable house by their hands and the hands of the believers so that it is eliminated and God's religion is made victorious over all religions. Without this level of understanding, we are not up to this challenge and have not prepared ourselves for Jihad yet. It is a Muslim's destiny to perform Jihad and work wherever he is and wherever he lands until the final hour comes, and there is no escape from that destiny except for those who choose to slack.[93]

Once you understand the goals and objectives of the Muslim Brotherhood, you will understand the goals and objectives of Barack Hussein Obama II.

To succeed and to thereby qualify as a true *Ikhwan* within the Muslim Brotherhood, Obama must sabotage our "miserable house" (now you know why Michelle called living in the White House "hell")[94] so that it is eliminated and Islam is made victorious over all religions. Do you understand now why Obama defended the development of the mosque at Ground Zero?

---

[93] Akram, Mohamed, *An Explanatory Memorandum on the General Strategic Goal for the Brotherhood in North America,* May 19, 1991, The Investigative Project on Terrorism
http://www.investigativeproject.org/document/id/20

[94] Michelle to Sarkozy's wife in Paris.

The beauty of his plan is its ability to dovetail the Cloward-Piven strategy,[95] the Marxist-Leninist strategy of violent, communist overthrow,[96] the looting of America for his crooked friends in international banking, and the Islamic goal of conquest over the "Great Satan," which is intended to usher in the reign of the Mahdi – the twelfth Imam, the Muslim messiah.

Is it possible to conclude that Obama is trying to impose Shari'a law on America? Absolutely. One needn't look beyond the appointment of Elena Kagan, Harvard's top Islamic activist, to the United States Supreme Court to reach this conclusion. When she was dean of the Harvard Law School, the National Review called her "the champion of Shari'a." Kagan accepted $20 million from Saudi prince Alwaleed bin Talal. You might remember this name, as his advisor, Khalid Al-Mansour, was the one who raised the money for Obama's Harvard tuition. Prince Talah, CAIR largest donor, is a person who blamed the attacks of 9/11 on American foreign policy. Kagan took the money to fund programs on Islam at Harvard. She also spearheaded the "Islamic Finance Project," a program aimed at mainstreaming Shari'a compliant finance in America. And she awarded the Harvard Medal of Freedom to the chief justice of the Supreme Court of Pakistan, Iftikhar Chaudhry, whose chief credential was his intention to implement Shari'a in Pakistan.

---

[95] Cloward, Richard; Piven, Frances (May 2, 1966), *"The Weight of the Poor: A Strategy to End Poverty",* (Originally published in *The Nation*).

[96] See generally, Kramer, Murphy, Courtois, Panne, Paczkowski, Bartosek, Margolin, *The Black Book of Communism: Crimes, Terror, Repression,* Harvard University Press, originally published as *Le Livre noir du communisme: Crimes, terreur, répression,* 1997.

Robert Spencer, the director of Jihad Watch, told The Daily Caller that "Kagan would knowingly and wittingly abet the advance of Shari'a." According to Spencer, Kagan will be a willing accomplice in the ongoing stealth jihad; the institution of Shari'a into non-Muslim societies via non-violent means, such as the courts and the mainstreaming of Islamic customs.[97] Let us make no mistake: Kagan was selected to serve on the Supreme Court because of her views on Shari'a. While this may say a lot about Elena Kagan, it says far more about Obama.

To make a further determination concerning Obama's *Ikhwan* status, consider his agenda for NASA, where they have been relegated from a space agency, to a propaganda agency whose directive is to create an Islamic history in space exploration in order to help Islamic nations "feel good" about their scientific accomplishments.[98] This directive is also consistent with the MB agenda to rewrite history no matter how distant from the truth.

Obama's ego is larger than every other Muslim on earth, as he is convinced he is "the one." Oprah affirmed this.[99] He has been deified worldwide since. This

---

[97] May, Caroline, *Critics allege Elena Kagan is sympathetic to Sharia law,* The Daily Caller, August 5, 2010.
http://dailycaller.com/2010/08/05/critics-allege-elena-kagan-is-sympathetic-to-sharia-law/#ixzz16A5Rn1zj

[98] York, Byron, *Obama's new mission for NASA: Reach out to Muslim world,* July 5, 2010, Washington Examiner,
http://www.washingtonexaminer.com/opinion/blogs/beltway-confidential/obamas-new-mission-for-nasa-reach-out-to-muslim-world-97785979.html#ixzz14qz8pEGn

[99] "I am here to tell you, Iowa, he is the one. He is the one!" Chung, Jen, *Oprah Calls Obama "The One",* Gothamist, the News, December 9, 2007.

worldview has caused Barry ("O") to seek out certain occult altars for their spiritual impartation, such as the Pergamum Altar, an altar that served as the birthplace of the deification of Caesar Augustus, the template for Hitler's Zeppelin Tribune, and the theogenous foundation for the DNC nominating podium in Denver in 2008. It makes no difference whether you believe in the spiritual authority of these altars. It is enough that Obama does.

Obama has taken several steps to cover his tracks, and his handlers have employed very serious people to scrub his background, but, like a backed-up toilet, Obama's past has left a stench that betrays its source of origin.

For instance, Obama put together an African American Religious Leadership Committee for his presidential campaign, almost all of whom were associates of Louis Farrakhan, the head of the Nation of Islam, the single largest Islamic group in the United States. You can smell the bathroom of this mosque from miles away.

Here is the roster: Rev. Jeremiah Wright, who has publicly honored Farrakhan and allowed him free access to his pulpit in Chicago; Willie Barrow, who said "I love my brother, Minister Louis Farrakhan;" Bishop Vashti McKenzie, Bishop Larry D. Trotter, Dr. Major L. Jemison, Dr. Joseph E. Lowery, and Rev. John Hunter, the coalition that put together Farrakhan's Million Man March. Friends of the Committee include Malik Shabazz (relationship to el Malik el Shabbaz, also known as Malcolm X is unknown) of the New Black Panther Party, well known for his racism and anti-Semitism who claimed Israel carried out the attacks of September 11; Leonard Jeffries who claimed Jews were behind the slave trade, that white people are an inferior race and who celebrated the Challenger Shuttle disaster as it "would stop whites from spreading their filth through the universe;" Al Sharpton, whose hate-filled rhetoric against Jews, Asians and white people helped lead to riots and murders in Crown Heights and Harlem; and Dr. Maulana Karenga who spent time in jail for torturing two women with a soldering iron.[100]

Of course we should never forget his Homeland Security transition team advisor, Major Nidal Malik Hasan, the man who killed 13 people and wounded 30 others at Fort Hood on November 5, 2009. The anniversary has passed, and still no trial – and, according to Obama's Department of Justice, it is not permissible to discuss this Palestinian's radical Islamic expressions before and during the shootings. Thou shalt not criticize a fellow *Ikhwan*.

To further illustrate Obama's Muslim Brotherhood membership, consider that Obama invited the leadership of the Muslim Brotherhood in Egypt to attend his speech back in 2009.[101] According to an article that appeared in the Atlantic:

> A sign that the Obama administration is willing to publicly challenge Egypt's commitment to parliamentary democracy: various Middle Eastern news sources report that **the administration insisted that at least 10 members of the Muslim Brotherhood, the country's chief opposition party, be allowed to attend his speech in Cairo on Thursday.** [Bold added]. The

---

[100] Sultan Knish, *Exclusive: Obama's Religious Leadership Committee Packed with Farrakhan Associates,* November 2, 2008
http://sultanknish.blogspot.com/2008/11/exclusive-obamas-religious-leadership.html

[101] *Muslim Brotherhood invited to Barack Hussein Obama's Speech in Cairo*, Atlas Shrugs, June 3, 2009.
http://atlasshrugs2000.typepad.com/atlas_shrugs/2009/06/muslim-brotherhood-invited-to-barch-hussein-obamas-spcech-in-cairo.html

brotherhood is a Salafist/Islamist party with branches in many countries, and it does not have a reputation for liberalism and has supported violent campaigns against Israel (and Egypt's own government). It has deep roots in the region and traces its intellectual lineage to Sayyid Qutb, a top American-educated Islamic intellectual who was executed -- or martyred -- by the Egyptian government in 1966. **The Brotherhood has direct links with Sunni groups like Hamas in the Palestinian territories**. [Bold added]. Its standing in Egypt has suffered as of late because of a crackdown by the Egyptian government and a growing frustration that it is too conservative (anti-women's rights, the whole gamut) for a modern Middle East. Still, it's the largest Sunni opposition party in the world, and it's clear that the Obama administration wants to engage the Sunnis -- even the less moderate Sunnis -- in his "Mutual Respect" tour. Hoping to tamp down criticism that by speaking in Egypt, Obama is giving legitimacy to Hosni Mubarak's quasi-dictatorship, the administration also invited leading human rights activists to the speech.[102]

Let's review: The Obama administration insisted that the leadership of the Muslim Brotherhood attend his speech – the speech where he gave an opening salutation in Arabic, proclaimed the Quran to be "holy" and quoted directly from it on at least seven occasions, and closed with

---

[102]Marc Ambinder, *"Brotherhood" Invited To Obama Speech By U.S.,* June 3, 2009, The Atlantic
http://www.theatlantic.com/politics/archive/2009/06/-brotherhood-invited-to-obama-speech-by-us/18693/

the phrase "I am one of you" in Arabic – in Cairo, Egypt in 2009.

The mere invitation to the group was all the green light the Brotherhood required to know that the American government would not act against them when they initiated revolution against the dictatorial regime of Hosni "Hoser" Mubarak. Is it possible to draw any conclusions from this behavior? If you do, you will not be alone.

According to the African press:

"WikiLeaks release of U.S. State Department diplomatic cables continues to expose Washington's Africa policy for its imperialistic designs. Various African states, those viewed as enemies and others considered allies, all face successive U.S. administrations' efforts for **economic control and political destabilization**. [Bold added]. These cables reveal that U.S. decisions led to displacement and deaths for millions of Africans."[103]

Deaths for millions of Africans. That is a loaded statement, especially if the underlying facts point to intentional acts on the part of the Obama administration to destabilize the region in order to bring about the collapse of the existing order, in favor of the New International Order (as distinct from the New World Order), or, as it is known in the inside circles of the Obama administration, the Worldwide Islamic Caliphate.

As we will see, Obama's involvement in the affairs of Egypt and the destabilization of the government there is

---

[103]Abayomi Azikiwe, *WikiLeaks reveals U.S. imperialism's role in Africa,* Pan-African News Wire, Dec. 18, 2010, Worker's World, http://www.workers.org/2010/world/africa_1223/

not his first foray into the horn of Africa. No. There is a little issue of ethnic genocide in Kenya with which Obama had no little part. Say what he may in later criticizing the Muslim Brotherhood: his actions are consistent with their empowerment, and let us judge him by what *he does*, not what he says.

Chapter Five

The pre-election crimes

Although Obama practiced a certain level of felonious activity prior to his run for the Presidency, the crimes committed during the campaign are sufficient to warrant impeachment, and the crimes since taking the office are beyond anything ever seen in the office before, and beyond the wildest nightmares of the average baseball-playing, apple-pie-eating American.

For instance, before taking office, Obama engaged in negotiations with al Qaeda privately to orchestrate a cease fire in Afghanistan in order to ensure our surrender and our withdrawal without dignity. That is a direct violation of the Logan Act and is tantamount to treason. Obama spent a cool million to get his "cousin" Raila Odinga elected as the President of Kenya in order that Odinga could impose Shari'a on Kenya in direct opposition to American interests in the region. He continued to support Odinga even after Odinga orchestrated ethnic genocide in Kenya, including the burning alive of 50 Christian women and children hunkered down in a small church. These actions to stir up such terror are typically referred to as ethnic genocide or ethnic cleansing and are internationally recognized as crimes against humanity. Odinga published his intent to engage in ethnic cleansing on the very same web page that bragged about the funding from "the friends of Senator Obama." Obama has never distanced himself from this conspiracy.

Obama claims he is an American and claims he was born in Hawaii. To prove this, he posted an image – not the actual document - of an invalidated Certification of Live Birth that has been shown to be a forgery (in fact, the forgery is self evident) on his Fightthesmears.com website. This COLB also appeared on the Daily Kos website early on in 2008. Once it was demonstrated by several forensic auditors that the COLB was a forgery, Obama produced a second, different Certification of Live Birth on the website that calls itself FactCheck.org, a so-called non-partisan organization created to check the accuracy of assertions made on the internet.

If one of these Certifications is bona fide, then necessarily the other is a forgery. However, both of these documents are forgeries. The placement of the forgery into the public eye for purposes of obtaining a federal job is a crime. These are obvious crimes that are not dependent upon any "birther" theory; he committed these crimes whether he was born in Hawaii, or hatched in an egg.

It is worth noting that at no point did he actually produce a document to a qualified forensic auditor within the federal government. As a matter of evidence, he has produced a forged photo-shopped *image* of a COLB based upon a generic template of the COLB produced by the state of Hawaii, without embossment; and several photographic *images* of a second COLB that appears to be embossed – although the embossment is backward to applicable standards that require the embossment to erupt out of the back to the front – and the unsworn testimony of two partisans that claim it was genuine. The production of internet images is simply not evidence.

Avoiding the birth certificate issue again, we have to consider the falsification of his social security number and his draft registration. You can't leave these out. Given that he was a Kenyan national and an Indonesian citizen before he decided to exclude those facts from the public eye in order to run for the Presidency, Obama had a problem meeting the simple requirements of being an American male – namely, possessing a social security number that was properly identified with a state (and not a number common to immigrants) and proof of draft registration. This proved to be difficult.

For instance, Steve Baldwin reports for Western Journalism, that Obama has sported multiple social security numbers. Importantly, two of the three numbers he used at Occidental College in California began with 999 – a number reserved for aliens in the US. Obama would have had such a number if he applied to Occidental as a foreign national under an F-1 visa, and he did not yet have a social security number. A 999 number would likely appear on his Indonesian passport as well.

Since deciding to claim that he was an American, Obama has used the SSN beginning with the numbers 042, as he did when he attended Harvard Law School. However, when he served as a Senator, he used a different SSN, beginning with 282. Apparently, there are 16 different SSNs associated with the name Barack Obama. By the way, the number he uses now was issued to someone in Connecticut during the time period 1976-1977. Obama was still at Punahou School in Hawaii at that time.[104]

Using a fake SSN number, or a number belonging to another person, is a form of perjury and fraud that is punishable under federal law. Under certain circumstances, a person using such a number can result in enhanced penalties. For instance, if a person signs a document that

[104] Baldwin, Steve, *The Mystery of Barack Obama Continues,* Western Center for Journalism, http://www.westernjournalism.com/exclusive-investigative-reports/the-mystery-of-barack-obama-continues/

requires both the SSN and a statement indicating that the person is signing under the penalty of perjury, the use of a false SSN can result in a conviction for perjury that can carry a five-year prison sentence and a fine of up to $40,000.[105] Obama's use of a false SSN is yet another high crime – a felony exposing him to another five years in prison, should he be convicted.

I-9 Fraud

Obama has likely filled out many federal forms in order to ensure his ability to get into the country, given the amount of international travel he did as a young person, including trips to Indonesia, Pakistan, India, Kenya and so on. He made reentry into the US on multiple occasions, and he could only have made such reentry with some form of documentation; it wasn't a US passport. Other forms were then provided. Providing a false SSN on such forms could also result in a five-year federal prison sentence and a maximum fine of $250,000.

Obama has almost certainly used a false SSN to obtain a mortgage and an auto loan or two. Investigators believe Obama has used multiple SSNs to obtain many bank loans. However, the use of a false SSN to obtain a loan from a federally chartered bank (which most are), can result in a conviction for bank fraud under 18 U.S.C. 1334. Prison time for this crime ranges upwards of 30 years, and the fine can be as high as $1 million.

Obama appears to be using the SSN of another person who is believed to be dead. Using the SSN of another person is punishable under federal law as identity theft and carries a maximum sentence of 15 years, under 18

---

[105] 18 U.S.C. 1621

U.S.C. 1028.[106] Obama's use of his current SSN is a whole series of federal crimes, which, when combined, exposes him to as much as 55 years in prison and over a million dollars in fines. There can be no doubt that such exposure most assuredly can be considered "high crimes."

Moving on to the issue of the draft registration: Debbie Schlussel has published Obama's Selective Service registration form that indicates his registration form was not submitted when he was younger as required, but rather in 2008 and then altered to look older. Apparently, somebody got in a hurry when they were forging the document and left the "Document Location Number" which demonstrates conclusively that the form used was from 2008, the same year his Certification of Live Birth from Hawaii surfaced. A falsified draft registration document is also a crime.[107]

This draft registration, NUMBER 08-970-606-32, the 08 representing the year 2008, was a little late to meet

---

[106] Federal Sentencing Guidelines Calculator

[107] *The Mystery of Barack Obama Continues ,Id.*

the statutory requirements for registration following the 18th birthday. Men who do not register with Selective Service before turning age 26 can be prosecuted and, if convicted, fined up to $250,000 and/or required to serve up to five years in prison.[108] In addition, men who fail to register, even if not prosecuted, will become ineligible for Student Financial Aid - including Pell Grants, College Work Study, Guaranteed Student/Plus Loans, and National Direct Student Loans; and Federal Job Training. The Job Training Partnership Act (JTPA) is only open to those men who register with Selective Service. Men who fail to register, even if not prosecuted, are ineligible for Federal Jobs, including jobs in the Executive Branch of the Federal government and the U.S. Postal Service. Finally and most importantly, men who fail to register if not American citizens lose eligibility to become U.S. Citizens, if the man first arrived in the U.S. before his 26th birthday.[109]

Not everyone is required to register for the draft. For instance, *nonimmigrant aliens in the U.S. on student,* visitor, tourist, or diplomatic *visas* are not required to register. If you are such an alien, and you enter the US after the age of 18, you may not have to register with Selective Service. If you are an illegal alien, the Selective Service will have no record of you, particularly if there is no state reporting a birth or showing a birth certificate on its records.

Given that Obama did not register for the draft until 2008, some 46 years after his birth, although he had been in

---

[108] 50 USC Sec. 1881g

[109] Longley, Robert, *Register for the Draft: It's Still the Law, Males 18 through 25 are required to register,* About.com Guide;
http://usgovinfo.about.com/od/defenseandsecurity/a/draftreg.htm

the United States since age 10 following his being made an Indonesian citizen, he has committed a felony that exposes him to a five year prison term and a $250,000 fine. That is the very definition of a high crime. More importantly, his failure to register makes him ineligible for Student Financial Aid, Federal Job Training, Federal Jobs in the Executive Branch of the Federal government, and finally, U.S. Citizenship.

Let's be obvious about this conclusion. If Obama cannot demonstrate that he registered with the Selective Service before his 26th birthday, given that he has never taken an oath of citizenship, then on his 26th birthday, he was permanently disqualified from ever becoming an American citizen. The only evidence of any draft registration for Obama is the document posted by Debbie Schlussel, seen above. This registration document is not sufficient to create a legal registration, as it was filed 20 years beyond its applicability. Instead, this registration is *prima facie* evidence of the crime of failing to register before reaching age 26.

Obama at one time was fairly clear-minded that his citizenship didn't require him to register for the draft. It is possible that he understood himself to be qualified to avoid the draft as a non-U.S. male in the country on a valid non-immigrant visa, such as an F-1 student visa. These records, if they ever existed in the US, have been destroyed ("scrubbed") earlier this year. To avoid the registration requirement, Obama would have needed to provide documentation indicating that he was admitted on an F-1 visa and attended school full-time beyond his 26th birthday. Acceptable documentation for this situation would include a copy of his I-20 form or a letter from the school he attended indicating his full-time attendance as a non-immigrant alien.

Obama turned 26 in 1987. He had already graduated from Columbia University; however, it doesn't appear as though he was in the country at that time. Either way, he cannot produce any records that Columbia provided the Selective Service with an I-20 form or a letter from the school. He can't produce anything, because even if there was something to produce, it has all been destroyed.

We can therefore reach the following conclusion: Obama either committed a crime as an American citizen by failing to register, which necessarily disqualifies him from holding a federal job, and in particular, a federal job in the executive branch; or Obama was an alien who didn't need to register because he was able to establish that he was an non-U.S. male in the country on a valid non-immigrant F-1 student visa and enrolled in school through to his 26th birthday (which would have been possible if he matriculated direct from Columbia University to Patrice Lamumba, and was registered at Patrice Lamumba through an American university). If the latter was the case, there would be no doubt that Obama was a non-U.S. male, and more importantly, such evidence would demonstrate that Obama knew he was a non-U.S. male during this entire period. That is, Obama knew he was not an American citizen at all material times. Non-Americans cannot hold the office of President.

However, Barack Obama is not the only one confused as to exactly who he is and where he was born. We will explore this issue a little more in detail in another chapter. Until then, let's see what has been published about him before his decision to jump in the race for the Presidency of the United States:

From the Honolulu Advertiser, January 8, 2006:[110]

---

[110] Screen capture courtesy of
http://www.oilforimmigration.org/facts/?p=3882

A close review of this article indicates that the writer had no compunction stating that, in reference to the two politicians being discussed, "both were born outside the country – Obama in Indonesia, Duckworth in Thailand – " It looks like, conspicuously, that before Obama decided to cover his off-shore birth with an Hawaiian alibi, the press in Hawaii was convinced he was "born outside the country." While they were not the only ones around the world who were convinced of an off-shore birth, it is equally important that there was, and is, no one in Hawaii who remembers his birth; no one. No one remembers the pregnant mother, and no one remembers the birth. In 2006, there was no one who came forward to challenge the Honolulu Advertiser on the claim that Obama was born in Indonesia, and that includes everyone who worked at the Punahou School who almost certainly read the article.

Consider the comments by the Sunday Standard in Kenya back in 2004, when they opened their story with "Kenyan born US Senate hopeful, Barack Obama:[111]

Kenyan-born Obama all set for US Senate

Kenyan-born US Senate hopeful, Barrack Obama, appeared set to take over the Illinois Senate seat after his main rival, Jack Ryan, dropped out of the race on Friday night amid a furor over lurid sex club allegations.

The allegations that horrified fellow Republicans and caused his once-promising candidacy to implode in four short days have given Obama a clear lead as Republicans struggled to fetch an alternative.

Ryan's campaign began to crumble on Monday following the release of embarrassing records from his divorce. In the records, his ex-wife, Boston Public actress Jeri Ryan, said her former husband took her to kinky sex clubs in Paris, New York and New Orleans.

Barrack Obama

"It's clear to me that a vigorous debate on the issues most likely could not take place if I remain in the race," Ryan, 44, said in a statement. "What would take place, rather, is a brutal, scorched-earth campaign – the kind of campaign that has turned off so many voters, the kind of politics I refuse to play."

Of course, in an Associated Press story in the New Times Online, Ghana saw fit to weigh in on the debate saying that "a Congressional Quarterly (CQ) politics monitored on BBC put the Kenyan born American ahead of his rival, Senator McCain."[112]

A couple of newspaper articles from the Associated Press should not prove too difficult to dismiss for someone willing to forge a birth certificate, grab up a dead man's social security number, scoop up a deceased child's birth

---

[111] http://web.archive.org/web/20040627142700/eastandard.net/headlines/news26060403.htm

[112] AP, Americans Decide Today. Go Obama!, November 4, 2008, newtimesonline.com http://www.modernghana.com/news2/189461/1/americans-decide-today-go-obama.html

certificate registration number, falsify a draft registration statement, and lie to the Illinois Bar Association. Just another day's work!

Let's throw in a third story, shall we? This time, from the Nigerian Observer, posted November 4, 2008, discussing the Kenyan-born Senator:

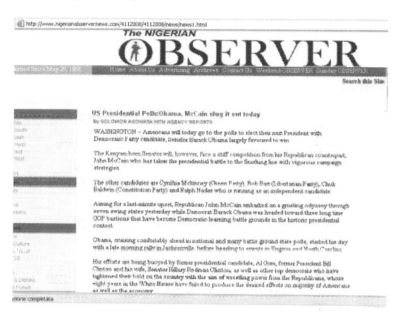

This is our starting point on the crimes of Obama before he took office. The issue of his nationality, his ineligibility to hold the Presidency, and now, his incompetence, are all material to an entire new series of high crimes and misdemeanors which followed the numerous misdemeanors, felonies and federal crimes listed above. We will also discuss the impeachable offenses that have taken place *since* taking the office of the Presidency; crimes which include misdemeanors (breaking and entering, simple theft, trespassing), high crimes (war crimes for the unauthorized killing of civilians in Afghanistan, Pakistan, Iraq and now Gaza), bribery (Joe Sestak, Andrew Romanoff, and Jim Matheson) and of course, treason (funding of Hamas, aiding and abetting the Muslim Brotherhood amongst our allies, aiding and abetting forces invading our southern border, and violations of Posse Comitatus).

Of all of these charges, the most wide-ranging issue in my mind is fraud. Minnesota Governor Pawlenty called him "one of the biggest bait-and-switch acts in history."[113] Former Speaker of the House Newt Gengrich has said Obama "is a person who is fundamentally out of touch with how the world works, who happened to have played a wonderful con, as a result of which he is now president. [Obama] is so outside our comprehension, that only if you understand Kenyan, anti-colonial behavior, can you begin to piece together [his actions]."[114]

The American public now knows he perpetrated a fraud. It is one thing to spread the truth, as many politicians have done in the past. It is another thing to hide your foreign nationality, your foreign birth, your foreign allegiance, and to disguise your ties to the Muslim Brotherhood, your active role in terrorism against the United States, your hatred for the United States and its laws, and your utter disregard for the Constitution. At some point, this rises above mere civil fraud, and reaches criminal fraud.

---

[113] Barr, Andy, *Tim Pawlenty: Barack Obama projecting 'weakness',* October 27, 2009
http://www.politico.com/news/stories/1009/28735.html

[114] Villa Marco, *Newt Gingrich: Obama Holds "Kenyan" Worldview,* InstaBlogs, September 13, 2010
http://marcovilla.instablogs.com/entry/newt-gingrich-obama-holds-kenyan-worldview/#ixzz14rVEP5Js

In the case of Barry Soetoro ("O"), now known as Barack Hussein Obama, his fraud has reached the high pinnacles of treason, and his treasonous acts are now contributing to the deaths of millions worldwide. Obama has blood on his hands in Kenya and Egypt, and will be responsible ultimately for the entire destabilization of the Middle East, the subsequent bloodbath that will be the war fought there, and the bloodbath that ensues worldwide among the allies of the various forces at war; that is, the millions who die when the allies of Islam fight the allies of the Zionists.

Shall we abide this fellow any longer in the highest office created under the Constitution?

Chapter Six

The Senatorial years

It is now necessary to consider the unlawful – the lawless – acts of Barack Hussein Obama, ignoring entirely the issue of his birth.

Violations of the Logan Act.

We begin with the Logan Act, 18 USC 953 - Sec. 953. Private correspondence with foreign governments:

> *Any citizen of the United States, wherever he may be, who, without authority of the United States, directly or indirectly commences or carries on any correspondence or intercourse with any foreign government or any officer or agent thereof, with intent to influence the measures or conduct of any foreign government or of any officer or agent thereof, in relation to any disputes or controversies with the United States, or to defeat the measures of the United States, shall be fined under this title or imprisoned not more than three years, or both. This section shall not abridge the right of a citizen to apply, himself or his agent, to any foreign government or the agents thereof for redress of any injury which he may have sustained from such government or any of its agents or subjects.*

1 Stat. 613, January 30, 1799, codified at 18 U.S.C. § 953 (2004)."

Although Stokely Carmichael (1967), Senators John Sparkman and George McGovern (1975), Rev. Jesse Jackson, (1984), House Speaker James Wright (1987/88), John Kerry (2005) and Nancy Pelosi (2007) have been accused of violation the Logan Act, no one has yet been prosecuted.

The Logan Act has been construed to create two general prohibitions. First, an unauthorized citizen may not, without the authority of the United States, directly or indirectly commence or carry on any correspondence or intercourse with any foreign government or any officer or agent thereof, with intent to influence the measures or conduct of any foreign government or of any officer or agent thereof, in relation to any disputes or controversies with the United States, and second, an unauthorized citizen may not do anything to defeat the measures of the United States; that is, no unauthorized citizen may work against the policies of the President and Executive Branch.

Prosecutorial discretion in the enforcement of this Act usually looks to the practicable capability of the actor to actually change foreign policy. If the actor is of insufficient stature, the Act will not be applied. However, if the actor is of sufficient stature within the political system of the United States, such as a high ranking member of the Senate, a rogue Vice President, or a Presidential candidate, the Act would have prosecutorial application.

Obama's Logan Act violation, re: al Qaeda

GeostrategyDirect.com, a newsletter published by Bill Gertz stated in a piece of February 3, 2009,[115] that

---

[115] GAFFNEY: S-U-B-M-I-S-S-I-O-N, Frank Gaffney, Washington Times, February 3, 2009

"Diplomatic sources said Barack Obama has engaged several Arab intermediaries to relay **messages to and from al Qaeda** in the months *before* his elections as the 44th U.S. president. The sources said al Qaeda **has offered what they termed a truce in exchange for a U.S. military withdrawal from Afghanistan**.

"For the last few months, Obama has been receiving and sending feelers to those close to al Qaeda on whether the group would end its terrorist campaign against the United States,' a diplomatic source said. 'Obama sees this as helpful to his plans to essentially withdraw from Afghanistan and Iraq during his first term in office.'

"If surrender in Afghanistan, Iraq and Iran were not enough, upcoming opportunities for Mr. Obama to exhibit American submission to Islam include ordering U.S. participation in the United Nations' 'Durban II' conference - thereby legitimating its Iranian-dictated, rabidly anti-Israel, anti-American, Holocaust-denying and 'Islamophobia' -banning agenda; adopting the program for undermining Israel promoted by longtime Friends-of-Barack Rashid Khalidi and Samantha Power (the latter just appointed a senior National Security Council official); and reversing the FBI's long-overdue decision to end its association with the Council on American Islamic Relations (CAIR), a prominent front organization of the Muslim Brotherhood (whose stated mission is 'to destroy America from within.')"

These are the facts as published, and which remain undisputed to this day. Now, let's take a look again at the elements of the Logan Act in relation to these facts as alleged:

Elements:

- Obama claims to be a Citizen of the United States

- He was never authorized to engage in discussions with al Qaeda prior to his election to the office of the Presidency
- He directly commenced and carried on correspondence or intercourse with members of al Qaeda
- He did so with the intent to influence the measures or conduct of any foreign government or of any officer or agent thereof, in relation to any disputes or controversies with the United States, or to defeat the measures of the United States.

You can conclude for yourself whether Obama's direct contacts with al Qaeda to deliberately subvert the express policies of the Bush administration in Afghanistan amount to a violation of the Logan Act occurred.

Obama's Logan Act violation, re: Odinga and Kenya

The most egregious actions of Senator Obama that appear to violate not only the Logan Act, but International Laws prohibiting ethnic cleansing and genocide, are those actions undertaken in support of the presidential campaign of Kenya's Raila Odinga – a purported cousin of Obama.

Obama, at the time a candidate for the Presidency of the United States with substantial standing in the polls – in other words, a qualifying individual under the Logan Act – made trips to Kenya to openly advocate for Odinga in his bid for the Presidency of Kenya.

Obama first visited Kenya to openly campaign for Odinga as a junior Senator from Illinois in 2006. His direct interference was so substantial that a spokesman for the Kenyan government called Obama a "stooge" for Odinga, and accused him of meddling inappropriately in Kenyan politics.[116]

Inappropriateness is not a block for Obama. Obama continued to support Odinga, even after Odinga began to execute on his post-election strategy to engage in ethnic violence should his political campaign fail.

Odinga put together a rather poorly put together website, which did two things: it first set out a list of cash contributors to the Odinga campaign, and on the same page, set forth his political agenda.

Here is a portion of the financial disclosure from that website:

Mr Zackaya Cheruyot	4,580,000
Mr Charles Onyancha	300,000
Fru Ltd Alexande Heyme	225,000
Dick Morris Associates (pro bono services)	21,335,000
Dr B Kosgey	2,570,000
Kirumu Simba League	21,750,000
Dr P Otuoma	250,000
Mr S Murungu (Kimiti)	8,500,000
Tony Teesta	21,500,000
Mr S B Sodi	130,000
Zuhedi group	20,000,000
Colourprint (peeterishops)	8,900,000
Anura Pereira	107,000,000
J Okungu	350,000
Tony Buckingham	8,000,000
Col Ted Spicer	17,000,000
Mr J Inusi	38,000,000
Kamani Family	45,000,000
COTU	42,666,600
Friends of Senator BO	85,000,000
PK Patel	4,528,123
United Business Association	76,000,000
Westlands Association	12,800,000

Working the currency translation, the contribution from Friends of Senator BO is one million USD. You can also see that Dick Morris Associates was a contributor.

---

[116] Obama-backed ally forged pact with radical Muslims, Aug 1, 2008, http://www.wnd.com/?pageId=71143#ixzz1KTx32T8f

From the same website (now scrubbed), we find the following statements of policy:

Ethnic Tensions/Violence as a last
Resort
To discourage voter participation in hostile areas
1. Continue pro-Majimbo utterances

1. Use ODM agents on the ground to engineer ethnic tensions in target areas

1. Support Kapondiis forces in Mt. Elgon

1. Leaflets targeting the Kikuyus, Kisiis, etc
Mid-Dec
Bring Alexandra Sibianei

The Odinga campaign website called for "Ethnic Tensions/Violence as a last Resort" in order to "discourage voter participation in hostile areas" by continuing "pro-Majimbo utterances," using ODM agents on the ground to "engineer ethnic tensions in target areas," supporting "Kapondiis forces in Mt. Elgon" and distributing leaflets "targeting the Kikuyus, Kisiis, etc" apparently in mid-December. One needn't wonder from what source the money was had to finance these objectives – the website clarifies that the friends of Senator BO was one of the top contributors, along with Sri Lankan/Cypriot Anura Pereira, a corrupt defense contractor who had previously stung the nation of Kenya for over a 4.1 billion Kenyan shillings in the construction of a military vessel. Obama's team gave a million USD; Pereira gave nearly 2 million.

On December 27, 2008, Odinga lost the presidential election. The Odinga team which included the Orange Democratic Party – a group that Odinga is now preparing to kick under the bus – then went to the policies of last resort.

Reuters reported on January 7, 2008, that Odinga and the Orange Democrats has orchestrated ethnic violence that killed over 1,000 people and displaced over 255,000. Kenya was hit by a wave of demonstrations and tribal clashes after Odinga lost the election, causing the worst crisis since independence from Britain in 1963.[117] The violence stopped only when President Kibaki invited Odinga to consolidate peace by means of a "national reconciliation," which included Odinga being appointed to the newly created position of Prime Minister.

The ethnically charged violence created shortages of food and water in parts of the country. Most of the bloodshed occurred in Kenya's Rift Valley province. For instance, in the city of Eldoret, a mob burned a Kenya Assemblies of God church to the ground on Tuesday, killing about 30 people trapped inside, an act of genocide.

These acts did not stop Obama in his support of Odinga, which by law makes him a co-conspirator, after the fact, in the international crime of genocide and crimes against humanity.

The term "genocide" was created or defined during the Nazi Holocaust and declared an international crime in the 1948 by the United Nations Convention on the Prevention and Punishment of the Crime of Genocide. The Convention defined genocide as any of the following acts committed with the intent to destroy, in whole or in part, a national, ethnical, racial, or religious group, as such:

a. Killing members of the group;
b. Causing serious bodily or mental harm to members of the group;

---

[117] Allistair Thomson and Daniel Wallis, *Up to 1,000 killed in Kenya crisis – Odinga,* Reuters, January 7, 2008.
http://www.reuters.com/article/2008/01/08/idUSL0743589._CH_.2400

c. Deliberately inflicting on the group conditions of life calculated to bring about its physical destruction in whole or in part;

d. Imposing measures intended to prevent births within the group;

e. Forcibly transferring children of the group to another group.

The "intent to destroy" particular groups is unique to the definition of genocide.

A closely related category of international law—"crimes against humanity"—is defined as widespread or systematic attacks against civilians.[118] An international treaty ratified on July 17, 1998, permanently established the International Criminal Court to prosecute genocide, crimes against humanity, and war crimes. The treaty reconfirmed the definition of genocide found in the 1948 UN Convention on the Prevention and Punishment of the Crime of Genocide. It also expanded the definition of crimes against humanity and prohibited these crimes during times of war or peace.

The treaty defines crimes against humanity as any of the following acts when committed as part of widespread or systematic attacks directed against a civilian population, with knowledge of the attack:

a. Murder;

b. Extermination;

c. Enslavement;

d. Deportation or forcible transfer of population;

e. Imprisonment or other severe deprivation of physical liberty in violation of fundamental rules of international law;

---

[118] *What is Genocide? An Evolving International Framework,* United States Holocaust Memorial Museum, 2008.
http://www.ushmm.org/genocide/pdf/timeline.pdf

f. Torture;

g. Rape, sexual slavery, enforced prostitution, forced pregnancy, enforced sterilization, or any other form of sexual violence of comparable gravity;

h. Persecution against any identifiable group or collectivity on political, racial, national, ethnic, cultural, religious, gender as defined in paragraph 3, or other grounds that are universally recognized as impermissible under international law, in connection with any act referred to in this paragraph or any crime within the jurisdiction of the Court;

i. Enforced disappearance of persons;

j. The crime of apartheid;

k. Other inhumane acts of a similar character intentionally causing great suffering, or serious injury to body or to mental or physical health.

Having funded Hamas in direct contravention with US law, Obama went on to directly fund a constitutional overthrow in Kenya. On August 6, 2010, Obama came public with his support of constitutional changes in Kenya, which his administration had promoted and funded, using $23 million in US tax dollars to pressure Kenya, in violation of Siljander amendment prohibiting the use of federal foreign aid funds to lobby for abortion.

Obama not only demanded that the constitution be amended to provide for abortion on demand, but also carved out space for Muslim khadi courts, which decide issues of family law in accord with Sharia law, when less than 12% of Kenya is Muslim.[119]

---

[119] *Obama funds Kenya's new constitution that pushes Sharia Law and Abortion*, Right Wing Extreme, August 7, 2010

Given what we now know about the law of genocide and crimes against humanity, the Logan Act seems trivial, doesn't it? Obama violates whatever law he so desires, and there is absolutely no consequence, whether it is the code of professional responsibility of the Illinois Bar Association, State Law, Federal Law, or even International Law.

Activities Affecting Armed Forces During War

18 U.S.C. 2388(a) Activities Affecting Armed Forces During War. (a) Whoever, when the United States is at war, willfully makes or conveys false reports or false statements with intent to interfere with the operation or success of the military or naval forces of the United States or to promote the success of its enemies; or

"Whoever, when the United States is at war, willfully causes or attempts to cause insubordination, disloyalty, mutiny, or refusal of duty, in the military or naval forces of the United States, or willfully obstructs the recruiting or enlistment service of the United States, to the injury of the service of the United States, or attempts to do so—Shall be fined under this title or imprisoned not more than twenty years, or both.

The false statement at issue is that Obama was constitutionally qualified to hold the office of the President pursuant to the relevant article of the US Constitution. First and foremost, this false statement was made by Nancy Pelosi and Howard Dean when they certified that Obama was constitutionally qualified to be on the ballot in Hawaii

http://www.rightwingextreme.us/index.php/News/Top-Stories/obama-funds-kenyas-new-constitution-that-pushes-sharia-law-and-abortion.html

However, Obama joined this false statement when he caused to be published the forged Certification of Live Birth on the Daily Kos (also a co-conspirator), and the second forged Certification of Live Birth on factcheck.org (additional co-conspirators).

Following the false statement, Obama went on to engage in negotiations with al Qaeda in Afghanistan, in order to interfere with the operation or success of the military or naval forces of the United States, and furthermore, to promote the success of its enemies, namely, the Taliban in Afghanistan.

The charge is similar to a charge of treason, in that the actions must take place when the nation is at war, and the indictment need not go further than to set forth the language of the statute which defines the offense, because intent is inferred from that actions alleged.[120]

Fraud and False Statements.

18 U.S.C. § 1002 - Fraud and False Statements - Possession of false papers to defraud United States, provides severe criminal penalties for fraud and false statements using false papers in order to defraud the United States, to wit:

(c) Whoever uses or attempts to use **any certificate** of arrival, declaration of intention, certificate of naturalization, certificate of citizenship **or other documentary evidence** . . . **of citizenship, or any duplicate or copy thereof**, knowing the same to have been procured by fraud or false evidence . . .; or

(d) Whoever knowingly **makes any false certificate** . . .; or

---

[120] *Schulze v. U.S.,* 259 F. 189; *United States v. Greathouse*, 2 Abb.U.S. 364, Fed. Cas. No. 15,254

(e) Whoever knowingly makes any false statement or claim that he is, or at any time has been, a citizen or national of the United States, with the intent to obtain on behalf of himself, . . ., any Federal or State benefit or service, or to engage unlawfully in employment in the United States;

Shall be fined under this title **or imprisoned** not more than **five years**, or both.

Also consider 18 U.S.C. § 1017 – Fraud and False Statements - Government seals wrongfully used and instruments wrongfully sealed. This federal statute also provides for five years in prison for "whoever fraudulently or wrongfully affixes or impresses the seal of any department or agency of the United States, to or upon any certificate," or "whoever knowingly and without lawful authority produces an identification document, authentication feature, or a false identification document.

However, the federal government takes identity fraud very seriously. Under 18 U.S.C. § 1028 - Fraud and related activity in connection with identification documents, authentication features, and information, the punishment for an offense under subsection (a) of this section is a fine or imprisonment for not more than 15 years, or both, **if the offense is** the production or transfer of an identification document, authentication feature, or false identification document that is or appears to be . . . **a birth certificate,** or a driver's license or personal identification card.

Obama is now a serial offender as to this statute. As burdensome as it is to post yet one more forgery, let's take a look at what I call the Adobe BC – that is, the long form birth certificate issued by some amateur forger at the White House.

Here's the most recent forgery:

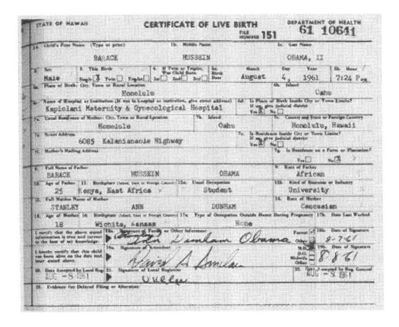

I am not going to go into how bad of a forgery this actually is, because there are literally hundreds of analyses on this certificate, and virtually every nation on earth knows it's a forgery. Here is Wayne Madsen's take:

> April 28, 2011 — World intelligence agencies: Obama's long form birth certificate a rank forger
>
> From intelligence agencies around the world, the verdict on President Obama's newly-released certificate of live birth from Hawaii is in: the certificate is a rank forgery on the same level as the Niger "yellow cake" uranium and Iraq Oil Ministry

forged documents. Intelligence and law enforcement services are experts on fake documents since they have to deal with large numbers of counterfeit documents, such as birth certificates, passports, identity cards and driver's licenses, as well as currency. Intelligence agencies are also experts at forging their own documents for their clandestine agents.

Within 24-hours of the release of the long form Certificate of Live Birth on April 27, intelligence agencies from Britain and China to Germany and Russia examined the document and concluded it was a forgery based on the fact that Barack H. Obama Sr.'s race, listed as "African," was a monumental error, considering that not only the United States, but other English-speaking nations described Africans and those of African descent as either "Negroes" or "blacks" in 1961.

In 1961, the U.S. Department of Health, Education, and Welfare classified non-Whites, who were not Asian, Eskimo, Aleut, Hawaiian, part-Hawaiian, or other "non-White," as "Negro." The U.S. Census Bureau also used the term "Asian and other Pacific Islander" in 1961, which included Filipino, Hawaiian, and part-Hawaiian. The Census Bureau, like HEW, used the term "Negro" to describe blacks and those of black descent. The term "mulatto," used to describe those of mixed white and black ancestry, ceased being used by the U.S. Census Bureau in 1918.

1961 Vital Statistics of the United States; U. S. Dept. of Health Education, and Welfare; Public Health Service; National Center for Health Statistics; National Vital Statistics Division;

Race and color

Births in the United States in 1961 are classified for vital statistics into white, Negro, American Indian, Chinese, Japanese, Aleut, Eskimo, Hawaiian and Part-Hawaiian (combined), and "other nonwhite."

The category "white" includes, in addition to persons reported as "white," those reported as Mexican or Puerto Rican. With one exception, a reported mixture of Negro with any other race is included in the Negro group; other mixed parentage is classified according to the race of the nonwhite parent and mixtures of nonwhite races to the race of the father. The exception refers to a mixture of Hawaiian and any other race, which is classified as Part-Hawaiian. In most tables a less detailed classification of "white" and "nonwhite" is used.

In the United Kingdom, the terms "black" and "Asian" were used in the 1961 census to describe those who were "non-white British" nationals. Barack Obama, Sr., as a citizen of the British Colony of Kenya, would have known that his British racial designation was "black" in 1961. The term "African" was not used as a racial designation in either the colony of Kenya or on the British mainland. In South Africa and other British colonies in Africa, "Coloured" was used to describe those of mixed white-black descent.

The consensus among intelligence agency experts is that the Obama long form Certificate of Live Birth was hastily manufactured by an amateur who never thought of using the standard race designation of Negro in Barack Obama, Sr.'s racial designation block on the form either due to ignorance or an attempt to be politically correct in 2011 by refusing to use an accepted term from 1961.[121]

Also see:

* http://www.huffingtonpost.com/dan-pashman/obamas birth-certificate-_b_854432.html
* http://atlasshrugs2000.typepad.com/atlas_shrugs/obamas_birth_certifcate_forgery/
* http://patriotupdate.com/6137/is-obama%E2%80%99s-birth-certificate-a-fake
* http://www.ihatethemedia.com/is-obama-long-form-birth-certificate-a-forgery
* http://www.favstocks.com/is-the-latest-obama-birth-certificate-long-form-a-forgery/2750538/
* http://lamecherry.blogspot.com/2008/08/proof-barack-obama-birth-certificate-is.html
* http://www.abovetopsecret.com/forum/thread694949/pg1
* http://www.infowars.com/new-obama-birth-certificate-is-a-forgery/

---

[121] Wayne Madsen Reports, April 28, 2011

- http://hotair.com/greenroom/archives/2011/04/27/is-the-birth-certificate-fake-the-games-have-begun/
- http://gatewaypundit.rightnetwork.com/2011/04/critics-obamas-latest-long-form-birth-certificate-is-a-fake/

Here is the Gateway Pundit analysis:[122]

> This is so maddening to listen to the media on this recent revelation... it's such an obvious fake.
>
> Look at the JPG... (which shows what you will see when opening the PDF in Illustrator and how to get there)... but to recap... if you open the PDF in Illustrator (instead of Photoshop) – Select the entire document and go to the Object menu and choose Clipping Mask > Release. Repeat as necessary until all clipping masks are released. Also open the Layer and turn off the visibility of each clipping group and you can see all the numerous places in which information was added (edited) into the form.
>
> Lastly, look at the attached 1961 sample image found on the Internet of a legitimate 1961 Hawaii Birth Certificate (which someone posted to show what a real certificate would look like from that year in Hawaii)... look at the marks on this Internet version and you can see this was the template for Obama's BC handiwork. The handwriting is exactly the same between posted Internet image and Obama's fake version — the placement of boxes

[122] Jim Hoft, Critics: *Obama's Latest Long-Form Birth Certificate Is a Fake ...Update: More Expert Opinion,* Gateway Pundit, April 27, 2011

and marks are in the exact same position, dates are where the modified clipping masks occur to adjust dates to fit for Obama, but the handwriting of dates match (except for the clipping mask changes). Even the Cert. number is only off by the last two digits (which…you guessed it… happens to be a clipping mask layer).

Finally, also wanted to make the point that regardless of where Obama is born, he's still not a Natural Born Citizen since both parents were not born on U.S. soil but I won't hold my breath waiting for the media to educate the public on this fact.

Enough belaboring the point. The Adobe BC, like the Certificates of Live Birth before, are forgeries, and no one in any law enforcement agency in the country is doing anything about it. All of the laws that were breached in the making of the Certificates of Live Birth were also breached in the making of this forgery. Mispersonation and fraud continue unabated, with no one to stop it. Such is the state of the union.

Obama prior to his election, initially caused to be produced the following forged Certification of Live Birth:

CERTIFICATION OF LIVE BIRTH

STATE OF HAWAII
HONOLULU

DEPARTMENT OF HEALTH
HAWAII U.S.A.

CERTIFICATE NO. ███████

CHILD'S NAME
BARACK HUSSEIN OBAMA II

DATE OF BIRTH
August 4, 1961

HOUR OF BIRTH
7:24 PM

SEX
MALE

CITY, TOWN OR LOCATION OF BIRTH
HONOLULU

ISLAND OF BIRTH
OAHU

COUNTY OF BIRTH
HONOLULU

MOTHER'S MAIDEN NAME
STANLEY ANN DUNHAM

MOTHER'S RACE
CAUCASIAN

FATHER'S NAME
BARACK HUSSEIN OBAMA

FATHER'S RACE
AFRICAN

DATE FILED BY REGISTRAR
August 8, 1961

ANY ALTERATIONS INVALIDATE THIS CERTIFICATE

This document has been determined to be a forgery by at least two internationally respected computer forensic auditors. The state of Hawaii has never validated this document as genuine. A preliminary audit is in order. There are some obvious things about this COLB. First, it provides on the bottom that "Any Alterations Invalidate This Certificate." A quick review indicates that the Certificate No. has been blacked out. It is therefore altered, and therefore invalid. Nonetheless, this is the document that Chris Matthews heralded as proof that Obama was born in Hawaii, and this is the document that Bill O'Reilly claimed was in his possession (he incorrectly called it a birth certificate).

There are other glaring deficiencies with this document as well, including the failure to evidence a raised embossed seal from the State of Hawaii (a clear indication of a faked document), and the signature of an Hawaiian

136

authority signing the seal. The document is not creased as a mailed document would be, and the "hard copy" was never produced – just an internet posting.

As we all know, if you get two different stories from a suspect, at least one of the stories is a lie. After the DNC and most of the news broadcasters had concluded that Obama was born in Hawaii based on this forgery, FactCheck.org released another internet image of a different document – a document that had a certificate number, claiming that this time, the Certification of Live Birth was genuine. However, this document, according to Dr. Ron Polland, PhD, was photo-shopped, printed on a transparency, and placed on security paper. This forgery was eventually replaced with a fraudulent document from the state of Hawaii, the publication of which was directed by co-conspirator Dr. Fukino.

Before reviewing this document, it is important to know that Barack Obama and William Ayers served together on the Philanthropic Woods Foundation Board, a foundation that funds FactCheck.org. The Daily Kos, Politico.com and FactCheck.org have worked together to attempt to obfuscate the entire birth certificate issue. As part of this obfuscation, a series of counterfeit Certifications of Live Birth, purportedly from the state of Hawaii, were created and promulgated on line, as if their placement on line would somehow constitute a legitimate release of the a vital record into the public arena. There are actually three COLBs. The first one is deficient on its face; the second one is the FactCheck forgery, and the third one is the cover document issued by Hawaii's Janice Fukino. Here is what FactCheck.org produced:

Magically, the black line over the Certificate Number is gone. This document is creased and it contains a state seal, although the seal and the whole document cannot be seen in the same photograph:

Above is a photograph of the so-called seal of Hawaii, which if forged is a significant element of a federal felony. The actual practice of Hawaii is to evidence a signature over the seal.

Two separate COLBs, and two separate images means at least one of them was a fraud, and between the two, document number one is a clear qualifier, although document number 2 has also been proven a fake. Take a look at 18 U.S.C. § 1028 one more time. The penalty for violating this statute with the intent to secure anything from the United States can be punishable with up to fifteen years in prison.

False Personation of Officer or Employee of the United States.

18 U.S.C. § 912 - False Personation of Officer or Employee of the United States. Whoever falsely assumes or pretends to be an officer or employee acting under the authority of the United States or any department, agency or officer thereof, and acts as such, or in such pretended character demands or obtains any money, paper, document, or thing of value, shall be fined under this title or imprisoned not more than three years, or both.

Being the son of a foreign national, Obama cannot be a natural born citizen under Article II, Section 1 of the US Constitution. He has therefore assumed the presidency fraudulently in order to obtain money and other things of value. Convictions have been upheld under this Federal Statute in several cases.[123]

Conspiracy to Commit Offense to Defraud the United States

---

[123] *U.S. v. Lepowitch*, 63 S.Ct. 914; *Lamar v. U.S.,* 36 S.Ct. 535

18 U.S.C. 371. Conspiracy to Commit Offense to Defraud the United States. If two or more persons conspire either to commit any offense against the United States, or to defraud the United States, or any agency thereof in any manner or for any purpose, and one or more of such persons do any act to effect the object of the conspiracy, each shall be fined under this title or imprisoned not more than five years, or both. If, however, the offense, the commission of which is the object of the conspiracy, is a misdemeanor only, the punishment for such conspiracy shall not exceed the maximum punishment provided for such misdemeanor.

This offense would include Obama and each and every person, who, having knowledge that Obama had a foreign born father, and yet made claims in support of Obama's charge that he was eligible would be liable under this statute

False Statement in Application and Use of Passport.

18 U.S.C. 1542 - False Statement in Application and Use of Passport.

"Whoever willfully and knowingly makes any false statement in an application for passport with intent to induce or secure the issuance of a passport under the authority of the United States, either for his own use or the use of another, contrary to the laws regulating the issuance of passports or the rules prescribed pursuant to such laws; or

"Whoever willfully and knowingly uses or attempts to use, or furnishes to another for use any passport the issue of which was secured in any way by reason of any false statement—Shall be fined under this title, imprisoned not more than 25 years (if the offense was committed to facilitate an act of international terrorism (as defined in section 2331 of this title)), 20 years (if the offense was committed to facilitate a drug trafficking crime (as defined in section 929 (a) of this title)), 10 years (in the case of the first or second such offense, if the offense was not committed to facilitate such an act of international terrorism or a drug trafficking crime), or 15 years (in the case of any other offense), or both."

Obama has posted his new passport online.[124] To obtain a passport lawfully, you must establish your American citizenship by supplying one of the following with your passport application, according to the State Department: 1A previously issued, undamaged U.S. Passport; 2) a Consular report of birth abroad or a certification of birth; 3) a Naturalization Certificate; 4) A Certificate of Citizenship; or 5) A Certified birth certificate issued by the city, county or state.

Although it is widely believed that the COLBs that are shown above are fraudulent, no court has allowed a jury to consider the certificate on the merits, denying standing to every single person who has brought suit. So, if the President tendered his falsified COLB to a bureaucrat to obtain his passport – particularly if that person was an ardent Obama supporter, it is unlikely the reviewer would question its authenticity.

The USJF analysis said: "To obtain a U.S. passport one must show a valid birth certificate or some other form of identification showing U.S. citizenship. Barack Obama would have to have furnished some sort of birth certificate or other document showing he is a citizen. Of course, even

---

[124] http://209.157.64.201/focus/f-news/2575721/posts

if he was not a natural born citizen, he could show naturalization or some other citizenship papers. However, if these documents are spurious, then he would be guilty pursuant to the first paragraph, and to then use his illegally obtained passport, he would also be guilty under the second paragraph as well."

False Personation of Citizen of the United States (18 U.S.C. 911).

It states: "Whoever falsely and willfully represents himself to be a citizen of the United States shall be fined under this title or imprisoned not more than three years, or both."

The analysis said: "If Mr. Obama is not a natural born citizen, then he must have other proof of United States citizenship. If he has neither of these, then as acting head of state he is holding himself out to be a citizen of the United States, and is therefore liable under this section as well."

Perjury (18 U.S.C. 1621).

It states: "Whoever—(1) having taken an oath before a competent tribunal, officer, or person, in any case in which a law of the United States authorizes an oath to be administered, that he will testify, declare, depose, or certify truly, or that any written testimony, declaration, deposition, or certificate by him subscribed, is true, willfully and contrary to such oath states or subscribes any material matter which he does not believe to be true; or

"(2) in any declaration, certificate, verification, or statement under penalty of perjury as permitted under section 1746 of title 28, United States Code, willfully subscribes as true any material matter which he does not believe to be true; is guilty of perjury and shall, except as otherwise expressly provided by law, be fined under this title or imprisoned not more than five years, or both. This section is applicable whether the statement or subscription is made within or without the United States."

The USJF analysis said: "Mr. Obama has taken the oath of office of POTUS, in front of Chief Justice of the U.S. Supreme Court, John Roberts, in which he promises to 'defend the Constitution'. As an illegal alien, or even a non-natural born citizen, he would be acting as an ineligible president. Furthermore, as an attorney, and a former professor of constitutional law, Barack Obama would have full knowledge of the requirements for an eligible candidate for the office of POTUS. This shows that he has willfully stated that he will and is acting contrary to his presidential oath."

The USJF document showed that all of the charges require a specific intent.

"Mr. Obama knows, or at least should know, the place of his birth and the status of his citizenship, as all, or nearly all, adults in the world do. He has, therefore, willfully and knowingly made repeated false claims as to his citizenship, and this makes him absolutely liable for the above mentioned crimes," the analysis said.

The organization's earlier research, now included in its appeal documentation, found that in 1968, the Peace and Freedom Party submitted the name of Eldridge Cleaver as a qualified candidate for president of the United States.

The then-California Secretary of State, Frank Jordan, found that, according to Mr. Cleaver's birth certificate, he was only 34 years old, one year shy of the 35 years of age needed to be on the ballot as a candidate for president. Jordan, using his administrative powers, threw him off the ballot.

The other is a court precedent in which the governor of North Dakota was removed from office after the state Supreme Court determined he did not meet the state constitution's eligibility requirements.

"Even though Obama was elected to this office, this ineligibility constitutes a legal disability for the office of president of the United States," the USJF brief states. "In *'State ex rel. Sathre v. Moodie*,' after Thomas H. Moodie was duly elected to the office of governor of the state of North Dakota, it was discovered that Thomas H. Moodie was not eligible for the position of governor, as he had not resided in the state for a requisite five years before running for office, and, because of that ineligibility, he was removed from office and replaced by the lieutenant governor," the brief explains.

North Dakota's historical archives document the case. The Democrat was nominated by his party for governor in 1934 and beat his Republican opponent, Lydia Langer.

"As soon as the election was over, there was talk of impeachment, but no charges were filed," the state's archives report. "After Moodie's inauguration on January 7, 1935, it was revealed that he had voted in a 1932 municipal election in Minnesota. In order to be eligible for governor, an individual has to have lived in the state for five consecutive years before the election. The State Supreme Court determined that Governor Moodie was ineligible to serve, and he was removed from office on February 16, 1935," the state reports.

The president's lawyers in many of the cases have said, and judges have agreed so far, that the courts simply don't have jurisdiction over a question of eligibility because of the Constitution's provision that president's must be removed by impeachment, which rests with Congress.

In one case, the president's lawyers argued, "The Constitution's commitment to the Electoral College of the responsibility to select the president includes the authority to decide whether a presidential candidate is qualified for office."

"The examination of a candidate's qualifications is an integral component of the electors' decision-making process. The Constitution also provides that, after the Electoral College has voted, further review of a presidential candidate's eligibility for office, to the extent such review is required, rests with Congress," the president's lawyers argued.

The Constitution, Article 2, Section 1, states, "No Person except a natural born Citizen, or a Citizen of the United States, at the time of the Adoption of this Constitution, shall be eligible to the Office of President."

However, none of the cases filed to date has been successful in reaching the plateau of legal discovery, so that information about Obama's birth could be obtained.

Besides Obama's actual birth documentation, the still-concealed documentation for him includes kindergarten records, Punahou school records, Occidental College records, Columbia University records, Columbia thesis, Harvard Law School records, Harvard Law Review articles, scholarly articles from the University of Chicago, passport, medical records, his files from his years as an Illinois state senator, his Illinois State Bar Association records, any baptism records, and his adoption records.

Another significant factor is the estimated $1.7 million Obama has spent on court cases to prevent any of the documentation of his life to be revealed to the public.

The "certification of live birth" posted online and widely touted as "Obama's birth certificate" is not a document, but an *image*, and does not in any way prove he was born in Hawaii, since the same "short-form" document is easily obtainable for children not born in Hawaii. The true "long-form" birth certificate – which includes information such as the name of the birth hospital and attending physician – is the only document that can prove Obama was born in Hawaii, but to date he has not permitted its release for public or press scrutiny.

Oddly, though congressional hearings were held to determine whether Sen. John McCain was constitutionally eligible to be president as a "natural born citizen," no controlling legal authority ever sought to verify Obama's claim to a Hawaiian birth.

Chapter Seven

Criminal Conspiracy to Defraud

18 U.S.C. § 371. Conspiracy to commit offense or to defraud United States:

If two or more persons conspire either to commit any offense against the United States, or to defraud the United States, or any agency thereof in any manner or for any purpose, and one or more of such persons do any act to effect the object of the conspiracy, each shall be fined under this title or imprisoned not more than five years, or both.

If, however, the offense, the commission of which is the object of the conspiracy, is a misdemeanor only, the punishment for such conspiracy shall not exceed the maximum punishment provided for such misdemeanor.

This is my kind of statute – something that has some teeth in it. A "conspiracy" is defined as the agreement between two or more persons to commit a crime or to perpetrate an illegal act. The end may be legal, but the planned means are illegal. For example, two persons making a plan to steal bread from a supermarket (illegal) to donate to a local food bank (legal) would be guilty of conspiracy. While intent is key in any federal conspiracy case, only "general intent" to violate the law is necessary; proof of the defendants' specific intent to violate the law is not needed, only an agreement to engage in an illegal act.

U.S.C. Title 18, Chapter 19 prohibits conspiracies to defraud the United States, conspiracies to impede or injure an officer, and conspiracies to commit violent crimes. However, conspiracy is prohibited in several other federal statutes. It is important to note that an actual crime is not necessary to prosecute a conspiracy case – only the stated intent to break the law. This means that even if the ultimate crime was not committed, the conspirators can be prosecuted under federal law. However, most states have laws that prevent conspiracy charges to be pressed if no actions were taken to actually carry out the conspiracy. This prevents people from effectively being prosecuted for having thoughts of breaking the law. While this caveat does prevent some conspiracy cases from going to court, it does not reduce the severity of a conspiracy claim. In many cases, conspiracy to commit a crime such as murder is regarded as a crime as severe as murder itself.

Conspiracy crimes can include conspiracy to engage in criminal activity such as money laundering, conspiracy to violate federal laws, or conspiracy to manufacture drugs or weapons. The federal maximum penalty for conspiracy is five years in prison; however, this may be compounded by other state and federal violations. Depending on the nature of the conspiracy, it may be prosecuted by different entities including the FBI, Department of Justice, or state and local law agencies.[125]

So what are the nuts and bolts of the conspiracy to violate 18 U.S.C. § 1002 - Fraud and False Statements - Possession of false papers to defraud United States?

Start with the fraudulent Certificate of Live Birth that first appeared on the Daily Kos and then again on Fightthesmears.com – the scanned image with the certificate number blacked out (making it invalid on its

---

[125] Criminal Law: Criminal Conspiracy - Federal Crimes & Consequences
http://criminal-law.freeadvice.com/criminal-law/criminal-conspiracy.htm

face). There have been many analyses proving this to be a forgery created in Microsoft's Photoshop. There is further evidence:

According to Atlas Shrugs, Jay McKinnon, a self-described Department of Homeland Security-trained document specialist, "implicated himself in the production of fake Hawaii birth certificate images similar to the one *endorsed as genuine* [italics added] by the Barack Obama campaign, and appearing on the same Daily Kos blog entry where the supposedly authentic document appears."

According to Altas Shrugs, "the evidence of forgery and manipulation of images of official documents, triggered by Israel Insider's revelation of the collection of Hawaii birth certificate images on the Photobucket site and the diligent detective work of independent investigative journalists (led by JimJ and Texas Darling) and imaging professionals such as Polarik in the three weeks since the publication of the images, implicate The Daily Kos, a "progressive" blog site, and the Obama campaign's "Fight the Smears" website, in misleading the public with official-looking but manipulated document images of doubtful provenance. Moreover, the blog and the campaign have been negligent in allowing the promotion of obviously forged and fake official documents together with the purported image of Obama's birth certificate."[126]   Well said.

Now let us consider the follow-up, second Certificate of Live Birth published on FactCheck.org's site and vouched for by Jess Henig and Joe Miller.   This

_____

[126] *omg -- BLOGGER ADMITS TO Obama Birth Certificate Forgery,* Altas Shrugs, July 4, 2008
http://atlasshrugs2000.typepad.com/atlas_shrugs/2008/07/omg----blogger.html

document has a certificate number and a pressed seal. Instead of being a plain Photoshop image, this one is photographed as an actual document (the document has otherwise not been released – only the photos of the document). In short, this image is a different image than the first. At least one of these is therefore a criminal forgery; however, the evidence will show that in fact, both of these are forgeries.

Here is the confession of Chanise Foxx:

"My name is Chanise Foxx. I work at an office supply store in Kenwood, IL. After nearly 3 years of silence and death threats to me and my family to stay quiet, I am compelled to come forward and tell the world my secret.

"I helped Obama campaign staffer Divorah Adler create a fake birth certificate for use in the famous Fact Check story to prove the world of Obama's birth in the 2008 election. Divorah approached me in early 2007 and held onto the birth certificate until she released it in August 2008.

"As I've been making fake IDs part-time for local college students for about eight years now, faking a birth certificate was actually quite easy. Our first step was to get our hands on someone else's birth certificate from Hawaii. We then created the stationary to match.

"Next, we had to create an embossed stamp and rubber signature stamp for Hawaiian officials. With the help of a high-resolution scanner at the store, I did most of my work at night when the place was vacant..."[127]

Okay, so we have a confession that the document was forged. We also have prima facie evidence that the document was forged. Janice Okubo, the Director of Hawaii's Department of Health, confirmed on February 23,

---

[127]   http://gatewaypundit.rightnetwork.com/2010/03/birther-article-at-free-republic-shuts-down-website/

2010 that the "Date filed by the State Registrar" is the date a record was received, and the date a file number is placed on a document such as a Certificate of Live Birth. There are Certificates of Live Birth issued to the Nordykes on August 11 which have numbers lower than Obama's, which was supposedly issued on August 8. There are no pre-numbered certificates. A certificate given a certificate number on Aug 8th (Obama's Factcheck COLB) would not be given a later number than a certificate given a number on Aug 11th. There is therefore no way that both the date filed and the certificate number can be correct on the Factcheck COLB. The COLB is thus proven to be a forgery on its face.[128]

Pursuant to this confession, we now have an interesting group of conspirators: The editorial staff at the Daily Kos, the staff at Fightthesmears.com and their bosses in the Obama campaign reaching all the way to Obama himself, Jay McKinnon, the Photo-shopper, Chanise Foxx, the forger, Divorah Adler, the actual perpetrator of the second forgery, acting in her capacity as an Obama campaign staffer, and of course, her boss, Barack Obama, who has principal liability for his agent under the doctrine of *respondeat superior*. Of course, he could have broken the conspiracy had he disavowed it and came forward to expose those who engaged in the conspiracy; but he didn't.

The issue of Obama's birth was given substantial cover and an air of authenticity where his revised Certificate of Live Birth vouched for by FactCheck.org. The claim of authenticity was made by two FactCheck.org employees Jess Henig and Joe Miller, pictured below. These two "got a chance to spend some time with the 'birth

[128]Butterdezillion, *DOH indirectly confirms: Factcheck COLB date filed and certificate number impossible*, February 23, 2010
http://www.freerepublic.com/focus/bloggers/2457491/posts?page

certificate,'" and they went on to "attest to the fact that it is real and three-dimensional and resides at the Obama headquarters in Chicago." What they claim they saw – a birth certificate – is not what they photographed.

The attempt to declare a Certification of Live Birth to be a Birth Certificate alone is a fraudulent and false statement. The failure to actually release the document to forensic auditors who could make an objective analysis is also fraudulent and insufficient to establish a vital record. Finally, the two FactCheck.org employees who were "granted access" to Obama's bogus Certification of Live Birth (COLB) became co-conspirators under federal law, if in fact the Certification of Live Birth they declared to be "genuine" is not. Neither Henig nor Miller are professional document examiners or forensic experts. They appear in their photos to be leftist academics, and the credentials support such a conclusion. Joe Miller is a Ph. D. in Political Philosophy. One wonders which philosophy he prefers. Henig has an M.A. in English Literature. Miller took the photographs, Henig wrote the claims.

FactCheck.org is a partisan organization and what LBG1 calls "part and parcel of the Annenberg

Foundation.[129] In 1995 Obama was appointed Board Chairman and President of the Annenberg Chicago Challenge, a "branch of the Annenberg Foundation". William Ayers, the former leader of the domestic terrorist group known as the Weathermen. The Weathermen was a small band of extreme leftists that conducted a bombing campaign against targets such as police headquarters, prisons and courthouses for three years, eventually concluding with the deaths of two police officers in 1981, when members of the Weathermen and Black Liberation Army stole $1 million from an armored car. It was their last action.[130]

Charges against Ayers were dropped after the FBI was accused of using illegal wiretaps. Ayers wrote in his 2001 book *Fugitive Days*, that he regretted that his group "didn't do enough" back then in regards to the almost 30 plus bombings his group took credit for. Ayers later became a professor in Chicago and the founder of the Chicago Annenberg Challenge (the CAC), an offshoot of the Annenberg Foundation.

Ayers co-chaired the Chicago Annenberg "Collaborative," which set education policy for the "Challenge." Obama was "authorized to delegate to the

---

[129] LBG1, *Obama, Bill Ayers, and FactCheck.Org: All Have Ties To Annenberg Foundation*, DBKB Reports, October 6, 2008; http://deathby1000papercuts.com/2008/10/obama-bill-ayers-and-factcheckorg-all-have-ties-to-annenberg-foundation/

[130] Baxter, Sarah, *'Terrorist' link puts Barack Obama under fire, Another dubious contact is dogging the Democrat hopeful,* The Sunday Times, April 13, 2008.
http://www.timesonline.co.uk/tol/news/world/us_and_americas/us_elections/article3736043.ece

Collaborative the development of collaborative projects and programs." Bill Ayers sat on the same board as Obama as an "ex officio member."

Obama and Ayers sat together on the board's Governance Committee, and Ayers and Obama were "part of a group of four instructed to draft the bylaws that would govern CAC." As Board Chair, Obama authorized the funding for Ayers educational projects, as well as projects of Ayers' "radical" friends. For instance, they "guided" funds to the Association of Community Organizations for Reform Now (ACORN).[131]

Factcheck.org was the organization chosen by the Obama campaign as the expert of whether Obama's birth certificate, which purported to prove that he's a citizen of the United States, was authentic. The parties joined to defraud the United States, the American people, the various Secretaries of State, the Electors, and the fifty states that put this imposter on the ballot.[132]

---

[131] Kurtz, Stanley, *Obama's Challenge, The campaign speaks to "Radicalism."* National Review Online, September 23, 2008. http://www.nationalreview.com/articles/225752/obamas-challenge/stanley-kurtz

[132] *Obama, Bill Ayers, and FactCheck.Org: All Have Ties To Annenberg Foundation, op. cit.*

Chapter Eight

Conspiracy to commit Federal Election Fraud

Given the facts of the 2008 election, it is now necessary to determine if Obama was part and parcel of the federal election laws prohibiting the intimidation of voters and the conspiracy to inhibit the civil right of voting as also prohibited by federal law. Consider 18 U.S.C. § 594. Intimidation of voters:

> *Whoever intimidates, threatens, coerces, or attempts to intimidate, threaten, or coerce, any other person for the purpose of interfering with the right of such other person to vote or to vote as he may choose, or of causing such other person to vote for, or not to vote for, any candidate for the office of President, Vice President, Presidential elector, Member of the Senate, Member of the House of Representatives, Delegate from the District of Columbia, or Resident Commissioner, at any election held solely or in part for the purpose of electing such candidate, shall be fined under this title or imprisoned not more than one year, or both.*

The federal crime of intimidation of voters is pretty clear. So are the facts surrounding the dismissal of charges against King Samir Shabazz. After a federal judge ordered default judgments against the New Black Panthers when party members refused to appear in court, the Obama administration nonetheless refused to prosecute the Panthers. According to Christian Adams, a former DOJ attorney, *the Obama administration* ordered the DOJ not to pursue voting-rights cases against black people, even though the DOJ trial team had won its case. The case was dismissed on May 15, 2009.[133]

For those who say it is about "race" with Obama, this action by the Obama Administration and US Attorney General Eric "We are a nation of cowards" Holder dismisses charges against Philadelphia Black Panthers member who engaged in threats and intimidation during the November 2008 Presidential election even though there were multiple eye witnesses and a videotape of the entire incident.[134]

Shabazz, who is one of the leaders of Philadelphia's New Black Panther Party, was filmed on Election Day 2008 with Jerry Jackson, wearing paramilitary uniforms, carrying nightsticks and blocking a doorway to a polling location to intimidate voters. A witness reported that Shabazz was brandishing a nightstick to threaten voters just 15 feet outside a Philadelphia polling location, which was, for purposes of federal law, alongside a highway.

"As I walked up, they closed ranks, next to each other," the witness told Fox News at the time. "So I walked directly in between them, went inside and found the poll watchers. They said they'd been here for about an hour. And they told us not to come outside because a black man is going to win this election no matter what."

---

[133] Schilling, Chelsea, *'Want freedom? Kill some crackers!' New Black Panther Obama DOJ refused to prosecute: 'I hate white people – all of them!'* WND TV, July 7, 2010.

[134] Sinclair, Larry, *Eric Holder / Obama refuses to prosecute 2 Black Guys with a nightclub,* The Obambi.com Blog May 30, 2009; http://obambi.wordpress.com/2009/05/30/eric-holder-obama-refuses-to-prosecute-2-black-guys-with-a-nightclub/

He said the man with a nightstick told him, "'We're tired of white supremacy,' and he starts tapping the nightstick in his hand. The men also hurled racial epithets such as "white devil" and "cracker" and told voters they should prepare to be "ruled by the black man." The two Black Panthers called a Republican poll worker a "race traitor" and told him there would be "hell to pay."[135] All of these facts were videotaped, and the defendants did not appear in court when summoned. A default judgment was entered and a conviction was certain.

Even under these circumstances, the Obama administration caused Eric Holder and the DOJ to dismiss the charges, and to walk away from all criminal sanctions.

18 U.S.C. § 241. Conspiracy against rights

If two or more persons conspire to injure, oppress, threaten, or intimidate any person in any State, Territory, Commonwealth, Possession, or District in the free exercise or enjoyment of any right or privilege secured to him by the Constitution or laws of the United States, or because of his having so exercised the same; or

If two or more persons go in disguise on the highway, or on the premises of another, with intent to prevent or hinder his free exercise or enjoyment of any right or privilege so secured—
They shall be fined under this title or imprisoned not more than ten years, or both; and if death results from the acts committed in violation of this section or if such acts include kidnapping or an attempt to kidnap, aggravated sexual abuse or an attempt to commit aggravated sexual abuse, or an attempt to kill, they shall be fined under this title or

---

[135] *'Want freedom? Kill some crackers!' New Black Panther Obama DOJ refused to prosecute: 'I hate white people – all of them!'*

imprisoned for any term of years or for life, or both, or may be sentenced to death.

Remember, a "conspiracy" is defined as the agreement between two or more persons to commit a crime or to perpetrate an illegal act. The end may be legal, but the planned means are illegal. An ongoing conspiracy can be joined, if the newly arrived person agrees that the illegal act should continue.

When you review the statement of the DOJ attorney who quit his job as a result of this decision, you will see that he makes it clear that the decision not to prosecute the New Black Panther Party members came directly from the Obama administration, who indicated there would not be any prosecution of Black political activists.

Some prosecutors would argue that the Obama administration has in fact joined the conspiracy to commit the crime of voter intimidation prohibited under the applicable federal statute, and when married with the conspiracy to deprive people of rights along the highway, the possibility of ten years in prison is on the table.

18 U.S.C. § 608. Absent uniformed services voters and overseas voters

(a) Whoever knowingly deprives or attempts to deprive any person of a right under the Uniformed and Overseas Citizens Absentee Voting Act shall be fined in accordance with this title or imprisoned not more than five years, or both.

(b) Whoever knowingly gives false information for the purpose of establishing the eligibility of any person to register or vote under the Uniformed and Overseas Citizens Absentee Voting Act, or pays or offers to pay, or accepts payment for registering or voting under such Act shall be

158

fined in accordance with this title or imprisoned not more than five years, or both

Those who are certain that they will not receive the votes of those men and women who are deployed in the service of the United States throughout the world have seen fit to delay the delivery of ballots to the troops to ensure that their votes cannot be received in time to have an effect on the election.

In the 2008 election, 98,000 military ballots of deployed Americans were mailed back to the U.S. but not counted.[136] This occurred even though the top commander of U.S. forces in Afghanistan, Maj. Gen. Jeffrey Schloesser, said the effort made was "the most significant drive probably in our nation's history" to make sure deployed Soldiers could vote. The U.S. military made a big push to help Soldiers request ballots, advertised the process with TV commercials, posters and ballot drives outside dining halls and recreations centers.

There are several federal statutes that address voter fraud, and there are essentially four types of federal election fraud. Federal statutes exist to combat the following:

- Schemes to purposely register voters who either do not exist, or who are known by the perpetrator to be ineligible to vote under applicable state law.
- Schemes to cast, record or fraudulently tabulate votes for voters who do not participate in the voting act at all. This includes such activities as schemes

---

[136] Thorton, Maggie M., *Military Votes Not Counted 98,000 Lost Military Ballots,* Truth on Target, October 27, 2010
http://truthontarget.blogspot.com/2010/10/military-votes-not-counted-98000-lost.html
http://military.rightpundits.com/2009/05/13/military-votes-not-counted-98000-lost-military-ballots/

by poll managers to stuff ballot boxes, schemes to impersonate nonvoting individuals either at the polls or via absent voter ballot, and schemes by vote canvassers to alter vote tallies.

- Schemes to corrupt the voting act of voters who do participate in the voting act to a limited extent. These include such things as schemes to assist voters in such a manner that the voter does not knowingly consent to electoral preferences that are placed on the ballot, schemes to pay voters for voting, schemes to intimidate voters through physical or economic means, schemes to cast multiple ballots, and schemes to induce voters to validate ballot documents (usually absentee ballots) by misrepresenting what the document is.

- Schemes to knowingly prevent qualified voters from voting. These include such activities as destroying voter registrations or ballots, preventing people known to be qualified to vote from doing so, and physically disrupting order within open polling locations.

Federal prosecution becomes possible and even advisable when there is a federal effect, when there is a violation of civil rights, when the Department of Justice becomes the prosecutor of last resort, or where there is a link to other federal crimes.

Federal prosecutors should step in when the objective of the conduct is to corrupt the outcome of a federal elective contest, or where the consequential effect of the corrupt conduct impacts upon the vote count for federal office.[137] When the object of the scheme is to discriminate against racial, ethnic or language minority groups, the

---

[137] *Anderson v. United States*, 411 U.S. 211 (1974).

voting rights of which have been specifically protected by federal statues such as the Voting Rights Act, 42 U.S.C. §1973 et seq., it is also proper for federal prosecutors to act.

Federalization is required in order to redress longstanding patterns of electoral fraud, either at the request of state or local authorities, or in the face of longstanding inaction by state authorities who appear to be unwilling or unable to respond under local law. Most state authorities are partisan operatives whose main function is to provide election results, notwithstanding the vote as actually cast. In addition, the federal authorities are now working with state and local authorities to ensure voter fraud. As Stalin said: "It is enough that the people know there was an election. The people who cast the votes decide nothing. The people who count the votes decide everything."[138]

Schemes by polling officers to violate their duty under state law to safeguard the integrity of the election process through purposefully allowing void ballots to be cast (stuffed) in the ballot box, or by intentionally rendering fraudulent vote tallies, can be prosecuted as civil rights violations under 18 U.S.C. 241 and 242.[139] These two statutes prohibit, among many other things, intentional denigration by public officers acting under color of law of the one-person-one-vote principle of the Equal Protection clause set forth in the Fifth and Fourteenth Amendments of the Constitution. Schemes to manipulate voting equipment and to stuff ballot boxes normally require physical access to voting equipment that can only be accessed by the

---

[138] http://wwwbrainyquote.com/quotes/authors/j/joseph_stalin.html#ixzz18v6M5L5C

[139] *U.S. v. Olinger,* 759 F.2d 1293 (7th Cir. 1985)

authority granted to them under state law, which satisfies the state actor jurisdictional requirement.

Making payment to register to vote is a violation of 42 U.S.C. §19731 (c), and schemes to stimulate or reward voter registration by offering or giving voters things of monetary value are conspiracies to violate the same act. In the case where the voter registers for both the state and the federal election, such a unified registration provides a sufficient federal nexus to allow the federal criminal statutes to attach.[140] Schemes to engage in fraudulent voter registration by providing election officials false information about a voter's eligibility is also a violation of the federal law and can result in federal prosecution, although there are limitations in nonfederal elections.

Obama's problems become more manifest when you consider the false registration information clause of 42 U.S.C. §19731(c). This act declares it to be a federal crime to provide false information concerning your name, address or period of residence in the voting district. Schemes to obtain and cast ballots that are materially defective in nonfederal elections can still be prosecuted under 18 U.S.C. §1341,[141] when the materially defective ballot amounts to fraud. Federal jurisdiction attaches if the mails are used to distribute the defective ballot, the mail being a federal instrumentality.

The mail fraud statute is used appropriately in election cases when the voter fraud is for the purpose of 1) securing a salary or valuable emoluments for a specific

---

[140] *United States v. Cianciulli,* 482 F.Supp. 585 (E.D. Pa. 1979)

[141] *McNally v. United States,* 483 U.S. 350 (1987)

candidate;[142] and 2) causing a local election jurisdiction to spend money to run an election that the defendants knew would produce a defective result.[143]

The Travel Act, 18 U.S.C. §1951, is a federal statute that makes it a felony to travel across state lines or to mail items intrastate in aid of activity that amounts to bribery under the law of one or more of the states involved in the interstate travel. Schemes to pay voters can be prosecuted under this statute in those states where paying voters is treated as a bribery offense. This activity can be prosecuted under Section 1951. Most vote buying schemes do not involve inter-state travel. However, they do often rely on the absentee voting process, and use the U.S. Mail. Thus the availability of the Travel Act allows for the federalization of vote buying schemes using the absentee balloting process.

Federal law also criminalizes election fraud when a federal candidate is on the ballot. 42 U.S.C. §1973i (c) prohibits specific types of voter fraud in an election where federal candidates are on the ballot. Most schemes work to provide election officials with false information concerning the voters' names, addresses, or their period of residence in the election district in order to qualify to vote, or schemes to pay voters to vote in a certain way. Under federal law, paying for a vote is criminalized if the payment was intended to influence the voter merely to participate in the

---

[142] *United States v. Cranberry,* 908 F.2d 278 (6th Cir. 1990); *United States v. Doherty,* 867 F.2d 47, 54-57 (1st Cir. 1989); *Ingber v. Enzor,* 644 F.Supp. 814, 815-816, aff'd 841 F.2d 450 (2d Cir. 1988)

[143] *United States v. DeFries,* 43 F.3d. 707 (D.C. Cir. 1995)

election. It does not require that the voter be paid to vote for federal candidates, or for any specific candidate.[144]

18 U.S.C. §597 prohibits making expenditures for the specific purpose of stimulating voters to cast ballots for candidates seeking the federal offices of Senator, Congressman or President. This statute requires specific intent to affect a specific election.

42 U.S.C. 1973i (e) prohibits voting more than once in elections where federal candidates are on the ballot. 42 U.S.C. §1973gg-10(2) prohibits furnishing any significantly false information to an election officer for the purpose of voting in a federal election. Whether a statement is significantly false is determined by whether its importance to voter eligibility under the law of the state in which the vote was tendered. 18 U.S.C. 594 prohibits intimidating voters for the specific purpose of inducing them to cast ballots for one or more federal officers (i.e. Senators, Congressman, and Presidents). 42 U.S.C. §1973gg-10(l) prohibits voter intimidation in any election where federal candidates are on the ballot regardless of the objective of the defendant to influence specific election contests. Under Section 594, *intimidation* is defined as actual duress caused by physical or economic threats.

Finally, 18 U.S.C. §608 prohibits all the above forms of election fraud when they occur in connection with votes cast by Americans living abroad under the provisions of the Uniformed and Overseas Citizens Absentee Voting Act, which in the principle means by which American citizens living abroad vote by absentee ballot.

---

[144] *United States v. Bowman,* 636 F.2d 1003 (5th/ll Cirs 1981); *Dansereau v. Ulmer,* (Ak. S.Ct. 1995)

Obama and ACORN

ACORN is an acronym for the Association of Community Organizations for Reform. They are staffed with ardent "communityists" or in the vernacular, "communists." This group has engaged in numerous instances of election fraud in multiple states, which will be discussed below. First, let's see if there is a conspiratorial relationship between Obama and this group.

According to the Los Angeles Times, Obama forged a path to the door of ACORN as a Chicago Community Organizer (a "Communityist") when he was working with the Developing Communities Project and Project Vote!. Supposedly, this occurred sometime in 1986, in between his Columbia graduation, just before his 26th birthday, and before his later trip(s) to Pakistan to visit his mother in Lahore.[145] As a Communityist with a stellar communist pedigree, Obama's duties were to organize demonstrations. National Review Online noted, "Part of Obama's work, it would appear, was to organize demonstrations, much in the mold of radical groups like ACORN."[146]

The Chicago leader of ACORN, Madeline Talbott, was duly impressed. She invited Obama to train her staff. Talbott was the one who led the Chicago chapter of ACORN to intimidate banks into making high-risk "subprime" loans to low-credit customers in Chicago. At one point, Talbott and ACORN protesters broke into a meeting of the Chicago City Council to demand a "living wage"

---

[145] Tayler, Letta; Herbert, Kieth, *Obama Forged Path As Chicago Community Organizer,* Los Angeles Times, March 2, 2008

[146] *Id.*

law, shouting and screaming as she was arrested for riot and disorderly conduct.

Although Project Vote! was registered as a 501(c)(3) tax exempt non-profit organization whose tax exempt status is dependent upon them not engaging in political activities, Project Vote! hired ACORN to run its voter registration drives, and all of its board members were either members or staff of ACORN.[147]

John Lund at the Wall Street Journal documented that Obama's ties to ACORN "are extensive." Lund calls Project Vote! an ACORN "partner" and notes that Obama was then selected as a top trainer for ACORN's Chicago conferences. It was Obama that represented ACORN in a key case where the Motor Voter Act was found to be constitutional. As a result of this case, ACORN workers have been able to flood election offices with bogus voter registrations which of course have led to bogus elections nationwide.[148]

By 2004, ACORN had a "Muscle for Money" program in full swing, where ACORN intimidated business into payment "protection" money in the form of grants. These programs are often known to law enforcement as extortion schemes. An ACORN operative that Lund refers to as "Ms. MonCrief" testified that in November 2007 a Project Vote! director Karyn Gillette told her that the Obama campaign had given them their donor lists. The key portion of this testimony includes the information that

---

[147] Strom, Stephanie, *Acorn Report Raises Issues of Legality,* October 21, 2008, The New York Times

[148] Lund, John, *An Acorn Whistleblower Testifies in Court: The group's ties to Obama are extensive, Wall Street Journal,* October 30, 2008
http://online.wsj.com/article/SB122533169940482893.html

certain donors who had maxed out were targeted for additional funding for voter registrations efforts. Project Vote! also received copies of donor lists from other Democratic campaigns as well as the 2004 DNC donor lists.

Another witness, according to Lund, was Gregory Hall, a former Acorn employee. Hall apparently was told on his very first day in 2006 to engage in deceptive fund-raising tactics. Mr. Hall has founded a group called Speaking Truth to Power to push for a full airing of ACORN's problems.[149] This is the group Obama represented as counsel in their suit against the state of Illinois to force it to implement the 1993 Motor Voter Law. Motor voter, which was the first law passed by the Clinton administration, mandated a nationwide postcard voter registration system in order to make voter registration easier. ACORN has been using these same motor voter cards to flood election offices with fraudulent registrations. The challenge to the law was based on the extent to which Federal law can mandate a state to take action regarding election law, which the Constitution of the United States delegates to the state. The court upheld the law as constitutional, and motor voter was implemented in Illinois in 2005.

It appears as though Obama had joined the conspiracy to engage in extortion, voter fraud, and wide ranging violations of federal election laws early on after leaving Harvard, ultimately riding the wave of stuffed ballots into the White House. Given the 16 years it took to develop, it really begs the question whether he was actually elected by the popular vote.

---

[149] *Id*

Woods Foundation

In 1993 Obama joined the board of the Woods Fund with Bill Ayres, where he remained until 2002. During his tenure there, he voted to invest $1 million into the Neighborhood Rejuvenation Partners, L.P., an organization partly controlled by convicted felon Tony Rezko. However, of interest here is Obama's continuous support of the Arab American Action Network, a militant anti-Israeli, Palestinian group. Abunimah, a co-founder of AAAN, also ran the Electronic Intifada, a website with substantial accusations against the so-called "apartheid state of Israel."

Obama also approved of grants to ACORN of $45,000 (2000), $30,000 (2001), $45,000 (2001), $30,000 (2002) and $40,000 (2002) from the Woods Fund.[150] Obama then went on to represent ACORN as their counsel in the Buycks-Roberson v. Citibank Federal Savings Bank case, where ACORN sued Citibank to force them to make more loans to marginally qualified African-American applicants in a race neutral way. Plaintiffs filed their class action lawsuit on July 6, 1994, alleging that Citibank had engaged in redlining practices in the Chicago metropolitan area in violation of the Equal Credit Opportunity Act (ECOA), 15 U.S.C. 1691; the Fair Housing Act, 42 U.S.C. 3601-3619; the Thirteenth Amendment to the U.S. Constitution; and 42 U.S.C. 1981, 1982. The Plaintiffs alleged that the Defendant-bank rejected loan applications of minority applicants while approving loan applications filed by white applicants with similar financial characteristics and credit histories. Plaintiffs sought injunctive relief, actual damages, and punitive damages.

---

[150] Rubin, Jennifer, *Obama and the Woods Fund,* September 10, 2008, Pajamas Media
http://pajamasmedia.com/blog/obama-and-the-woods-fund/

Although U.S. District Court Judge Ruben Castillo certified the Plaintiffs' suit as a class action on June 30, 1995, *Buycks-Roberson v. Citibank Fed. Sav. Bank,* 162 F.R.D. 322 (N.D. Ill. 1995) and granted Plaintiffs' motion to compel discovery of a sample of Defendant-bank's loan application files, *Buycks-Roberson v. Citibank Fed. Sav. Bank*, 162 F.R.D. 338 (N.D. Ill. 1995), the parties voluntarily dismissed the case on May 12, 1998, pursuant to a settlement agreement. After obtaining a settlement in the Citibank litigation, ACORN used its subsidiary organization ACORN Housing, a nationwide organization with offices in more than 30 U.S. cities, to push the group's radical agenda to get subprime home buyers mortgages under the most favorable terms possible.

Annenberg Challenge

In 1995, Bill Ayers co-founded the Chicago Annenberg Challenge with a $50 million grant program for the Chicago public schools. Ayers selected Obama to be the first chairman of the board of the Chicago Annenberg Challenge, a position Obama held for eight years, until 2003, a period during which Ayers remained active with the Challenge.[151] Mr. Obama and Mr. Ayers worked as a team to advance the CAC agenda. CAC disbursed money through various far-left community organizers, such as the Association of Community Organizations for Reform Now (ACORN). According to Kurtz, As CAC chairman, Mr.

---

[151] Kurtz, Stanley, *Obama and Ayers Pushed Radicalism On Schools,* Wall Street Journal, September 23, 2008

http://online.wsj.com/article/SB122212856075765367.html?mod=djem EditorialPage

Obama was lending moral and financial support to Mr. Ayers and his radical circle.[152]

Speaking of circles. Consider that FactCheck.org, the website that vouched for the second form of the Certification of Live Birth is owned by Annenberg Public Policy Center, a Division, or Project, of the Annenberg Foundation.[153]

FactCheck.org, working in conjunction through the Annenberg group of funding agents, including the CAC, ACORN, and the Obama campaign, joined in the effort to defraud the voters by attesting to the eligibility of Obama by means of an artifice of fraud, the Chenise Foxx forged Certificate of Live Birth.

To date, only Chenise Foxx has come forward to expose the conspiracy. All of the others remain engaged in conspiracy to engage in election fraud, in violation of U.S.C. §1973i (c), 18 U.S.C. §597, 42 U.S.C. 1973i (e) and 42 U.S.C. §1973gg-10(2).

---

[152] Kurtz, *op. cit.*

[153] Terry's Blog, *Factcheck.org, The Annenberg Foundation, and Barack Obama,* September 10, 2008

Chapter Nine

Federal crimes – bribery

18 U.S.C. § 201. Bribery of public officials and witnesses

(a) *For the purpose of this section—*

> *(1)* *the term "public official" means Member of Congress, Delegate, or Resident Commissioner, either before or after such official has qualified, or an officer or employee or person acting for or on behalf of the United States, or any department, agency or branch of Government thereof, including the District of Columbia, in any official function, under or by authority of any such department, agency, or branch of Government, or a juror;*

> *(2)* *the term "person who has been selected to be a public official" means any person who has been nominated or appointed to be a public official, or has been officially informed that such person will be so nominated or appointed; and*

> *(3)* *the term "official act" means any decision or action on any question, matter, cause, suit, proceeding or controversy, which may at any time be pending, or which may by law be brought before any public official, in such official's official capacity, or in such official's place of trust or profit.*

(b) Whoever—

> *(1)* *directly or indirectly, corruptly **gives, offers or promises anything of value** to any public official or*

171

*person who has been selected to be a public official, or offers or promises any public official or any person who has been selected to be a public official to give anything of value to any other person or entity, **with intent**—*

*(A) **to influence any official act**; or*

*(B) **to influence such public official** or person who has been selected to be a public official **to commit or aid in committing, or collude in, or allow, any fraud, or make opportunity for the commission of any fraud, on the United States**; or*

(C) to induce such public official or such person who has been selected to be a public official to do or omit to do any act in violation of the lawful duty of such official or person;

*(2) **being a public official or person selected to be a public official, directly or indirectly, corruptly demands, seeks, receives, accepts, or agrees to receive or accept anything of value personally or for any other person or entity, in return for**:*

*(A) **being influenced** in the performance of any official act;*

*(B) **being influenced to commit or aid in committing, or to collude in, or allow, any fraud, or make opportunity for the commission of any fraud, on the United States**; or*

(C) being induced to do or omit to do any act in violation of the official duty of such official or person;

*(3) directly or indirectly, corruptly **gives, offers, or promises anything of value** to any person, or offers or promises such person to give anything of value to any other person or entity, **with intent to influence the testimony under oath** or affirmation of such*

first-mentioned person as a witness upon a trial, hearing, or other proceeding, before any court, any committee of either House or both Houses of Congress, or any agency, commission, or officer authorized by the laws of the United States to hear evidence or take testimony, or with intent to influence such person to absent himself therefrom;

(4) directly or indirectly, corruptly demands, seeks, receives, accepts, or agrees to receive or accept anything of value personally or for any other person or entity in return for being influenced in testimony under oath or affirmation as a witness upon any such trial, hearing, or other proceeding, or in return for absenting himself therefrom;

shall be fined *under this title or not more than three times the monetary equivalent of the thing of value, whichever is greater,* **_or imprisoned for not more than fifteen years_***, or both,* **and _may be disqualified from holding any office of honor, trust, or profit under the United States_***.*

(c) Whoever—

(1) otherwise than as provided by law for the proper discharge of official duty—

(A) directly or indirectly gives, offers, or promises anything of value to any public official, former public official, or person selected to be a public official, for or because of any official act performed or to be performed by such public official, former public official, or person selected to be a public official; or

(B) being a public official, former public official, or person selected to be a public official, otherwise than as provided by law for the proper discharge of official duty, directly or indirectly demands, seeks,

173

receives, accepts, or agrees to receive or accept anything of value personally for or because of any official act performed or to be performed by such official or person;

(2) directly or indirectly, gives, offers, or promises anything of value to any person, for or because of the testimony under oath or affirmation given or to be given by such person as a witness upon a trial, hearing, or other proceeding, before any court, any committee of either House or both Houses of Congress, or any agency, commission, or officer authorized by the laws of the United States to hear evidence or take testimony, or for or because of such person's absence therefrom;

(3) directly or indirectly, demands, seeks, receives, accepts, or agrees to receive or accept anything of value personally for or because of the testimony under oath or affirmation given or to be given by such person as a witness upon any such trial, hearing, or other proceeding, or for or because of such person's absence therefrom;

shall be fined under this title or imprisoned for not more than two years, or both.

(d) Paragraphs (3) and (4) of subsection (b) and paragraphs (2) and (3) of subsection (c) shall not be construed to prohibit the payment or receipt of witness fees provided by law, or the payment, by the party upon whose behalf a witness is called and receipt by a witness, of the reasonable cost of travel and subsistence incurred and the reasonable value of time lost in attendance at any such trial, hearing, or proceeding, or in the case of expert witnesses, a reasonable fee for time spent in the preparation of such opinion, and in appearing and testifying.

(e) *The offenses and penalties prescribed in this section are separate from and in addition to those prescribed in sections 1503, 1504, and 1505 of this title.*

18 U.S.C. § 210. **Offer to procure appointive public office.**

__Whoever pays or offers or promises any money or thing of value, to any person, firm, or corporation in consideration of the use or promise to use any influence to procure any appointive office or place under the United States for any person, shall be fined under this title or imprisoned not more than one year,__ [bold added] *or both.*

Well, who knew this was a crime? Apparently no one at the White House, as we will soon see. Those of you who have read this far are also aware of the federal conspiracy laws, so every offense that is laid out here, when joined by others who have knowledge of the crime, becomes also conspiracy to effect the same crime. So, for instance, when the justice department has knowledge that the crime has been committed and then fails to prosecute it, they join in the perpetration of the crime as conspirators.

18 U.S.C. § 211. **Acceptance or solicitation to obtain appointive public office**

*Whoever **solicits or receives,*** [bold added] *either as a political contribution, or for personal emolument, any money or thing of value, in consideration of the promise of support or use of influence in obtaining for any person any appointive office or place under the United States, shall be fined under this title or imprisoned not more than one year, or both.*

*Whoever **solicits or receives anything of value** [bold added] in consideration of aiding a person to obtain employment under the United States either by referring his name to an executive department or agency of the United States or by requiring the payment of a fee because such person has secured such employment shall be fined under this title, or imprisoned not more than one year, or both. This section shall not apply to such services rendered by an employment agency pursuant to the written request of an executive department or agency of the United States.*

On January 5, 2011, the following was posted on several financial websites:

1st CASPER for JAN 5th: "Slush fund accounts have been located and seized from within the ..." Due to the secrecy involved in how the following was uncovered WE will honor certain request to avoid those details. Slush fund accounts have been located and seized from within the greatest criminal organization in world history and their Bank, WE refer of course to THE VATICAN. The accounts were deeply buried but not deep enough. The source of funds for these accounts in most every instance was/is the U.S. Treasury Department. There was no expectation these accounts would ever be located or the funds found much less repaid to Treasury. In other words THE MONEY WAS STOLEN FROM THE U.S. TREASURY AND THE AMERICAN PEOPLE and any other source" they" could lay hands on. Owners of these Slush Fund Accounts include John Roberts and Tiny Tim Geithner. The top echelon of the Vatican including the Pope and several Cardinals. Obama, Michelle and each of their children. Michelle's mother. The Bushes and the Clintons including the Clintons daughter. Joe Biden. The U.S. Provost Marshal and several Military Chiefs

of Staff. The head of HLS, Janet Napalitano. Several U.S. Judicial Officers, i.e. Judges. Several Senators and Congressmen .Also the JAG.

Let's discuss this evidence for just a second. Consider yourselves to be the greater Grand Jury in the court of public opinion. In a courtroom, this evidence is likely inadmissible, as it is difficult to verify. Nonetheless, such evidence would be something a grand jury could consider in the course of amassing admissible evidence, as it is evidence designed to lead to the discovery of admissible evidence. It certainly is sufficient to establish a reasonable suspicion of wrongdoing, and should there be any corroborating evidence – say for instance that the Vatican banks were not spotless, or worse, that they had a history of securing secret accounts for politicians, such evidence may cumulatively create probable cause for a thorough and extensive investigation.

I remind you that the Vatican is its own country. Apparently, Italian prosecutors have been looking into money laundering at the Vatican for some time.[154] Last year, they seized $30 million from the Institute of Religious Operations (IOR), which was allegedly being used by Italian residents to hide fraud and tax evasion.[155] This wasn't the first time that the Vatican bank was found in fraud scandals, but this time, it was uncovered by the financial intelligence office at the Bank of Italy. The IOR, which manages bank accounts for Roman Catholic

---

[154] AFP, *Italian prosecutors probe Vatican bank for money laundering,* September 21, 2010
http://www.google.com/hostednews/afp/article/ALeqM5h6itasF4u_kY
e5AIRUiFT_ic-LCg

[155] *Id.*

religious orders and associations, is not bound by the same regulation as Italian financial institutions.

To give you an idea how the Vatican bank is viewed in Italy, consider that the Italian authorities have long worked to place the Holy See on a *money laundering and terrorism white list*. The Bank of Italy has told other Italian banks they should deal with IOR as if it was a non-European Union bank.

Now, of course, things continue to perk. The Global Post is making its own inquiry, given that the Vatican is the only branch of the Istituto per le Opere di Religione, (IOR), otherwise known as the Vatican bank. Its ATM uses Latin.[156] Supposedly, only Vatican employees and religious institutions are allowed to open accounts in the bank, yet its chief, economist Ettore Gotti Tedeschi, is under investigation for money laundering by Italian and EU authorities.

The IOR's holdings are estimated at 5 billion Euros, but IOR doesn't publish a budget or an annual report. Its biggest asset is its secrecy, as all of the accounts within are identified only by number; that is, they are numbered accounts, and its secrecy has been used for unholy goals.
Some of them have been documented in full. Gianluigi Nuzzi, the author of "Vaticano SPA," gained access to Monsignor Renato Dardozzi's archive, and found the bank involved in money-laundering for Italian politicians and mafia bosses. Apparently, the IOR had laundered bribes that it held in ciphered accounts for Catholic politicians. It is noteworthy that the head of the American branch of IOR, Illinois-born cardinal Paul Casimir Marcinkus, was forced

---

[156] *Chatter: What we're hearing.* Global Post, January 25, 2011
http://www.globalpost.com/notebook/global/110125/chatter-what-were-hearing

to resort to Vatican immunity to avoid prosecution by Italian judges. He died "unexpectedly" in 2006.[157]

18 U.S.C. § 216. Penalties and injunctions

(a) The punishment for an offense under section 203, 204, 205, 207, 208, or 209 of this title is the following:

(1) Whoever engages in the conduct constituting the offense shall be imprisoned for not more than one year or fined in the amount set forth in this title, or both.

(2) Whoever willfully engages in the conduct constituting the offense shall be imprisoned for not more than five years or fined in the amount set forth in this title, or both.

(b) The Attorney General may bring a civil action in the appropriate United States district court against any person who engages in conduct constituting an offense under section 203, 204, 205, 207, 208, or 209 of this title and, upon proof of such conduct by a preponderance of the evidence, such person shall be subject to a civil penalty of not more than $50,000 for each violation or the amount of compensation which the person received or offered for the prohibited conduct, whichever amount is greater. The imposition of a civil penalty under this subsection does not preclude any other criminal or civil statutory, common law, or administrative remedy, which is available by law to the United States or any other person.

(c) If the Attorney General has reason to believe that a person is engaging in conduct constituting an offense under

---

[157] Alessandro Speciale, *Unmasking the Vatican's bank: The mysterious Istituto per le Opere di Religione responds to anti-money-laundering laws.* Global Post, January 25, 2011
http://www.globalpost.com/dispatch/italy/110124/vatican-bank-ior-money-laundering

section 203, 204, 205, 207, 208, or 209 of this title, the Attorney General may petition an appropriate United States district court for an order prohibiting that person from engaging in such conduct. The court may issue an order prohibiting that person from engaging in such conduct if the court finds that the conduct constitutes such an offense. The filing of a petition under this section does not preclude any other remedy which is available by law to the United States or any other person.

18 U.S.C. § 599. Promise of appointment by candidate

Whoever, being a candidate, directly or indirectly promises or pledges the appointment, or the use of his influence or support for the appointment of any person to any public or private position or employment, for the purpose of procuring support in his candidacy shall be fined under this title or imprisoned not more than one year, or both; and if the violation was willful, shall be fined under this title or imprisoned not more than two years, or both.

18 U.S.C. § 600. Promise of employment or other benefit for political activity

__Whoever, directly or indirectly, promises any employment, position, compensation, contract, appointment, or other benefit, provided for or made possible in whole or in part by any Act of Congress, or any special consideration in obtaining any such benefit, to any person as consideration, favor, or reward for any political activity or for the support of or opposition to any candidate or any political party in connection with any general or special election to any political office, or in connection with any__

180

primary election or political convention or caucus held to select candidates for any political office, shall be fined under this title or imprisoned not more than one year, or both.

Were these statutes violated by the acts of Obama in the events now known as "The Louisiana Purchase," the "Cornhusker Kickback," and the "$5 billion Medicaid set-aside for Florida"? The Louisiana Purchase refers to a special provision given to Louisiana Senator Mary Landrieu, D-La in exchange for her vote on Obamacare. Charles Krauthammer explained that a certain $100 million provision put into the Senate version of health care legislation to favor undecided Democratic senators, specifically Sen. Mary Landrieu, D-La., represents a different brand of politics from what Obama advertised. [158] U.S. Congressman Bart Stupak (D-Wisconsin) was also accused of taking a "kickback" for changing his vote on Obamacare, even after it became obvious that the bill was loaded with federal funding for abortion. His district later received funding for three airports. [159]

According to Senator Bill Nelson, taxpayer money was used as a virtual slush fund to buy swing votes. For instance $2,000,000,000: ($2 billion) is the approximate

---

[158] Poor, Jeff, *Krauthammer on Landrieu $100 Million 'Louisiana Purchase' Buyoff: 'It's a New Kind of Business as Usual'*, Newsbusters, November 21, 2009
http://newsbusters.org/blogs/jeff-poor/2009/11/21/krauthammer-landrieu-100-million-louisiana-purchase-buyoff-its-new-kind-b#ixzz19Tg5W1Be

[159] STUPAK ANNOUNCES $726,409 FOR AIRPORTS IN ALPENA, DELTA AND CHIPPEWA COUNTIES
http://www.house.gov/list/speech/mi01_stupak/morenews/20100319faa grant.html

amount of money that House Appropriations Chairman David Obey (D-WI) earmarked related to his son's lobbying efforts.[160] Craig Obey is "a top lobbyist for the nonprofit group" that received a roughly $2 billion component of the "Stimulus" package. $3,700,000,000: ($3.7 billion) is the estimated value of various defense contracts awarded to a company controlled by the husband of Rep Diane Feinstein (D-CA). Despite an obvious conflict-of-interest as a member of the Military Construction Appropriations subcommittee, Sen. Feinstein voted for appropriations worth billions to her husband's firms. $4,190,000,000: ($4.19 billion) is the amount of money in the so-called "Stimulus" package devoted to fraudulent voter registration ACORN group under the auspices of "Community Stabilization Activities." ACORN is currently the subject of a RICO suit in Ohio. Good thing Obama was not connected to this group. Unlike Republicans, Democrats are above the law.

Within the Obama administration, corruption is rampant. Former chief of staff Rahm Emanuel exercised the full power of Obama's office to reach out to Rep. Joe Sestak, Pennsylvania Democrat, to offer a high-ranking job in the hopes of persuading Mr. Sestak to pull out of the primary against Sen. Arlen Specter. That is a violation of 18 U.S.C. § 600. It was Mr. Emanuel who offered another government position to Andrew Romanoff to do the same in the Colorado Democratic Senate primary. That is a violation of 18 U.S.C. § 600. And it was Mr. Emanuel - as the trial of former Illinois Gov. Rod Blagojevich has revealed - who acted as the go-between to try to have Valerie Jarrett parachuted into Mr. Obama's former Senate

---

160

http://news.yahoo.com/s/ap/20090129/ap_on_go_co/stimulus_national _parks_2 .

seat. That is a violation of 18 U.S.C. § 600. The only question was: What did Mr. Blagojevich want in exchange?[161] All of these acts are the acts of the agent Emanuel on behalf of the principal Obama under the doctrine of *respondeat superior*. In response to Emanuel's actions, he was soon named (the word I think Al Gore Democrats are looking for is selected) as the new mayor of Chicago, notwithstanding the fact that he is an Israeli citizen, member of the IDF and does not have sufficient residency in Chicago to occupy the post. Being legally eligible for an elected position is a legal standard that well-bribed judges are just no longer willing to enforce.

Obama twisted arms, begged, borrowed and coerced members of Congress to pass ObamaCare. Then the Obama administration went on to offer federal jobs for political purposes to two Democratic candidates. Obama and members of his administration directly violated federal law by offering federal jobs to Rep. Joe Sestak and former Colorado legislator Andrew Romanoff. Congress has an obligation to call for the appointment of a special prosecutor to investigate this corruption. We shall see if they do.

Title 18, Chapter 11, Section 211 of the United States Code states that "Whoever solicits or receives ... any....thing of value, in consideration of the promise of support or use of influence in obtaining for any person any appointive office or place under the United States, shall be fined under this title or imprisoned not more than one year, or both."

---

[161] Kuhner, Jeffrey T., *KUHNER: President's socialist takeover must be stopped*, Washington Times, July 22, 2010
http://www.washingtontimes.com/news/2010/jul/22/the-case-for-impeachment-142967590/

The Obama administration offered the two Democratic primary candidates, Joe Sestak and Andrew Romanoff, high profile jobs which included the Secretary of the Navy and a position within the U.S. Agency for International Development (that is USAID). In return for these favors the two were to withdraw from their Senate challenges to Obama's allies, Sen. Arlen Specter in Pennsylvania and Sen. Michael Bennet in Colorado.

The Denver Post reported that "Jim Messina, President Barack Obama's deputy chief of staff and a storied fixer in the White House political shop, suggested a place for Romanoff might be found in the administration and offered specific suggestions, according to several sources who described the communication to The Denver Post. Romanoff turned down the overture, which included mention of a job at USAID, the foreign aid agency, sources said."[162]

In February, Pennsylvania Congressman Joe Sestak launched a new charge of bribery by accusing the Obama White House of offering him the Secretary of the Navy job in exchange for his agreeing to abandon his race against Specter. The Philadelphia Inquirer reports that this exchange occurred during a TV interview with Comcast anchor Larry Kane: "'Was it secretary of the Navy?' Kane asked. 'No comment,' Sestak said. 'Was it [the job] high-ranking?' Kane asked. Sestak said yes, but added that he would 'never leave' the Senate race for a deal."[163]

---

[162] Booth, Michael, *Romanoff confirms White House job discussions,* Denver Post, June 3, 2020
http://www.denverpost.com/election/ci_15213784#ixzz19TpYctDJ

[163] Larry Kane Report, May 28, 2010
http://www.larrykane.com/2010/05/28/the-joe-sestak-question-anatomy-of-an-interview-that-spread-like-wildfire/

Sestak has later confirmed that yes, he was offered a job, but he has been unwilling to go into greater details. After stonewalling and avoiding the question for weeks, White House Press Secretary Robert Gibbs stated that he talked to people in the White House about the claim and that, "I'm told whatever conversations have been had are not problematic." He added that the incident is "in the past."

Sestak's opponent in the primary, Sen. Arlen Specter (D-Pa.) and Rep. Darrell Issa (R-Calif.), the top Republican on the House Oversight and Government Reform Committee, both said this week that if Sestak's claim is true, such a job offer could constitute a federal crime. Specter specifically said it would constitute bribery, while Issa referenced three sections of the U.S. code on the matter.[164]

Obama tried to influence Democratic Congressman Jim Matheson, who voted against the initial health bill, by appointing his brother Scott M. Matheson, Jr. to the Tenth Circuit Court of Appeals, another violation of federal law both on the part of Obama and on the part of Scott M. Matheson, Jr. I'm certain he will be capable of objective decision making in the spirit of due process and substantive justice under the Constitution. The offering of a federal job in order to affect an election constitutes a direct violation of federal law and must be investigated.

According to Representative Darell Issa, the top Republican on the House Oversight and Government

---

[164] Lucas, Fred, *Two Members of Congress Say That If Administration Offered Sestak Job to Drop Senate Race It Could Be a Crime,* CNS News, March 11, 2010
http://www.cnsnews.com/node/62670

Reform Committee, who has called for a special prosecutor to probe these allegations: "What you have is a credible allegation by a member of Congress of a felony," Issa told Fox News. "It is a felony to offer somebody a federal job in order to get them to affect an election."

Chapter Ten

Is Obama an Agent of a Foreign Principal?

Another high crime that emerges given the actions of this foreign national, undisclosed Muslim Brotherhood member, is the crime of being unregistered as an agent of a foreign principal. Here is the statute:

18 U.S.C. § 219. Officers and employees acting as agents of foreign principals

(a) Whoever, being a public official, is or acts as an agent of a foreign principal required to register under the Foreign Agents Registration Act of 1938 or a lobbyist required to register under the Lobbying Disclosure Act of 1995 in connection with the representation of a foreign entity, as defined in section 3(6) of that Act shall be fined under this title or imprisoned for not more than two years, or both.

(b) Nothing in this section shall apply to the employment of any agent of a foreign principal as a special Government employee in any case in which the head of the employing agency certifies that such employment is required in the national interest. A copy of any certification under this paragraph shall be forwarded by the head of such agency to the Attorney General who shall cause the same to be filed with the registration statement and other documents filed by such agent, and made available for public inspection in accordance with section 6 of the Foreign Agents Registration Act of 1938, as amended.

(c) For the purpose of this section "public official" means Member of Congress, Delegate, or Resident Commissioner, either before or after he has qualified, or

an officer or employee or person acting for or on behalf of the United States, *or any department, agency, or branch of Government thereof, including the District of Columbia, in any official function, under or by authority of any such department, agency, or branch of Government.*

22 U.S.C. § 611. Definitions

As used in and for the purposes of this subchapter—

(a) The term "person" includes an individual, partnership, association, corporation, organization, or any other combination of individuals;

(b) The term "foreign principal" includes—

(1) a government of a foreign country and a foreign political party;

(2) a person outside of the United States, unless it is established that such person is an individual and a citizen of and domiciled within the United States, or that such person is not an individual and is organized under or created by the laws of the United States or of any State or other place subject to the jurisdiction of the United States and has its principal place of business within the United States; and

(3) a partnership, association, corporation, organization, or other combination of persons organized under the laws of or having its principal place of business in a foreign country.

*(c) Expect as provided in subsection (d) of this section, **the term "agent of a foreign principal" means—***

*(1) **any person who acts** as an agent, representative, employee, or servant, or any person who acts in any other capacity **at the order, request, or under the direction or control, of a foreign principal** or of a person any of whose activities are directly or indirectly supervised, directed, controlled, financed, or subsidized in*

whole or in major part by a foreign principal, and who directly or through any other person—

(i) engages within the United States in political activities for or in the interests of such foreign principal;

(ii) acts within the United States as a public relations counsel, publicity agent, information-service employee or political consultant for or in the interests of such foreign principal;

(iii) **within the United States solicits, collects, disburses, or dispenses contributions, loans, money, or other things of value for or in the interest of such foreign principal;** *or*

(iv) within the United States represents the interests of such foreign principal before any agency or official of the Government of the United States; and

(2) any person who agrees, consents, assumes or purports to act as, or who is or holds himself out to be, whether or not pursuant to contractual relationship, an agent of a foreign principal as defined in clause (1) of this subsection.

(d) The term "agent of a foreign principal" does not include any news or press service or association organized under the laws of the United States or of any State or other place subject to the jurisdiction of the United States, or any newspaper, magazine, periodical, or other publication for which there is on file with the United States Postal Service information in compliance with section 3611 of title 39, published in the United States, solely by virtue of any bona fide news or journalistic activities, including the solicitation or acceptance of advertisements, subscriptions, or other compensation therefor, so long as it is at least 80 per centum beneficially owned by, and its officers and directors, if any, are citizens of the United States, and such news or press service or association,

newspaper, magazine, periodical, or other publication, is not owned, directed, supervised, controlled, subsidized, or financed, and none of its policies are determined by any foreign principal defined in subsection (b) of this section, or by any agent of a foreign principal required to register under this subchapter;

*(e) **The term "government of a foreign country" includes any person or group of persons exercising sovereign de facto or de jure political jurisdiction over any country, other than the United States, or over any part of such country, and includes any subdivision of any such group and any group or agency to which such sovereign de facto or de jure authority or functions are directly or indirectly delegated**. Such term shall include any faction or body of insurgents within a country assuming to exercise governmental authority whether such faction or body of insurgents has or has not been recognized by the United States;*

(f) The term "foreign political party" includes any organization or any other combination of individuals in a country other than the United States, or any unit or branch thereof, having for an aim or purpose, or which is engaged in any activity devoted in whole or in part to, the establishment, administration, control, or acquisition of administration or control, of a government of a foreign country or a subdivision thereof, or the furtherance or influencing of the political or public interests, policies, or relations of a government of a foreign country or a subdivision thereof;

*(g) The term **"public-relations counsel" includes any person who engages directly or indirectly in informing, advising, or in any way representing a principal in any public relations matter pertaining to***

190

political or public interests, policies, or relations of such principal;

(h) The term *"publicity agent"* includes any person who engages directly or indirectly in the publication or dissemination of oral, visual, graphic, written, or pictorial information or matter of any kind, including publication by means of advertising, books, periodicals, newspapers, lectures, broadcasts, motion pictures, or otherwise;

(i) The term *"information-service employee"* includes any person who is engaged in furnishing, disseminating, or publishing accounts, descriptions, information, or data with respect to the political, industrial, employment, economic, social, cultural, or other benefits, advantages, facts, or conditions of any country other than the United States or of any government of a foreign country or of a foreign political party or of a partnership, association, corporation, organization, or other combination of individuals organized under the laws of, or having its principal place of business in, a foreign country;

(j) Repealed. Pub. L. 104–65, § 9(1)(A), Dec. 19, 1995, 109 Stat. 699.

(k) The term *"registration statement"* means the registration statement required to be filed with the Attorney General under section 612 (a) of this title, and any supplements thereto required to be filed under section 612 (b) of this title, and includes all documents and papers required to be filed therewith or amendatory thereof or supplemental thereto, whether attached thereto or incorporated therein by reference;

(l) The term *"American republic"* includes any of the states which were signatory to the Final Act of the Second Meeting of the Ministers of Foreign Affairs of the American Republics at Havana, Cuba, July 30, 1940;

(m) The term "United States", when used in a geographical sense, includes the several States, the District of Columbia, the Territories, the Canal Zone, the insular possessions, and all other places now or hereafter subject to the civil or military jurisdiction of the United States;

(n) The term "prints" means newspapers and periodicals, books, pamphlets, sheet music, visiting cards, address cards, printing proofs, engravings, photographs, pictures, drawings, plans, maps, patterns to be cut out, catalogs, prospectuses, advertisements, and printed, engraved, lithographed, or autographed notices of various kinds, and, in general, all impressions or reproductions obtained on paper or other material assimilable to paper, on parchment or on cardboard, by means of printing, engraving, lithography, autography, or any other easily recognizable mechanical process, with the exception of the copying press, stamps with movable or immovable type, and the typewriter;

(o) The term "political activities" means any activity that the person engaging in believes will, or that the person intends to, in any way influence any agency or official of the Government of the United States or any section of the public within the United States with reference to formulating, adopting, or changing the domestic or foreign policies of the United States or with reference to the political or public interests, policies, or relations of a government of a foreign country or a foreign political party;

(p) The term "political consultant" means any person who engages in informing or advising any other person with reference to the domestic or foreign policies of the United States or the political or public interest, policies, or relations of a foreign country or of a foreign political party.

192

The Foreign Agents Registration Act is an act that requires people and organizations that are under foreign control ("agents of a foreign principal") to register with the Department of Justice when acting on behalf of foreign interests. This law defines the agent of a foreign principal as someone who 1) engages in political activities for or in the interests of a foreign principal; 2) acts in a public relations capacity for a foreign principal; 3) solicits or dispenses anything of value within the United States for a foreign principal; or 4) represents the interests of a foreign principal before any agency or official of the U.S. government.

I guess this begs the question as to allegiance, ultimately. There are two factual issues before us in a glaring way: First, is the million dollars that was raised in the United States and then given to Obama's cousin in Kenya, a certain Raila Odinga, who, when he failed to obtain the Presidency in the regularly scheduled election engaged in ethnic-cleansing and tribal genocide as he was advised to do following the same basic threat that has regularly appeared in the American press should Obama be indicted for his high crimes, and otherwise removed from office.

For instance, the *screaming skull* James Carville told Anderson Cooper that riots were likely if Obama were to lose.[165] Fox news' reporter Tom Sullivan also predicted that African-Americans would be rioting in the streets

[165] Gladnick, P.J., *James Carville Hints at Riots If Obama Loses Election,* Newsbusters, October 08, 2008
http://newsbusters.org/blogs/p-j-gladnick/2008/10/08/james-carville-hints-riots-if-obama-loses#ixzz19TzcFqpo

similar to what happened after the O.J. trial in the 1990s.[166] Africans did riot in the streets of Kenya following Odinga's loss, killing about 1,000 people and displacing 250,000. Odinga is now the Prime Minister, thanks to Obama's win in the US. The Obama campaign – the Friends of Senator Obama – directly funded Odinga in the amount of $1 million USD. This funding was set forth on Odinga's website, just above the mission statement indicating that if he lost, they would engage in ethnic violence; which they did on both counts. Obama's joining of this campaign makes him a conspirator to commit ethnic cleansing, to do so in a foreign country which is arguably a war crime, and appeared on Odinga's behalf on several occasions before the election, using his American campaign dollars to do so, all in violation of the Foreign Agents Registration Act.

In addition, we have the issue of *the direct funding to Hamas* following his inauguration, when, by executive order, he moved more than $20 million into Gaza with expedience – almost like he was paying someone back or paying a commission (maybe for funds raised). This act of directly funding Hamas – an entity on the designated terrorist list – and doing so with American dollars is also a violation of the Foreign Agents Registration Act.

Now there is the question of the bow to the Saudi King. If in fact this was an act of fealty, as everyone in the entire world took it, then he expressed himself as an agent of a foreign principal. As I have argued above, Obama is an undisclosed Ikhwan – a member of the Muslim Brotherhood engaged in economic jihad against the United States in order to bring about the Islamic conquest of the nation. Given the bow, and given the work his mother was engaged while she lived in Pakistan under the Ul Haq

---

[166]Murphy, Logan, *FOXNews' Tom Sullivan: Blacks Will Riot If Obama Loses, Crooks and Liars,* March 19, 2008

regime, his loyalties are distinctly Sunni. Iran's Ahmadinijad finally deciphered this loyalty and came to understand what that meant – that Obama's loyalties are to the Saudi kingdom – the Sunni state in direct opposition to the Shiite state, which is almost all of Iran and most of Iraq.

If this is true, then Obama would be willing to go to war with Iran in order to destroy the possibility of Shiite hegemony over the region and to empower the Sunni hegemony. If this is true, Obama would be willing to abandon his vendetta against Israel, if it means that Hezbollah – an Iranian agent stationed in Lebanon – would gain a foothold at the expense of Saudi Arabia. It is not enough to simply conclude that Obama is a Muslim Brother; it is also requisite on the student of history to conclude that he is a Sunni Muslim brother, whose fundamental allegiance is to the Muslim Brotherhood first, the Saudi kingdom second, and then to the sycophants of the New World Order.

How is this working itself out now? The entirety Sunni world is in insurgency, except he who established his alliance with Obama early on – namely Erdoğan in Turkey. Turkey, for those of you who are students of the seventh head of the beast – the one that suffered the fatal head wound – you would know that the modern nation of Turkey, whose capitol is Istanbul, is all that remains of the Ottoman Empire – the Caliphate – that collapsed into a secular state in 1924 under Ataturk. Constantinople, its capitol, did not become Istanbul officially until 1930. The collapse of the Caliphate is known in the Muslim world as the fatal head wound. Should the Ottoman Empire rise again, one could say that the seventh head of the beast has been miraculously healed of its fatal head wound. This is scripturally significant, but I will leave it to you the reader to go and find it.

The Muslim Brotherhood is now an activated asset, and its well-scripted insurgency has been planned since 1924, when the Brotherhood first formed with a stated purpose to recreate the Caliphate. Under the tutelage of Ikhwan Obama, the time to act is now, especially if Americans actually figure out who he is before the 2012 election. Virtually the entire Sunni world is inflamed with the bloodlust of revolution, and American troops and naval armadas are poised throughout the region. Some of the bribed among the media may try to claim that the US has deployed its military assets to protect "the peace" but, in reality, we are there to prevent Israel from stopping the unification of Neo-Ottoman Empire, a feat which will be accomplished in just weeks.

Students of scripture will know that by means of a pact with Sheol, the leadership of the Jewish nation of Israel will make agreement that will allow for international control over the old city of Jerusalem and the Mount of Olives in exchange for the construction of the third temple. This too is coming very soon. This deal will be constructed in order to house the seat of power in the new Caliphate in the city which is the very center – the epicenter – of the political world: Yerushaliym.

As we contemplate this agenda in the hands of Obama, let us now ask the question how such actions are consistent with the United States Constitution. Can you show me?

Chapter Eleven

Obama – Citizen of the Commonwealth

During the course of 2008 Presidential campaign, it was necessary for Barack Obama to be placed on the ballot of the fifty states. To do so, it was necessary that he be certified to do so pursuant to state law. In the state of Washington, as with 47 other states, an affirmation by the Democrat National Committee that he had been duly nominated was sufficient for him to obtain ballot status. There were two states that presented difficulties: Hawaii and Arizona. Here is what Barack Obama presented to the state of Arizona:

Let's read the applicable parts of the affirmation again:

"I am a natural born citizen of the United States, am at least thirty-five years of age, and have been a resident within the United States for at least fourteen years." This affirmation was signed by Barack Obama under the statement "I do solemnly swear or affirm that all the information in this Nomination Paper is true, that as to these and all other qualifications, I am qualified to hold the office that I seek, having fulfilled the United States constitutional requirements for holding said office. I further swear or affirm that I have fulfilled Arizona's statutory requirements for placing my name on its Presidential Preference Election ballot." This was signed on November 30, 2007 and received on December 13, 2007.

To meet the constitutional requirements for holding the office of President, the candidate must meet the provisions of Article II, Section 1, to wit:

> *No person except a natural born Citizen, or a Citizen of the United States, at the time of the Adoption of this Constitution, shall be eligible to the Office of President; neither shall any Person be eligible to that Office who shall not have attained to the Age of thirty-five Years, and been fourteen Years a Resident within the United States.*

This affirmation was sworn to and made before the Certification of Live Birth had been presented and before the phony draft registration document had been posted. One now wonders which answer is more untrue – that he is a "natural born citizen" or that he is "qualified to hold the office" he sought.

If it is shown that he is not a natural born citizen, Arizona has a separate case for perjury against Obama, and if he is removed under Article 25 for incompetence, a second charge may lie. Of course, the debate has continued as to exactly what is a "natural born citizen" as compared with "native born citizen" and "naturalized citizen." In the case of Obama, it is first necessary to establish "citizen."

On August 6, 2008, the Rocky Mountain News retracted its online published statement that Barack Obama held dual United States-Kenyan citizenship.[167] RMN had run the story earlier in the week stating that Barack Obama

---

[167] The Rocky, *Things you might not know about Barack Obama*, August 6, 2008
http://www.rockymountainnews.com/news/2008/aug/06/things-you-might-not-know-about-barack-obama/

"Holds both American and Kenyan (since 1963) citizenship" as one of the items listed in the story.

FactCheck.org, the organization whose operatives Jess Henig and Joe Miller vouched for the forged COLB as a Birth Certificate, weighed in on the topic, arguing that Obama held both U.S. and Kenyan citizenship as a child, "but lost his Kenyan citizenship automatically on his 23rd birthday.[168] In this piece, Joe Miller, a PhD in Political Philosophy, makes no argument to establish Barack's supposed American citizenship, but argues that the citizenship of Barack Obama (senior) was governed by the British Nationality Act of 1948. The '48 Act states:

> **British Nationality Act of 1948 (Part II, Section 5):** Subject to the provisions of this section, a person born after the commencement of this Act shall be a citizen of the United Kingdom and Colonies by descent if his father is a citizen of the United Kingdom and Colonies at the time of the birth.

To reiterate: FactCheck.org, a partisan organization engaged to provide cover for Obama in his quest to cover the actual circumstances of his birth made the claim on August 29, 2008, that Barack Obama was a British citizen at birth. This claim was repeated on Obama's own website, Fightthesmears.com, on the same page that displayed the forged, invalidated COLB is "Barack Obama's Official

---

[168] Miller, Joe, *He held both U.S. and Kenyan citizenship as a child, but lost his Kenyan citizenship automatically on his 23rd birthday*, FactCheck.org, August 29, 2008.
http://www.factcheck.org/askfactcheck/does_barack_obama_have_ken yan_citizenship.html

Birth Certificate."[169] Of course, for FactCheck operatives, none of whom are lawyers, misconstruing the law was no problem. FactCheck's Joe Miller makes the statement that "Obama did in fact have Kenyan citizenship after 1963,"[170] but then cites to the Kenyan constitution to indicate that Obama's Kenya citizenship automatically ended on Obama's 21st birthday, August 4, 1982.

However, New Jersey attorney Leo Donofrio researched the issue to obtain an accurate understanding of the law, and FactCheck was required to correct its "facts" to conclude that Obama's citizenship in Kenya would expire only two years *following* his 21st birthday, or on August 4, 1984, not 1982.

FactCheck then conceded that the operative date for Obama's termination of Kenyan citizenship was actually August 4, 1984. Miller then makes the bare naked, unsubstantiated factual statement that "Sen. Obama has neither renounced his U.S. citizenship nor sworn an oath of allegiance to Kenya."[171] Miller should be number one on the deposition list to determine exactly how he knows this.

Donofrio then argues that because of the option, Obama obtained citizenship of the United Kingdom and the Commonwealth of Nations, pursuant to the British Nationality Act of 1981.[172] Section 37 of the British

---

[169] *The Truth About Barack's Birth Certificate,* Fightthesmears.com
http://fightthesmears.com/articles/5/birthcertificate

[170] *He held both U.S. and Kenyan citizenship as a child, but lost his Kenyan citizenship automatically on his 23rd birthday , Id.*

[171] *Id.*

[172] Donofrio, Leo, *CONFIRMED: Factcheck.org Published Bogus Fact Regarding Obama's Kenyan Citizenship*, September 1, 2009; Posted on Tuesday, September 01, 2009 4:20:00 PM by Vincent Jappi
http://www.freerepublic.com/focus/bloggers/2329845/posts

Nationality Act of 1981 (effective January 1, 1983), made all citizens of commonwealth nations who had British Subjects before commencement of the Act, Commonwealth Citizens. Kenya, although independent, was a Commonwealth nation, and Obama was a Kenyan citizen by his own admission through to August 4, 1984. Twenty months earlier, Obama was deemed a citizen of the Commonwealth of Nations – that is to say, the equivalent of a *British Subject*, now called a *Commonwealth Citizen*.

Contrary to this issue of law, FactCheck's Joe Miller claimed in his disclosure that Obama's British citizenship terminated on December 12, 1963, when Kenya gained its independence from the United Kingdom. He cites no factual or legal basis for this conclusion. Donofrio counters again, demonstrating that under the British Nationality Act of 1948, Obama's citizenship under the United Kingdom continued unabated.[173] Donofrio concludes that Obama could put the issue to rest by disavowing his other citizenships, including his Commonwealth Citizenship. To date, Obama has not taken such a step, because to do so would mean admitting dual citizenship. Consequently, he remains a citizen of the Commonwealth – a subject of the Queen.

His Commonwealth Citizenship is not sufficient to render a complete determination as to the actual citizenship of Obama. His paternal citizenship status, no matter where he was born, is as described above. His maternal citizenship is then the question. Can Barack Obama establish by means of his mother's American citizenship at the time of his birth that he is eligible to claim American citizenship?

---

[173] *Id.*

A certain amount of history is necessary to obtain a complete understanding of the passing of citizenship. Before the year 1934, American citizenship did not pass to the child through the mother, period. There were no exceptions. The child's citizenship was determined by the citizenship of the child's father. The political incorrectness of it all is difficult for the historians, because when it comes to the issue of citizenship as initially established in this country, there were most certainly considerations that we would now label as both sexist and racist. The infamous *Dred Scott* case,[174] while rendering a distasteful conclusion of law, sets forth a comprehensive understanding of citizenship within the United States just prior to the Civil War the decision helped to ignite. Some of these were cured by the enactment of the Fourteenth Amendment, and some required a continuous stream of Congressional Acts on Nationalization to remove the elements of what we would call sexism in establishing citizenship. The Fourteenth Amendment provides in relevant part as follows:

> *1. All persons born or naturalized in the United States, and subject to the jurisdiction thereof, are citizens of the United States and of the State wherein they reside.*

The Fourteenth Amendment was duly considered in the seminal case on natural born and native born citizenship, *Wong Kim Ark*[175] and the case made no relevant discussion concerning whether the citizenship passed through the mother in lieu of the father – rather, the discussion included both parents.

---

[174] *Dred Scott v. Sandford,* 60 U.S. 393 (1857)

[175] *United States v. Wong Kim Ark,* 169 U.S. 649 (1898)

For purposes of this discussion, we will assume that Stanley Ann Obama was in fact married to Barack Hussein Obama at the time of the birth of Barack Hussein Obama II, and that BHO II was born in Honolulu, Hawaii. His birth has yet to be factually established with substantive evidence of birth, such as a long form birth certificate.

The young Obama obtained another citizenship, however. Obama's mother, Stanley Ann Obama (Dunham), divorced Barack Obama Sr. on March 20, 1964, when Obama was still 2 years old. She then remarried an Indonesian native named Soetoro on March 24, 1965, when Obama was 3 years old. On July 20, 1966, Lolo Soetoro left Hawaii, where he had been attending the University of Hawaii, to return to Indonesia for work. On June 29, 1967, Stanley Ann Dunham applied to the U.S. Department of State to amend her U.S. Passport No. F777788 to change her name from Stanley Ann Dunham to her married name, Stanley Ann Soetoro. Stanley Ann Soetoro then left Honolulu, Hawaii via Japan Airlines, and moved to Jakarta, Indonesia in October, 1967, with her son in tow, according to her passport records, using U.S. Passport No. 777788.[176]

Obama attended school in Indonesia, registered as Barry Soetoro ("O") (as discussed in Chapter One), an Indonesian national of an Islamic faith. The record indicates that Barry Soetoro, formerly known as Barack Hussein Obama II, became an Indonesian citizen very early during his stay in Indonesia, and while he was still a minor.

Obama failed to naturalize as a citizen of the US after his 18th birthday but before his 26th birthday; failed to

---

[176] Corsi, Jerome R., *Old papers tell different tales on Obama's past; Articles from 1990 cast doubt on president's 'official' childhood story*, WorldNetDaily, November 21, 2010.
http://www.wnd.com/index.php?fa=PAGE.view&pageId=230829

confirm his Kenyan citizenship within two years of his 21st birthday, and by operation of law, became a Citizen of the Commonwealth (UK) in 1983. He has one other citizenship in Indonesia. Otherwise, he is subject to the jurisdiction of the Crown.

If Obama knows that he is a British subject, and if fact is operating (at least in part) on behalf of the Crown to manipulate the US currency, destroy the economies of scale in the US and the underlying infrastructure in order to bring about a New World Order – or so he has led the Crown to believe, then he walks completely in the spirit of the man of perdition, otherwise known as Judas Iscariot; because the New World Order, like the anti-war left, Code Pink, Rev. Wright, Bill Ayres, Tony Rezko, Rod Blagoyovitch, Hosni Mubarek, Louis Farrakhan, Saudi King Abdullah, Moammar Qaddafi, and the nation of Israel, will be kicked under the bus.

Chapter Twelve

Treason - An Undisclosed Jihadist Building the New International Caliphate

Al-Tabari's (d. 923) famous tafsir (an exegesis of the Koran) is a standard and authoritative reference work in the entire Muslim world. Regarding 3:28, he writes: "If you [Muslims] are under their [infidels'] authority, fearing for yourselves, behave loyally to them, with your tongue, while harboring inner animosity for them. ... Allah has forbidden believers from being friendly or on intimate terms with the infidels in place of believers — except when infidels are above them [in authority]. In such a scenario, let them act friendly towards them." Regarding 3:28, Ibn Kathir (d. 1373, second in authority only to Tabari) writes, "Whoever at any time or place fears their [infidels'] evil may protect himself through outward show." As proof of this, he quotes Muhammad's close companion, Abu Darda, who said, "Let us smile to the face of some people [non-Muslims] while our hearts curse them"; another companion, al-Hassan, said, "Doing taqiyya [lying] is acceptable till the Day of Judgment [i.e., in perpetuity].[177]

Obama's agenda seeks to accomplish the following three objectives: 1) Cripple the economy of the United States, and consequently the economies of the trilateral financial world; 2) Empower and authorize reestablish the Neo-Ottoman Empire; and 3) Secure Jerusalem from the Israelis.

---

[177] Ibraham, Raymond, *War and Peace – and Deceit – in Islam.*

206

Crippling the economy of the United States

The only restraint this fellow ("O") has on federal spending is ink and paper. He has driven the deficit to unsustainable limits, exhausting all sources of credit and forcing the Federal Reserve to buy its own debt. Even Federal Reserve Chairman Ben Bernanke admitted that an audit of the FR could result in the collapse of the dollar because of the fraudulent internal workings of the promissory note system in worldwide application. We now suffer from depression-level unemployment, collapsing economies of scale and a GDP that has fallen by one-third since January, 2008. The dollar is in such a precarious position, that the nation's credit rating has been prepared for a downgrade, the biggest warning coming from Moody's in December, 2010. Yet, Obama seeks to increase the debt ceiling and has pushed the IMF – an institution whose corporate headquarters are mere blocks from the White House – to call for a new international currency as the world money standard.

Obama's solution? Spend another $3 trillion a year on socialized medicine, seize the financial industry, seize the automobile industry, seize the health care industry, and gut manufacturing and industry through the implementation of his fraudulent "green jobs" scheme. The grabbing up of corporations by government for purposes of ownership and management, while allowing the goods to stay priced in the public market in known within political science circles as *economic fascism*. The idea of spending without any concept of limitation is a monetary policy consistent with the policies of Robert Mugabe in Zimbabwe.

Mugabe created a hyperinflation of the currency in Zimbabwe in the early 2000s, shortly after Mugabe authorized the confiscation of white-owned farmland and

207

ated Zimbabwe's debts to the International ....ry Fund. This hyperinflation persisted through to 2009. Figures from November 2008 estimated Zimbabwe's annual inflation rate at 89.7 sextillion (10^{21}) percent. By December 2008, annual inflation was estimated at 6.5 quindecillion novemdecillion percent (6.5 x 10^{108}%, the equivalent of 6 quinquatrigintillion 500 quattuortrigintillion percent, or 65 followed by 107 zeros – 65 million googol percent). In April 2009, Zimbabwe abandoned printing of the Zimbabwean dollar, and the South African rand and US dollar became the standard currencies for exchange. As of 2011 the currency has not been reintroduced yet. Yes it was a problem, but you've got to love that rate of inflation!

Obama's practice of Mugabean economics has allowed the federal government to spend all of the wealth we have in the United States and all of the wealth we ever will have, and he did so in less than six months from his inauguration. He continues to harbor a desire to spend additional trillions in order to further the entitlements of his cronies at the expense of national sovereignty, and it appears as though he is siphoning off billions into personal accounts at the same time he is doing this.

However, for those who think he is working to redistribute wealth from the haves to the have-less, consider that he is simply working to completely destroy America's economy and its economic future, and he expects to take Western Europe and the ASEAN economies with us. This is *intentional destruction,* because the New Islamic Caliphate cannot rise to the world's only superpower if the United States remains healthy. Obama is the *agent provocateur* of Islamic economic jihad against the West, and he is working clandestine operations to secure the fortunes of Islam at the expense of the West and the New World Order.

As David Jonsson wrote in 2006: "Islamic Economics is the stealth sword of Islam. It is more powerful than the Weapons of Mass Destruction and terrorism. It is immune to negotiation. The stealth sword is being applied for the Islamization of the West and the whole world. The goal is to create the *"Islamic kingdom of God on earth."* The implementation of *Shari'a* law would have a dramatic affect on your life and that of the entire Western Civilization. Understand the nature of the evil and do not be blindsided."[178]

Jonsson goes on to write that "Islamic economics has an impact on your life, whether you are a banker, investing in the stock market, selling a home, buying a car, purchasing food, buying a suit or a dress, or just trying to make sense of the current events. Islamic economics and Islamic banking are primary Islamist strategies to condition the West to accept *Shari'a* law as a basis for all life in all nations."[179]

It is important to recognize that the crippling of the American economy is part and parcel of the goal to establish a Shari'a economic system not just over this nation, but worldwide. Jonsson said back in 2006 that "the Islamic movement is an idea movement" that "at the present time the leader(s) has not been identified." I think the leader has now been identified, as he and his staff are working tirelessly to achieve the ends of this economic jihad against America and the West.

---

[178] David J. Jonsson, *Islamic Economics and Shariah Law: A Plan for World Domination,* December 21, 2006.
http://www.salemthesoldier.us/jonsson_shariah_economics.html

[179] *Op. cit.*

As Jonsson put it: "The people in the West who are trying to construct a new socialism, a de-Marxified alternative to the politics of pure individualism, share the views of Islamist economists. These Westerners also accept the market as the essential driving-force of any economy, but they too wish to set it within a man-made moral framework that will ensure support for the weak through the compassion and self-discipline of the strong. What communism tried and failed to achieve through the state, one Islamic economist has written, 'is to be established through the agency of man himself.' It would be a good slogan for the possible new socialism of the twenty-first century. As we will see, these principles are being promoted broadly in the West. This merging of ideologies is a powerful force in today's political environment. This merging is taking the form of a *Marxist/Leftist - Islamist Alliance*."[180]

As a student of political science, I am not inclined to lump the Marxist/Leftist with the Islamist as quickly as Jonsson. Islamists are Islamists, top to bottom, and they will accommodate Marxism as long as it goes along with Shari'a.

Ye Shall Know Them By Their Fruits

Barack Hussein Obama tried to ensconce to the office of the presidency on January 21, 2009. Following his botched inauguration, BHO took his first official act, which was to call Palestinian President Mahmoud Abbas, and to assure him that he intended "to work with him *as partners* [italics added] to establish a durable peace in the

---

[180] *Op. cit.*

region."[181] Technically, this was not an official act, because Obama had not yet given a proper oath.[182] Because he wasn't properly installed, the act was yet another violation of the Logan Act.

The day after Obama actually succeeded in giving the oath to take the presidency, on January 22, 2009, he issued an executive order to halt terrorist court proceedings at the U.S. Navy base in Cuba. As a consequence, on February 5, 2009, the Pentagon's senior judge overseeing terror trials at Guantanamo Bay dropped charges against an al-Qaida suspect in the 2000 USS Cole bombing, Abd al-Rahim al-Nashiri. His case was the last active Guantanamo war crimes case.[183]

The following day, on February 6, 2009, the Islamabad High Court in Pakistan freed nuclear scientist Abdul Qadeer Khan from house arrest.[184] Dr. Khan is the father of Pakistan's nuclear program and had confessed to transferring nuclear secrets to other countries (Iran, Libya and North Korea) in 2004. President Musharraf had pardoned Dr. Khan but the latter was under house arrest

---

[181] Reuters, *Obama's first call abroad to Palestine: Official - New president vows to seek 'durable' Mideast peace in Mahmoud Abbas call,* Reuters January 21, 2009
http://www.vancouversun.com/Life/Obama+first+call+abroad+Palestine/1202283/story.html#ixzz16GH0DJzQ

[182] Martin, Jonathan, *Obama retakes oath of office,* Politico, January 21, 2009.
http://www.politico.com/news/stories/0109/17778.html

[183] Jakes, Lara, Associated Press, *Charges dropped vs. suspect in 2000 USS Cole blast,* February 5, 2009
http://peakoilpetroleumandpreciousmetals.yuku.com/topic/6991/t/Obama-Pardons-USS-Cole-Bomber.html?page=-1

[184] *Pakistan nuclear scientist 'free',* BBC News, February 6, 2009.

since his confession. The release of Dr. Khan was contingent upon a secret 'agreement' reached between him and the government.[185] Dr. Khan is unquestionably an Islamic fundamentalist. Here is his statement on his release: "Let them talk. Are they happy with our God? Are they happy with our Prophet? Are they happy with our leaders? Never, so why should we bother what they say about us?"[186] Obama was silent. More importantly, Obama had taken no affirmative steps to ensure that Dr. Khan remained secure under house arrest. Khan has since been elevated to the status of national hero, and Musharraf has been kicked under the bus.

In case you missed the point, on April 1, 2009 – that's correct, April fool's day, Obama, the descendent of an Assyrian Bedouin tribesman[187] from the village of Bir al-Maksour in the Israeli region of Galilee[188] used the opportunity of his first meeting with the Saudi King to

---

[185] Madhavi, *A.Q. Khan - From Release to Reverence,* The Trajectory, September 8, 2009
http://thetrajectory.com/blogs/index.php/2009/09/aq-khan-from-release-to-reverence/comment-page-1/

[186] *Id.*

[187] Bir al-Maksour council member Abdul Rahman Sheikh Abdullah's mother said that a relative Obama's Kenyan grandmother had once been employed as a migrant worker in the 1930s in the British Mandate of Palestine, and married a local Bedouin girl, with whom he later returned home. Haaretz Service, *Report: Galilee Bedouin claim Obama as lost member of tribe,* November 13, 2008.
http://www.haaretz.com/news/report-galilee-bedouin-claim-obama-as-lost-member-of-tribe-1.257171

[188] *8,000 Bedouins Claim to Be Obama's Lost Tribe,* Journal of the Turkish Weekly, November 14, 2008
http://www.turkishweekly.net/news/61270/8-000-bedouins-claim-to-be-obama-s-lost-tribe.html

greet him with a full bow from the waist, expressing ultimate fealty.[189]

A few days later, on April 5, 2009, Obama told Europe to admit Islamic Turkey into the EU, much to the consternation of the Europeans.[190] Says Pamela Geller, "it is becoming increasingly clear that Obama's two main objectives are to break the back of America and advance the global goals of Islam."

Turkey's Prime Minister Recep Tayyip Erdoğan rejected attempts to call Turkey the representative of moderate Islam. "It is unacceptable for us to agree with such a definition. Turkey has never been a country to represent such a concept. Moreover, Islam cannot be classified as moderate or not," Erdoğan said, speaking at the Oxford Centre for Islamic Studies last Thursday.[191] In short, Obama demanded that Europe accept Turkey as an EU member while Turkey's Prime Minister proclaimed Turkey to be a radical Islamic state.

The following day while giving a speech in Turkey, before expressing his reverence for Islam with his walk through the Hagia Sofia, formerly the Red Mosque and now a museum, and the Blue Mosque, Obama said that we

---

[189] Unruh, Bob, *Obama bows to Saudi king; Greeting called 'most unbecoming for president of the United States',* April 2, 2009, WorldNetDaily
http://www.wnd.com/?pageId=93696

[190] Geller, Pamela, *OBAMA TO EU: EMBRACE ISLAMIC TURKEY INTO EU SARKOZY WARNS OBAMA: STFU & MYOB,* Atlas Shrugs, April 5, 2009
http://atlasshrugs2000.typepad.com/atlas_shrugs/2009/04/obama-to-eu-embrace-islamic-turkey-into-eu-sarkozy-warns-obama-stfu-myob.html

[191] *Id.*

Americans "do not consider ourselves a Christian nation, or a Muslim nation, but rather, a nation of citizens who are, uh, bound by a set of values."[192] This statement begs a number of questions, such as: how does the non-American Obama speak for "we Americans"? Since he didn't even know there were only 50 states, not 57,[193] how would he know if we were Christian or not? Finally, uh, just what set of values is he discussing?

That is not the only stupid remark made during this speech. He also said "We do not consider ourselves a Christian nation, a Jewish nation or a Muslim nation. *uh uh...* we consider ourselves uh uh a nation of *uh* citizens."[194] Speak for yourself, if you can! Before you declare yourself a "citizen", please do us all the favor of producing the birth certificate demonstrating a qualifying birth.

Why slow yourself down? The same day Obama was making remarks about America being a nation of

---

[192] Eidsmoe, Joe, *Obama: American Not a Christian Nation*, New American, April 15, 2009

[193] "It is wonderful to be back in Oregon," Obama said. "Over the last 15 months, we've traveled to every corner of the United States. I've now been in 57 states? I think one left to go. Alaska and Hawaii, I was not allowed to go to even though I really wanted to visit, but my staff would not justify it." And Sarah Palin is stupid?! Malcolm, Andrew, *Barack Obama wants to be president of these 57 United States,* LA Times, May 9, 2008.
http://latimesblogs.latimes.com/washington/2008/05/barack-obama-wa.html

[194] Geller, Pamela, *President Hussein: "We Are Not A Christian Nation",* April 6, 2009
http://atlasshrugs2000.typepad.com/atlas_shrugs/2009/04/president-hussein-we-are-not-a-christian-nation.html

citizens (and not Americans), he appointed the first hijab-clad person to his staff, when he appointed Dalia Mogahed as Executive Director, Gallup Center for Muslim Studies in Washington, DC as an additional member to the Advisory Council on Faith-Based and Neighborhood Partnerships.[195] Dalia Mogahed has alarmed the world with her "moderate" approach to Islam. For instance, in an interview with Sheik Yusuf Qaradawi, she made the statement: "Many have claimed that terrorists have 'hijacked Islam'. I disagree. I think Islam is safe and thriving in the lives of Muslims around the world. What the terrorists have been allowed to take over are Muslim grievances."[196]

Mogahed stirred up a rat's nest in Britain as well, when she appeared on a British television show which was hosted by by Ibtihal Bsis, a member of the extremist Hizb ut Tahrir party to talk about Shari'a Law, claiming that the Western view of Shari'a was "oversimplified" and the majority of women around the world associate it with "gender justice." Hizb ut Tahrir believes in the non-violent destruction of Western democracy and the creation of an Islamic state under Shari'a Law across the world.[197]

---

[195] Office of the Press Secretary, the White House, President Obama Announces Additional Members of Advisory Council on Faith-Based and Neighborhood Partnerships, April 6, 2009.
http://www.whitehouse.gov/the_press_office/President-Obama-Announces-Additional-Members-of-Advisory-Council-on-Faith-Based-and-Neighborhood-Partnerships/

[196] Qasim, Muhammed, *Obama's Muslim Advisor (Exclusive)*, IslamOnline.net, April 28, 2009
http://www.islamonline.net/servlet/Satellite?c=Article_C&cid=123988
8438065&pagename=Zone-English-News/NWELayout

[197] Gilligan, Andrew; Spillius, Alex, *Barack Obama adviser says Sharia Law is misunderstood,* Telegraph.Co.UK, October 8, 2009

Candice Salima holds no punches when she declares categorically that Barack Obama appointed Dalia Mogahed to promote Sharia Law in America.[198] While she may be the first to wear the veil in the White House, she will not be the last appointment Obama made to promote Shari'a Law in America.

He began with a Homeland Security transition team that included terrorist and jihadist Major Nidal Hasan; he appointed Jack Brennan number 2 at HSA – an infidel who converted to Islam while stationed in Saudi Arabia, who speaks Arabic fluently and who refers to Jerusalem as al Quds; he appointed Ali Khan to the number 3 position at HSA. Khan is a *hafiz* – someone who has memorized the entire Quran in Arabic.

As of the end of January 2011, Obama's work with the Muslim Brotherhood within the nation of Egypt emerged. Obama's operatives were meeting secretly with a senior leader of Muslim Brotherhood on January 31, 2001 in anticipation of the overthrow of Hosni Mubarak.[199] According to the Telegraph, Frank Wisner, a consigliore of the Obama administration and former ambassador to Egypt, held a secret meeting with Issam El-Erian, a senior leader of the Muslim Brotherhood at the American embassy in

http://www.telegraph.co.uk/news/worldnews/northamerica/usa/baracko bama/6274387/Obama-adviser-says-Sharia-Law-is-misunderstood.html

[198] Salima, Candice, *Dalia Mogahed Appointed to Promote Sharia Law in America*, Zimbio, October 16, 2009
http://www.zimbio.com/War+on+Terrorism/articles/7Yno0aitOuw/Dali a+Mogahed+Appointed+Promote+Sharia+Law

[199] Aaron Klein, *U.S. 'held secret meeting with Muslim Brotherhood' - Discussed fall of Egypt with group dedicated to Islam's global spread*, February 1,2011, WorldNetDaily
http://www.wnd.com/?pageId=258405#ixzz1CmVxrK5X

Cairo. The Egyptians have stated openly that they believe the political aspects of the insurgency are being coordinated by the U.S. State Department and the Obama administration.

Wikileaks released a series of U.S. diplomatic dispatches showing that the State Department was pressing the Egyptian government to release dissidents who would work to agitate the ongoing insurgency. In the meantime the White House was calling for an orderly transition at the first sign of the insurgency – almost as if they were in on it.

US Department of Justice Assistant Attorney General Thomas Perez will soon be advising the Muslim Brotherhood on how to takeover and run Egypt. Gustav Torres, the Executive Director of Perez's former organization is also teaming up with the Muslim Brotherhood to overthrow the existing pro-American Egyptian government, ignoring the organic pro-democracy movement of pro-U.S. demonstrators.

Torres leads a group called The Organizers Forum, whose board of directors includes Mary Gonzales, Associate Director of the Gamaliel Foundation; and Wade Rathke, Chief Organizer of ACORN just to name a couple.

Obama and his friends are taking a position totally contrary to the pre-existing and long-standing policies of the American government to the consternation of all of our allies in Africa, Asia and the Middle East. Who can predict who Obama will next kick under the bus? (If you are a leader in one of those countries, let me give you a tip: if you are not a Sunni brother in on Obama's plan to resuscitate the Ottoman Empire, then you are next to go under the tires of the bus – *and darling, you know who you are*).

Before Obama, the United States was vitally interested in having the Muslim Brotherhood listed as a

Specially Designated Terrorist Organization. The Muslim Brotherhood is the progenitor cell of Islamic terrorism worldwide, having founded HAMAS and converting al Qaida. Ayman al Zwahiri, al Qaida's number two behind Osama bin Laden, was a leader in the Egyptian Muslim Brotherhood. The Brotherhood was outlawed in Egypt and was the entity responsible for the assassination of Anwar Sadat, and the attempted assassination of President Hosni Mubarak in 1995. The Egyptian Muslim Brotherhood also spawned Mohamed Atta, the ringleader of the September 11 attacks.

Obama – the *Ikhwan* – made clear his intentions soon after he seized control of the reins of power in the United States. He overruled his own Secret Service directives to personally invite 10 members of the Muslim Brotherhood's parliamentary bloc to attend his pro-Islamic, Quran praising, "I'm a Muslim" speech in Cairo in 2009, setting the stage by deed to let the Brotherhood know that the U.S. would not stand in the way of an MB overthrow in Egypt

Believe what you want. The facts speak at a volume far in excess of the filthy, despicable, sin-infested lies of the bribed members of the media and the corrupted members of Congress pretending they care about America.

Chapter Thirteen

The Treasonous Support of Hamas

Treason is defined both in the Constitution of the United States and in the United States Code. Let's take a look:

Article 3, Section 3

Treason against the United States, shall consist only in levying War against them, or in adhering to their Enemies, giving them Aid and Comfort. No Person shall be convicted of Treason unless on the Testimony of two Witnesses to the same overt Act, or on Confession in open Court.

The Congress shall have power to declare the Punishment of Treason, but no Attainder of Treason shall work Corruption of Blood, or Forfeiture except during the Life of the Person attainted.

Congress has taken additional steps to criminalize treason under the United States Code:

18 U.S.C. § 2381. Treason

Whoever, owing allegiance to the United States, levies war against them or adheres to their enemies, giving them aid and comfort within the United States or elsewhere, is guilty of treason and shall suffer death, or shall be imprisoned not less than five years and fined under this title but not less than $10,000; and shall be incapable of holding any office under the United States.

For purposes of our discussion, we will also reach beyond treason to misprision of treason, a federal law which criminalizes the act of knowing about the commission of treason and failing to disclose the same.

219

Congress has also codified this as a high crime and is defined under the United States Code as follows:

18 U.S.C. § 2382. Misprision of treason

Whoever, owing allegiance to the United States and having knowledge of the commission of any treason against them, conceals and does not, as soon as may be, disclose and make known the same to the President or to some judge of the United States, or to the governor or to some judge or justice of a particular State, is guilty of misprision of treason and shall be fined under this title or imprisoned not more than seven years, or both

Treason as discussed herein will concentrate on the *adhering to their Enemies, giving them Aid and Comfort* clause appearing in the constitution and the *adheres to their enemies, giving them aid and comfort* clause set forth in the United States Code.

One of our enemies is Hamas. Hamas is placed by the USA on the terrorist groups list (European Union recognizes only the military wing of Hamas as a terrorist organization). Groups that are placed on the terrorist group list are at war with the United States, and giving them aid and comfort is by definition an act of treason.

Obama's ties to Hamas make it an organization worthy of consideration. For instance, as early as May, 2008, Obama explained that he understood why Hamas supported his bid for the presidency, saying "This is a guy who spent some time in the Muslim world, has a middle name of Hussein and appears more worldly and has called for talks with people, and so he's not going to be engaging in the same sort of cowboy diplomacy as George Bush." Ahmed Yousef, a political adviser to Hamas, told an interviewer on WABC radio that "We like Mr. Obama" and "we hope that he will win the election."[200]   This support was a little more than just an endorsement. On April 26, 2008, WorldNetDaily reported that Hatem El-Hady, the former chairman of an Islamic charity that was closed by the US because of its terrorist fundraising and its ties to Hamas, managed a page on the Obama official website, listing Michelle Obama as one of three "friends."[201]

Obama's relationship to Hatem El-Hady is also something worthy of further inquiry. Before using his fundraising talents for Obama, Hatem El-Hady was the chairman of the Toledo, Ohio-based Islamic charity, Kindhearts.

After 9/11, the Benevolence International Foundation (BIF), Global Relief Foundation (GRF) and Holy Land Foundation for Relief and Development (HLF) were closed down, each accused of funneling millions of dollars to Al-Qaeda and/or Hamas. A handful of the leaders of the groups were taken into custody. Again for emphasis: the leaders of the groups listed above were taken into custody *for funneling money – millions of dollars   to Al-Qaeda and Hamas.* However, Khaled Smaili, the public relations representative for GRF, escaped prosecution, and

[200] Saul, Michael, *Barack Obama 'understands' Hamas view*, NYDailyNews, May 13, 2008
 http://www.nydailynews.com/news/politics/2008/05/13/2008-05-13_barack_obama_understands_hamas_view.html#ixzz16H7FEuPb

[201] *Obama's website quietly ditches Hamas supporter; Page for terrorist fundraiser suddenly disappears after drawing attention*, WorldNetDaily, April 26, 2008
http://www.wnd.com/?pageId=62653

followed these closures with the creation of KindHearts in January of 2002.[202]

KindHearts, in turn, was closed by the US Government for terrorist fundraising in February of 2006 – that is to say, *for funneling money to Al-Qaeda and Hamas*. KindHearts was an arm of the Holy Land Foundation and the Global Relief Foundation, and supported terrorism "behind the façade of charitable giving," according to Stuart Levy, Treasury Undersecretary for Terrorism and Financial Intelligence.[203]

El-Hady's KindHearts was a fundraising front for Hamas, and El-Hady had hired as its fundraising specialist Mohammed El-Mezain, Hamas's designated bag man in the US.[204] KindHeart's Director of Domestic Programs was Khalifah Ramadan, an operative for the Council on American Islamic Relations (CAIR) and the Islamic Society of North America (ISNA); another representative was Omar Shahin, an Imam for the Islamic Center of Tucson (ICT), the former home of numerous terror operatives, including Wael Jelaidan, who later helped found Al-Qaeda.[205]

---

[202] Kaufman, Joe, *The Black Hearts of KindHearts,* FrontPageMagazine.com, March 14, 2006
http://archive.frontpagemag.com/readArticle.aspx?ARTID=5236

[203] Poole, Patrick, *Terrorist Fundraisers for Obama,* FrontPageMagazine.com, April 23, 2008
http://archive.frontpagemag.com/readArticle.aspx?ARTID=30693

[204] *Id.*

[205] Kaufman, Joe, *The Black Hearts of KindHearts,* FrontPageMagazine.com, March 14, 2006
http://archive.frontpagemag.com/readArticle.aspx?ARTID=5236

El-Hady's "friends" page also included: Wagdy Ghuneim, an Egyptian cleric, who at a rally at Brooklyn College, in May of 1998, attempted to persuade the crowd to support violent jihad and labeled Jews as "descendants of the apes"; Hatem Bazian, an Islamic Studies instructor and a member of the faculty of Near Eastern Studies at UC Berkley, who, in April of 2004, during a San Francisco anti-war rally, called for an "intifada" against the United States; and Haytham Maghawri, who collected funds and sent them to Hamas and other Salafi groups. One of the recipients of KindHearts' funding was Specially Designated Global Terrorist (SDGT) Usama Hamdan, a leader of Hamas in Lebanon, and the South Asia Division Coordinator for KindHearts was Zulfiqar Ali Shah, an al-Qaeda operative working with the Tablighi Jamaat organization, an al-Qaeda recruitment group.[206]

El-Hady controlled a webpage on the official Obama campaign website that listed Michelle Obama as one of its three "friends."

So just how bad is Hamas? The name Hamas is an abbreviation of the Arabic words *Harakat al-Muqawama al-Islamiya*, meaning Islamic Resistance.[207]

Hamas emerged as an organization in the late 1960s, when it seceded as an independent wing of the Muslim Fraternity.[208] In 1978, the future Hamas was registered by Israeli authorities as a religious non-profit organization, under name of *Al Mujama*, headed by the leader of Muslim

---

[206] *Id.*

[207] Webman, Esther, *Anti-semitic motifs in the ideology of Hizballah and Hamas,* Project for the Study of Anti-Semitism, 1994.

[208] Heine Peter, *Terror in Allahs Namen*, Extremistische Krafte im Islam, Freiburg 2001.

Fraternity in Gaza Region, named Sheikh Ahmed Yassin (the Blind Sheikh). The activity of *Al Mujama* during 1980s was primarily promoting radical Islamic views among Cisjordanian Arabs, especially at social institutions and at universities, however, Yassin was an arms smuggler who was arrested and jailed in 1983 by Israeli authorities.[209]

Hamas began its militant activity in December 1987, after the outburst of *Intifada*, because several Cisjordanian Arabs were killed in a traffic accident involving an Israeli driver. This event led Yassin to organize with six other Palestinians the militant version of Hamas, picking up members and supporters among Cisjordanian Arabs throughout Israel. Hamas used its acronym in print for the first time in 1987 in a flyer that accused the Mossad (Israeli intelligence service) of undermining the morality of Islamic youth.

At that time, there were several armed Palestinian organizations already in action, including the Palestine Liberation Organization and Islamic Jihad or the Popular Front for the Liberation of Palestine – PFLP. Hamas, however, entered the fray as a radical organization that categorically excluded any compromise with Israel, refusing to ever recognize the state of Israel.

In 1989, members of Hamas attacked and killed two Israeli soldiers. The Israel Defense Forces (IDF) immediately arrested Yassin, tried him, convicted him, and sentenced him to life in prison. Four hundred Hamas activists were also deported to South Lebanon, which was occupied at that time by Israeli forces.

---

[209] Jarzabek, Jaroslaw, *Hamas*, HatikvahMagazyn Kultury Zedowskioj, November   2003

In 1992, the military branch of Hamas, the *Izz ad-Din al-Qassam* Brigades, was created.[210] The Brigades were established to provide Hamas with an armed option to support its political objectives. Although Hamas' main power base is the Gaza Strip, it has substantial support in the West Bank as well. The Brigades are also known as the Executive Force, and are an armed element of the military wing and operate independently of the other sections of Hamas. They are divided into a number of independent and specialized cells.

The Brigades have a substantial weapons inventory of light automatic weapons and grenades, improvised rockets, mortars, bombs, suicide belts and explosives. The Brigades fire 'Qassam' rockets and mortar shells into Israel on a regular basis. There have been over 8,000 strikes against the town of S'derot, Israel, since the 2006 election, and over 3,000 since Israel withdrew from the Gaza and returned the area to Hamas control exclusively.[211] The group engages in military style training, including training in Iran and Syria.

The Brigades, with two other groups, were responsible for the action which led to the death of two Israeli soldiers and the kidnapping of Corporal Gilat Shalit in June 2006.[212]

Because the Brigades are directly preparing, planning, assisting in or fostering the doing of terrorist acts, the

---

[210] *Hamas's Izz al-Din al-Qassam Brigades*, Australian National Security, What Governments Are Doing, Australian Government, February 22, 2010.

[211] This is the author's own reference, having visited S'derot in May of 2010.

[212] *Hamas's Izz al-Din al-Qassam Brigade, Id.*

Australian Government has concluded that the acts attributable to the Brigades are terrorist acts as they:

- are done with the intention of advancing a political cause, namely, destruction of the state of Israel, and establishment of an Islamic state in the current Israel, Gaza Strip and West Bank;
- are intended to coerce or influence by intimidation the governments of foreign countries, including Israel and/or intimidate the Israeli public; and
- constitute acts which cause serious physical harm to persons, including death, as well as serious damage to property.[213]

Hamas' *Izz al-Din al-Qassam* Brigades (the Brigades) have been proscribed as a terrorist organization by the government of the United Kingdom. Hamas itself, and including the Brigades, has been proscribed as a terrorist organization by the governments of the United States and Canada. Hamas is also listed by the European Union for the purposes of its anti-terrorism financing measures.

During the 1990s the al-Qassam Brigades conducted many attacks against civilians and the Israeli military. From April 1993 these included suicide bombings, for which Hamas became well-known internationally.[214] The Brigades' Yahya Ayash who was reputed to have been the mastermind of most of the early suicide attacks, was assassinated by the Israeli secret service in early 1996.[215]

---

[213] *Id.*

[214] *Palestinian territories: Inside Hamas,* PBS Frontline: World, May 9, 2006)

[215] Baruch Kimmerling & Joel S. Migdal, *The Palestinian people: a history.*

Hamas also opposed the Oslo accords,[216] and engaged in a new series of suicide attacks against Israeli targets following their ratification. Hamas used as its *raison d'etre* the February 1994 massacre by Baruch Goldstein of 30 Muslims in the Ma'arat Machpelah, a temple built by Herod over the gravesite of Abraham, Sarah, Isaac, Rachel and Jacob, which is sometimes a Hebron mosque, and at other times, a Jewish Synagogue,[217] an attack apparently in retaliation for the mindless slaughter and maiming of the Jewish families living in Hebron in 1929.[218] These Jewish men, women and children were slaughtered because of a rumor instigated by the Grand Mufti of Jerusalem that the Jews were cooking their food in the blood of slaughtered Palestinian infants. The Grand

---

[216] The Accords, signed in September, 1993, provided for the creation of a Palestinian National Authority (PNA). The Palestinian Authority would have responsibility for the administration of the territory under its control. The Accords also called for the withdrawal of the Israel Defense Forces (IDF) from parts of the Gaza Strip and West Bank.

It was anticipated that this arrangement would last for a five-year interim period during which a permanent agreement would be negotiated (beginning no later than May 1996). Permanent issues such as positions on Jerusalem, Palestinian refugees, Israeli settlements, security and borders were deliberately left to be decided at a later stage. Interim Palestinian self-government was to be granted by Israel in phases.

[217] *Massacre in Hebron,* TIME Domestic, March 28, 1994 Volume 143, No. 13.

[218] Sixty-seven Jews were killed on 23 and 24 August 1929 in Hebron, then part of the British Mandate of Palestine, by Arabs incited to violence by rumors instigated by the Grand Mufti of Jerusalem that Jews were massacring Arabs in Jerusalem and seizing control of Muslim holy places. Shira Schoenberg, *The Hebron Massacre of 1929*, Jewish Virtual Library

Mufti would later come to recommend the Final Solution to Adolf Hitler.

In September 1997, Israeli agents in Jordan attempted but failed to assassinate Hamas leader Khaled Mashaal, which lead to soured relations between the two countries and the subsequent release of Sheikh Yassin (the "Blind Sheikh"), Hamas's spiritual leader, from an Israeli prison. Two years later Hamas was banned in Jordan, reportedly in part at the request of the United States, Israel, and the Palestinian Authority, and part due to the rise of Syrian and Iranian control emerging under Hezbollah.[219]

Jordan's King Abdullah feared the activities of Hamas and its Jordanian allies would jeopardize peace negotiations with Israel, and accused Hamas of engaging in illegitimate activities within Jordan.[220] In mid-September 1999, authorities arrested Hamas leaders Khaled Mashaal and Ibrahim Ghosheh on their return from a visit to Iran, and charged them with being members of an illegal organization, storing weapons, conducting military exercises, and using Jordan as a training base. Hamas leaders denied the charges. Mashaal was exiled and eventually settled in Syria.[221]

Hamas was organized primarily in mosques, using an emphasis on the jihad portions of the Quran as a main source of propaganda. During the 1990s and early 2000s, the organization conducted numerous suicide bombings and other attacks directed against Israel.

---

[219] Baruch Kimmerling & Joel S. Migdal, *The Palestinian people: a history, op. cit.*

[220] *Id.*

[221] *Supra.*

In 2003, Israel's Prime Minister Ariel Sharon, having duly notified the leadership of the Palestinian Authority in advance, entered the surface of the Temple Mount, launching the *second intifada*. This intifada ultimately culminated with the death of Yassir Arafat and a power struggle within the West Bank and Gaza.

In the election of January, 2006, Hamas secured a majority of the seats in the Palestinian parliament, making Hamas the lawful authority in both the West Bank and the Gaza.[222] The ruling members of Fatah were not prepared to accept such a fate, and a series of violent clashes resulted in Hamas became the ruling authority in Gaza only[223] without dissent from Fatah,[224] while Hamas members have been ousted from government positions in the West Bank.[225]

Following the 2006 elections, the long standing animosity between Hamas and Fatah rose in intensity until Hamas killed hundreds of Fatah members and supporters in Gaza. In June 2007, elected Hamas officials were ousted from their positions in the PA government in the West Bank and replaced by rival Fatah members and independents. Hamas has since retained control of the Gaza Strip. Both Israel and Egypt then imposed an economic blockade on Gaza, and sealed the borders to prevent the smuggling of weapons into the Gaza. After gaining control of Gaza, Hamas and its militias launched rocket attacks

---

[222] The American Chronicle, *The largest and most influential Palestinian political party, Fatah, electing new leadership.*

[223] *The Gangs of Gaza,* Newsweek, June 26, 2006.

[224] al-Mughrabi, Nidal and Assadi, Mohammed. *Palestinian in-fighting provokes despair, frustration,* Reuters, October 3, 2006.

[225] *The Palestinian National Unity Government.* February 24, 2007. http://www.canadafreepress.com/2007/inss022407.htm.

upon Israel, which slowed down for a short period after Egypt brokered a ceasefire. The ink dried, and Hamas began shelling S'derot again with mortar fire and Kasam rockets, such that, in December, 2008, Israel launched a targeted invasion of Gaza, attacking armories and launching areas. Israel then withdrew its forces in mid-January, 2009.

Hamas, conversely, continued to engage in yet another round of arrests and executions of Fatah members in Gaza following the withdrawal of Israeli forces from Gaza in January 2009.

Hamas is a Muslim fundamentalist organization – an organization that focuses on Islamic extremism in the teaching of jihad. Its radicalism distinguishes Hamas from the other Palestinian organizations, including those organizations that function in the West Bank, by the degree of its extremism. Radicalization under the Quran and the teachings of the Islamic Hadith within schools and mosques where Cisjordanian Arabs attend, coupled with Iranian and US funding, are the primary reasons for the radical religious behavior, resulting in growing support for Islamic fundamentalists and terrorists.

The main goals of Hamas activists are set forth in the *Hamas Pledge*, a document published on August 18, 1988: "Israel will remain only as long (…) as it will not be demolished by Islam."

Article 6 of the Hamas Pledge declares that the main aim of the organization is "raising Allah's banner over every inch of Palestinian land" which, according to Hamas, is the "holy property of Muslims" and declares that the liberation of "Palestinian land" is an individual duty of every Muslim.

Hamas claims in the Pledge that Jews are usurping rights to Palestinian soil and proclaiming Jihad, alerting every Allah believer to fight against Jewish country. Su statements are the very definition of Islamic extremism, and acting on such dictates is well-defined as acts of terrorism.

Article 13 expressly condemns peace talks. Hamas declares that peace talks are "against the rules of Islamic Resistance," and international participation in such peace process is "employing non-believers as judges in a country of Islam."

Hamas believes and teaches that "there is no other solution to Palestinian problem as Jihad only, and peace talks are just a waste of time." Hamas has condemned the Camp David accords and subsequent peace treaty as an Egyptian betrayal and an attempt to divide the Arabic world. The Pledge also includes many parts discussing the inevitable extermination of Jews ("Judgment Day will not come before Muslims kill Jews"), and blaming the Jews for wars, revolutions and world Zionist plot.

Hamas engages primarily in military actions and terrorist attacks, prepared by its military wing, *Izz el-Din al-Qassam* Brigade. The brigades are divided into five independent detachments. Military actions on a large scale have been conducted since 1992, and consist of the kidnapping and killing of Israeli soldiers, attacks with firearms onto military targets and onto Jewish settlements within occupied territories, and bomb attacks (setting blasts into public places, using car traps, etc.). In April of 1994 Hamas conducted its first suicidal bomb attack.

According to a study from 2000, around 70% of Cirjordanian Arabs support suicide/homicide bombings as a means of fighting with Israel. There have been about 90 suicide attacks, conducted mainly by Hamas and Islamic Jihad.

Financial support for Hamas comes from Arabic

s and foundations located in Europe and North ...ch as the Foundation for Development and Help of Palestine in Great Britain, the Holy Land Foundation in the USA (in December 2001 its assets were taken over by American authorities as part of their war on terrorism), and the Al-Aksa Foundation in Germany, with branches in Belgium and the Netherlands. Large sums are also given by foundations and private donors from Saudi Arabia and other Arabian countries. Iran is also a primary funding agent.

Hamas was placed by the USA on the terrorist groups list (European Union recognizes only the military wing of Hamas as a terrorist organization). Groups that are placed on the terrorist group list are at war with the United States, and giving them aid and comfort is by the constitutional definition and act of treason.

On February 24, 2009, Obama announced a NINE HUNDRED MILLION DOLLAR ($900,000,000.00) funding in aid for rebuilding the Hamas-controlled Gaza Strip. That is to say, *Obama funneled millions of dollars to Hamas*. Hamas was very happy that its fundraising efforts for the presidential campaign provided such a windfall.[226] The lion's share of the funds were to be controlled by the United Nations Relief and Work Agency, or UNWRA, which administers aid to millions of Palestinian "refugees" in the Gaza Strip and West Bank. According to Klein, Hamas has a close relationship with UNWRA, and the agency openly employs a large number of Hamas members, including some of the group's most senior terrorists.[227]

---

[226] Klein, Aaron, *Hamas 'happy' with Obama's $900 million pledge; Funds earmarked for U.N. agency that openly employs terrorists,* WorldNetDaily, February 24, 2009

[227] *Id.*

Here's another early act of Obama in furtherance of the Muslim Brotherhood agenda, done under the darkness of *taqiya* on behalf of *jihad*, in the name of Allah. On January 27, 2009, five days following his corrected oath of office,[228] Obama issues the following Executive Order:

Presidential Determination No. 2009-15 of January 27, 2009[229]

Unexpected Urgent Refugee and Migration Needs Related To Gaza

Memorandum for the Secretary of State

By the authority vested in me by the Constitution and the laws of the United States, including section 2(c)(1) of the Migration and Refugee Assistance Act of 1962 (the "Act"), as amended (22 U.S.C. 2601), I hereby determine, pursuant to section 2(c)(1) of the Act, that it is important to the national interest to furnish assistance under the Act in an amount not to exceed $20.3 million from the United States Emergency Refugee and Migration Assistance Fund for the purpose of meeting unexpected and urgent refugee and migration needs, including by contributions to international, governmental, and nongovernmental organizations and payment of administrative expenses of Bureau of Population, Refugees, and Migration of the

---

[228] The President shall . . .take the following Oath or Affirmation:--"I do solemnly swear (or affirm) that I will faithfully execute the Office of President of the United States, and will to the best of my Ability, preserve, protect and defend the Constitution of the United States." U.S. Constitution, Article II, Section 1.

[229] Federal Register: February 4, 2009 (Volume 74, Number 22)] [Presidential Documents][Page 6115]From the Federal Register Online via GPO Access [wais.access.gpo.gov] [DOCID:fr04fe09-106]

Department of State, related to humanitarian needs of Palestinian refugees and conflict victims in Gaza.
You are authorized and directed to publish this memorandum in the Federal Register.
(Presidential Sig.)
THE WHITE HOUSE,
Washington, January 27, 2009

While the President may have the authority to direct funds under the United States Emergency Refugee and Migration Assistance Fund, he does not have authority to commit treason, to wit:

> *Treason against the United States, shall consist only in levying War against them, or in adhering to their Enemies, giving them Aid and Comfort. No Person shall be convicted of Treason unless on the Testimony of two Witnesses to the same overt Act, or on Confession in open Court.*[230]

As to the $900 million in U.S. funds in November, 2010, that Obama and Secretary of State Hillary Clinton promised to the PLO: Mahmoud Abbas, the head of the Palestine Authority (PA) and the PLO and Tayeb Abd Al-Rahim are the leaders of these organizations.[231] The PA now has so little authority, Abbas is considering dissolving it.[232] However, of the $900 million coming in, at least half

---

[230] U.S. Constitution, Article III, Sec. 3

[231] RWBNews, *Obama approves $900 MILLION to Palestine in the latest Mid-East Peace talks,* December 5, 2010
http://redwhitebluenews.com/?p=8523

[232] Miskin, Maayana, *Most PA Money Goes to Hamas-run Gaza, Abbas Admits,* Arutz Sheva, December 5, 2010
http://www.israelnationalnews.com/News/News.aspx/140963

with go to Hamas in the Gaza Strip.[233] It is well understood that Abbas cannot throw free and fair elections in the West Bank because he fears that Hamas, which won overwhelmingly in Gaza, would post a similar win in the West Bank. Those loyal to the PA in Gaza have been summarily executed by members of Hamas in those periods when militants in the Gaza stop shelling civilians in the Israeli cities (in undisputed lands) that abut the Gaza Strip.

Abbas and the Palestinian Authority continue to pay a monthly salary to 77,000 Gaza residents who formerly worked for the Fatah-led PA that was overturned in a bloody Hamas coup in 2007. PA money also covers the cost of fuel for the Gaza power plant, the district's water, many of the medicines in Gaza hospitals. A total of 58% of the PA's funds go to Gaza.[234] Of the $900 million, $522 million of it is going directly to Hamas in the form of a salary – think of it as a professional stipend to free up those hours when preparing a mortar launch on S'derot may be the order of the day.

There are 1.5 million people living in the Gaza Strip. 1.2 million of them support Hamas. 400,000 of them *are* Hamas.

[233] *Id,*

[234] *Id.*

Chapter Fourteen

Empowering Turkey and the Ottoman Empire

Does Obama seek to further the ambitions of the Turks to reestablish the Caliphate – the Ottoman Empire, and is he working in a clandestine way to accomplish this goal as a closet jihadist working on behalf of Islam and the Muslim Brotherhood at the expense of the West? Let's see if the facts as they can be readily found play any of this out.

On December 7, 2009, Obama met with Turkey's Erdoğan to discuss "strategies for Turkey's further involvement in Afghanistan and Pakistan."[235] Turkey expects to reassert its influence over Tadzhikistan, Uzbekistan, Kyrgyzstan, Kazakhstan, Turkmenistan, Afghanistan and Pakistan by introducing a "secular" Islamic model over the top of the Taliban fundamental model.

The Islamic nations of Tadzhikistan, Uzbekistan, Kyrgyzstan, Kazakhstan, Turkmenistan, Afghanistan and Pakistan are all intended to fall under Turkish influence and control as the Ottoman alliances are recreated in furtherance of reestablishing the Islamic Kingdom under a single Caliph –the nations of Islam united under a new Caliphate. This influence may also reach well into Russia herself, including the Islamic Oblasts of Dagestan, Chechnya, Ingushetia, Kabardino-Balkaria and Cherkassy.

This does not complete the authorization to rebuild, however. When Obama met with Erdoğan at the G-20

---

[235]   http://www.hurriyetdailynews.com/n.php?n=obama-to-welcome-turkish-prime-minister-to-white-house-on-2009-10-30

summit, additional strategies were discussed.[236] There was discussion about the Upper Karabakh – a disjointed piece of property to the south of Armenia, claimed by both Armenia and Azerbaijan, but occupied currently by Armenia. The willingness to discuss Turkey's influence on the Upper Karabakh while ignoring the issue of genocide against the Armenians in the last hours of the Ottoman Empire speaks volumes.

Erdoğan must have considered himself empowered, because when he left the G-20, he proceeded to New York where he attended a reception given on the occasion of the 40th anniversary of the foundation of the Organization of the Islamic Conference, OIC, and held talks with UN Secretary General Ban Ki-moon.

Since that time, and with the full permission and authority of the United States' Executive Branch, Erdoğan has formed a high level cooperation council with Pakistan on October 25, 2009, consolidated Turkey's alliance with Muslim Azerbaijan, calling the Azeri flag and territories "holy" (Dar-es-salaam) on October 23, 2009, which is tantamount to a declaration of jihad against Armenia (a Christian nation).

But in case you think this is the worst of it, consider that on October 16, 2009, Turkey signed accords with Iraq for regional integration.[237] Under these 48 accords, visa requirements and trans-border restrictions are all but abolished as though the two nations were . . . one empire.

Let's continue, shall we? On October 13, 2009, Turkey signed a 38 point accord with Syria that ended visa

---

[236] http://wwwtrtenglish.com/trtinternatinal/en/newsDetail.aspx?
HaberKodu=3e413a41-a9c2-440d-b74e-b329932c2e3b

[237]   http://merryabla64.wordpress.com/2009/10/16/turkey-iraq-sign-accords-for-regional-integration/

restrictions and travel between the two countries. The arrangement is more or less borderless. The vehicle used for this accord was something called the Turkey-Syria High Level Strategic Cooperation Council.[238]

Although this covenant with the many was established in the fall of 2009, it has been recently reiterated.

Securing Jerusalem from the Israelis

However, no sooner did Erdoğan wrap up the initial phase of the alliance between Turkey and Azerbaijan, Syria, Iraq, Iran, Tadzhikistan, Uzbekistan, Kyrgyzstan, Kazakhstan, Turkmenistan, Afghanistan and Pakistan (the nations ending with "Stan" are referred to in the bible as the lands of "Magog"), then Ban Ki-moon starts to press for international control over Jerusalem.[239]

Ban Ki-moon is pushing to make Jerusalem the capitol of both the Palestinian state and Israel, in order to make the holy sites acceptable to all. He stressed that the international community does not recognize Israel's annexation of East Jerusalem.

To make matters worse, Obama now wants a cram down, forcing the Israelis to accept the creation of Jerusalem as the capitol of the new Palestinian state as a unilateral move without Israeli approval.[240]

The One is moving well along his agenda, which is *inconsistent* with the agenda of his mentors, a total

---

[238] http://www.interesclub.org/home/3417.html?task=view

[239] http://www.scoop.co.nz/stories/WO0910/S00421.htm

[240] Klein, Aaron, *Obama green-lights Arab land grab*, WorldNetDaily, November 15, 2009.

violation of his duty to the United States of America, a betrayal of his oath of office, and a betrayal of the Western world. He is on the precipice of completely destroying the American economy for generations. He has already launched Turkey into a full court press to reestablish the Islamic Caliphate whose capitol will be Jerusalem, and he is well underway to securing Jerusalem from the Israelis, notwithstanding their objections.

When Obama began his denounce America tour while kowtowing to the Muslims whose agents attacked our largest city and our capitol city, he spoke in Ankara, Turkey and in Cairo, Egypt to make the claim that America "is not and never will be at war with Islam." Spoken like a true Ikhwan. However, his statement is buttressed by decades of anti-Christian, pro-Muslim policies of one US administration after another giving credence to Muslims and their terrorist progeny at the expense of Christian, Jews, and civilization in general.

America – an enemy of Christianity?

According to Mordechai Nisan, "America has been at war with Christians who are at war with Muslims, while the United States has accepted the defeat and death of Christians at the hands of Muslims." Nisan makes the argument that because of the "special relationship" of the US with Saudi Arabia that has been in place for at least 70 years, the Saudis have been allowed to promote a radical form of Islam all over the world.[241] The incorporation of Turkey into the NATO alliance in 1952 was a special

---

[241] Nisan, Mordechai, *Commentary: U.S. Has Long Sided with Arab World,* October 11, 2010

accommodation to the Saudis that was the result of this relationship, as is the decades-long alliance with the radical Islamic nation of Pakistan

Obama has a particular, pro-Islamic inclination, and when it comes to the rivalries between Muslims and Christians, the federal government has continually sided with Muslims, beginning with the Nixon administration's support of the Turkish invasion of Cyprus, continuing through the war crimes that was the Bosnian/Kosovo conflict under Clinton, to Obama's bowing to the Saudi king.

The Balkans have been a problem for Europe since the Ottomans first invaded in the 15th century. Albania, the Kosovoan portion of Serbia, Macedonia, Montenegro and Bosnia-Herzegovina - predominantly Muslim nations for the last five centuries, - presented a particularly difficult proposition to the Austrian-Hungarian empire. The assassination of the Archduke Ferdinand in Sarajevo, Bosnia was the impetus that set off the powder keg we call World War 1. Only under the brutal dictatorship of Tito was the region unified (with the exclusion of Albania), and then only under communism. Once Tito died and glasnost and perestroika prevailed in the USSR, the unified communist enclave known as Yugoslavia broke apart into its traditional regional states. Civil war followed, and the Christians in Serbia found themselves fighting against not only the indigenous Muslim populations in the various states, but also imported Mujahedeen from the Afghan-Russian wars.

The war in Bosnia and Croatia from 1992-95 and in Kosovo from 1996-99 pitted these ethnic and religious communities against each other in the former boundaries of Yugoslavia, which had ceased to exist in the early 1990s. Orthodox Christian Serbs were forced to flee as refugees

240

from Catholic Croatia, and Muslim-dominated Bosnia-Herzegovina. With the help of direct NATO interference, Serbia was also forced to withdraw from its own Muslim-dominated territory of Kosovo. The worldwide propaganda, promoted vociferously by U.S. Secretary of State Madelyn Albright, portrayed the Serbs as aggressors, murderers, and rapists.

As Nisan points out, "the United States supported the adversaries and enemies of the Serb people, offering them moral sanction and military advice, arms and money; by contrast, the Serbs were defamed, ultimately charged with war crimes and "ethnic cleansing" at the International Criminal Court in the Hague. The sweeping obliteration of Serbian religious history and life in Kosovo was consummated with the destruction of monasteries and the desecration of churches, as Serbs ran for their lives."[242]

America chose Islam over Christianity throughout the Balkans during this conflict, allowing both the Saudis and the Iranians to assist Muslim jihadist fighting Serbs throughout the region. It was American bombers who, without any defined national interest, bombed Serb civilian targets, strafed Belgrade, and destroyed the Chinese embassy in the Serbian capitol in 1995, under the Presidency of Bill Clinton, the approval and demand of Madelyn Albright, and the command of General Wesley Clark. America reversed the hegemony of Christendom over the continent of Europe for the first time since the 1500s.

In June, 1593, the power of the Ottoman Empire began its long decline, with its defeat in the Battle of Sisak (now in modern Croatia). This battle began on June 22, 1593, where 5,000 Christian Croats defended the fortress of

---

[242] *Commentary: U.S. Has Long Sided with Arab World, Supra*

Sisak against 12,000 Turks. With the assistance of artillery, the smaller force decimated the Turks, and when the Turks found themselves ambushed between two rivers, they panicked and attempted to flee, resulting in a complete rout. This marked the beginning of the end for the Ottoman Empire which culminated with "the fatal head wound" in the collapse of the Ottoman Empire in 1924. American policy has since reversed this decline with pro-Muslim policies, and Obama now works to restore the Ottomans in a neo-Ottoman caliphate.

For instance, in 1995 the Americans formulated the Dayton Agreement, an agreement intended to end fighting in Bosnia between the majority Muslims and the minority Serbs. This agreement was devised after NATO bombed Serb civilian targets with impunity, effectively softening Serb resistance to Muslim forces in Bosnia. American bombers also strafed Belgrade, the capital of Serbia, and made it a point to "accidentally" bomb the Chinese embassy therein. Saudis and Iranians were assisting the Muslim jihadists in the area, which were also reinforced with former members of Afghan Mujahedeen (then formulated as al Qaeda). Democratic leadership in America also chose to give political feet to Islamic forces in the Balkans at the expense of Christians, which has contributed to the strengthening and expansion of Islam in Europe.

Although Obama confirmed this covenant with many in the name of consistency with long-standing U.S. foreign policy, the relationship between the executive branch of the U.S. government and the Saudis has been in place long before GWB held hands with the Saudi king, or before Obama bowed and kissed the ring. Obama actually gave voice to U.S. policy in religiously-defined conflicts, because American-Islamic compatibility was a central aspect of Washington's conduct long before Obama made it central to the American political creed.

The Levant – a swath of territory running from south-eastern Europe across Asia Minor and toward the eastern Mediterranean basin- was conquered and controlled by the Turkish Ottoman Empire for centuries until WWI when the Ottomans, having sided with the Germans and the Austrians, found itself on the losing side. The collapse of the empire followed the genocide launched by the Turks against the Armenians, and resulted in the Ottomans ceding control of the area we now call the middle east to the French in the case of what we now refer to as Lebanon and Syria, and to the British in the case of what we call Iraq, Kuwait, Jordan, and of course Israel.

As a result of the desires of American oil interests, in 1900, a radical sect of Muslim extremists in the Arabian Peninsula were developed and funded to initiate a breakaway rebellion to the Ottoman control over the oil sands in Arabia. This unlawful rebellion was successful, and in 1901 resulted in the creation of the kingdom of Saudi Arabia, a kingdom controlled by Sunni Wahabist Muslim extremists who have instituted a fundamental version of Shari'a law that is the most intolerant society on earth for religious diversity. Wikileaks has since disclosed that the American intelligence organizations recognize that Saudi Arabia is the single largest funder of Islamic terrorism on earth; that donors in Saudi Arabia "continue to constitute a source of funding to Sunni extremist groups worldwide, especially during the Hajj and Ramadan."[243]

---

[243] Lister, Tim, *WikiLeaks cables assess terrorism funding in Saudi Arabia, Gulf states,* CNN World, December 06, 2010. http://articles.cnn.com/2010-12-06/world/wikileaks.terrorism.funding_1_saudi-arabia-terrorist-funding-terrorist-groups?_s=PM:WORLD

Obama's confirmation of the pro-Islamic policies of the American government can be best understood by looking at a few precedents, the actions of the United States in Cyprus, Lebanon, and Israel. A quick review indicates that Obama was correct in declaring that America is no longer a Christian country.

Cyprus

When the Turks invaded Cyprus in 1974 and took the northern third of the Island from Greece in order to declare the Turkish Republic of Cyprus, the act of war and premeditated aggression was taken by Turkey when Turkey was an American ally and a NATO member-country. The United States supplied Turkey with arms and funding for this escapade. At the time, only about twenty percent of the population in Cyprus was Turkish Muslim. Fearing a Greek takeover of the island which could harm the Muslim minority, Turkey used military force to implement a policy of "ethnic cleansing" that evicted 200,000 Greek Cypriots from their property. Christian churches and cemeteries in Northern Cyprus were desecrated by Muslims.

Lebanon

The United States in 1976, under President Carter, dealt secretly with the Palestine Liberation Organization (PLO) and its operatives to evict Lebanese Christians from Lebanon through a mass evacuation and emigration scheme during the civil war that began in 1975 between the Maronite Christians, the alien Palestinians and the illegally occupying Syrians. Christian villages and urban neighborhoods were mercilessly targeted, and they suffered significant civilian fatalities, slaughter and devastation. In 1989, the US sealed the fate of Lebanese Christians with the Taif Accord, an accord that demoted the office of the Presidency and elevate the Muslim-held offices of Prime Minister and the Speaker of the Legislature. The accord also defined Lebanon as an Arab country in close relations with Syria. The ancient Christians of Lebanon were abandoned.

Israel

Although American media interests have continually labeled the US as "Israel's best friend" claiming that the two countries enjoy a strategic relationship, the United States has often been a great adversary of Israel's national interests and rights. For instance, since 1967, Washington has opposed Israel's retention of territories captured in the Six Day War.

The Six Day War occurred in June of 1967. On the third day of the Six Day War, an Israeli paratrooper announced that the Temple Mount had been regained. On June 7 of that year, Israeli troops moved into the Old City and stood at the Western Wall (Wailing Wall) for prayer, where Rabbi Shlomo Goren declared:

"We have taken the city of God. We are entering the Messianic era for the Jewish people, and I promise to the Christian world that what we are responsible for we will take care of."[244] The city of Jerusalem was reunified and the Star of David flew again from its ramparts.

---

[244]Dolphin, Lambert, *Moving Towards a Third Jewish Temple,* July 9, 1997

However, on Saturday June 17, 1967, shortly after the end of the Six Day War, Israeli Defense minister Moshe Dayan negotiated the removal of the Israeli flag from the top of the Dome of the Rock with five leaders of the Supreme Muslim Council (the Waqf). Dayan went on to negotiate away the victory of Israel over Jerusalem and made further concessions, such as granting administrative control over the Temple Mount to the Supreme Muslim Council - the Jordanian Waqf. Prayer by Jews was prohibited, and Dayan refused to allow any Jewish identification with Judaism's holiest site.[245] Dayan was quoted as saying that the Temple Mount was "a historic site relating to past memory."

The Waqf to this day does not accept the reunification of Jerusalem. Islamic preachers during the regular Friday day of prayer on the Mount regularly and routinely denounce Israel the right of the Jews to exist, frequently delivering inflammatory polemics designed to foster Arab hatred towards the Jews.

During this war, the United States had a plan to intervene militarily in the Middle East, including an attack on Israel, if it believed that the integrity of any nation in the region was threatened. The US seriously considered military intervention against Israel, as well as against Arab nations in the event of a war. The relationship of the US to Israel is actually variable. The State Department tends to favor Arab states, while presidents pay lip-service to the "special relationship" with Israel. This idea was exemplified by the evasive behavior of the U.S. government in the critical period preceding the Six Day War.

---

[245] *Op cit.*

When Israeli diplomat Abba Eban sought US intervention to pressure Egypt not to proceed against Israel in the spring of 1967, he got nothing. He was turned down by Secretary of State Dean Rusk He was turned down by Secretary of Defense Robert McNamara, and he was turned down by President Johnson. The US would not commit itself to the defense of Israel for constitutional reasons. After the six day war, the US added insult to injury by failing to agree to Israeli requests for rearmament.

The diplomatic corps of the US at that time considered Israel a liability and an "unviable client state." Following the Israeli victory in the six day war, the US Senate even discussed the idea of terminating the tax deductible status of Jewish charities in the US, in order to deprive Israel of its independence of action.

The US prepared to recoup its loss of status with the Saudis following the war, by trading on its influence with Israel in order to put the US in a position to recover the "land of the Arabs" for the Arabs. Diplomats of the U.S. diplomatic service and State Department were categorically "Arabist" and anti-Israeli even before the inception of the state of Israel. The State Department told Truman that a Zionist state would support the USSR and be a communist state. Only as a result of the Israeli victory in the Six Day war did the US come to view Israel as a strategic asset.

America then used Israeli strength to gain a foothold in the Middle East, used Israeli intelligence to enhance US operations in the Middle East, and used Israel as a silent but vital ally in the 1991 Desert Storm war against Iraq. However, in 1993, under yet another Democrat President, the US sought and obtained the so-called Oslo Accord – a reaffirmation of the arbitrary boundary lines of U.N. Resolution S.181 (the '49

247

boundaries), designed to create a Palestinian state in the CisJordan region of the Levant.

Under the presidency of GW Bush, Israel pushed ahead in agreement with the US for the "Road Map" two-state plan, a plan that like the Oslo Accord would create a Palestinian state on the old '49 borders. Israelis who have not entered into this covenant of death[246] (בְּרִית מָוֶת) understand that Israel's survival will be endangered if the Palestinians have a state on the mountains above Israel, while intertwined with the hatred and hostility from neighboring Arab and Muslim countries.

The US presses Israel at all turns, arming the Palestinians, funding Hamas, and relentlessly seeking ways to clobber Israel into submission. Arabs are never expected to accept responsibility for murderous terrorism. The U.S. has directly supervised the military training and arming of the Palestinian Authority. The United States actually spurs on war in its support of CisJordanian Muslims against Jews, while paying lip service to the goal and fruits of peace.

It would be equally naïve to believe that the US supports "Palestinians" to the exclusion of Jews. The US supports Muslim Palestinians to the exclusion of Christian Palestinians, and through its political demands and funding allows the majority Muslim element to oppress, persecute and intimidate Christian Palestinians, allowing for the eviction of Christian Palestinians from Bethlehem, the murdering of converts to Christianity, and the ransacking and torching of Palestinian Christian homes. Such actions have never been criticized by US diplomats or its propaganda ministers in state-run media.

---

[246] Isaiah 28:14-15

The lying dogs of the American media system have raised the alarm over the 1982 Christian Lebanese massacre of Palestinian Muslims in Sabra and Shatila in Beirut, and the Christian Serb massacre of Bosnian Muslims in Srebrenica in 1995, while ignoring the Turkish Cypriot Muslim massacre of Greek Christian Cypriots in Palekythro and the Turkish bombing of Kyrenian civilians in 1974. The media ignored the Palestinian massacre of Lebanese Christians in Damour and Ayshiyyah in 1976, the Bosnian Muslim slaughter of withdrawing Serb Christian soldiers on Dobrovoljacka Street in Sarajevo in 1992, and has completely forgotten about the Palestinian terrorist bomb-attack murdering 21 Israelis at the Maxim Restaurant in Haifa in 2003.

The martyrdom of Christians in today's world is unimaginable. Christians are the most persecuted religious group in the world. More people have lost their lives for their Christianity since 1900 than in all the previous centuries combined. During the twentieth century more of them died, as a result of persecutions, than in all the preceding nineteen hundreds since the birth of Christ. Christians are subjected to slavery, torture and murder. All over the world there are about 200 million followers of Christ suffering these barbarities today. The average number of Christian martyrs per year worldwide is 163,000. According to a 1998 report by the Helsinki International Federation for Human Rights, 19 European countries violate religious liberty.[247]

To carefully understand the full scope of Obama's unconditional support for the rising neo-Ottoman empire, consider that the Turks have acted as instigators and aggressors in the Balkans, aggressors in Cyprus, and

---

[247] http://www.liferesearchuniversal.com/etstats2.html

recently assumed the role of patron of the Palestinian people's war against Israel. Turkey was the funding agent behind the Mavi Marmara naval incident (the "Gaza Flotilla") in May 2010, and has abandoned its alliance with Israel to become an ally of Islamic Iran.

Then the president of Brazil, the largest US ally in Latin America, and the prime minister of Turkey, for more than half a century the Muslim anchor of NATO, were photographed raising hands together with Mahmoud Ahmadinejad, the rabid anti-American President of Iran. Brazil and Turkey went out of their way to give cover for Iran's nuclear ambitions, and Turkey deliberately undermined US efforts to curb Iran's nuclear program.[248]

Let's see if you can answer the question why Obama would give carte blanche to Turkey's prime minister under these circumstances.

[248] Krauthammer, Charles, *The Fruit of Obama's Weakness – Brazil & Turkey Allied With Iran Against USA,* The Washington Post's Writers Group, May 21, 2010

Chapter Fifteen

Ineligible at Birth

Verily, verily, I say unto you, He that entereth not by the
door into the sheepfold,
but climbeth up some other way,
the same is a thief and a robber. John 10:1.

Obama's ineligibility became an issue again in 2011, until it was eclipsed by the release of the Adobe BC – the "birth certificate" – a forgery acceptable to the media without further verification of any sort. Before the release, many states were considering legislation to require proof of eligibility, especially after Hawaii's newly elected Governor, Neil Abercrombie, reopened the can of worms as to the question of exactly where "Zero" was born.

Instead of helping Obama, Abercrombie managed to verify the testimony of Tim Adams, the former senior elections clerk for the city and county of Honolulu in 2008, who stated well before Abercrombie's election that no long-form, hospital-generated birth certificate for Obama was on file with the Hawaii Department of Health and that neither Honolulu hospital, Queens Medical Center or Kapiolani Medical Center, has any record that Obama was born there.

It begs the question what notation Abercrombie actually discovered. According to The Brazil Times,[249] the Governor's exhaustive search revealed that Barack Obama's

---

[249] *The Accidental Birther or Born in the U.S.A.?* The Brazil Times, Sunday, January 23, 2011.
http://www.thebraziltimes.com/blogs/1487/entry/39434/

white grandparents registered his live birth. The grandparents were persons who could claim his birth to be Hawaiian. This is the birth record that has supposedly been produced to establish the President's eligibility to hold the office of the President. The failure to produce a medical birth record anywhere in Hawaii, neither in any government office nor in any Hawaiian hospital brought into question not only his eligibility, but also raised the issue whether he was even an American citizen. Given the fraudulent nature of the forged BC, the question remains open.

The Brazil Times gives Governor Abercrombie credit for discovering that Obama's grandparents, Stanley and Madelyn Dunham, could have made an in-person report of a Hawaiian birth in 1961 even if the infant Barack Obama Jr. had been foreign-born. Similarly, the newspaper announcements of Obama's birth do not prove he was born in Hawaii, since they could have been triggered by the grandparents registering the birth as Hawaiian, even if the baby was born elsewhere. Moreover, the address reported in the newspaper birth announcements was the home of Obama's grandparents, Stanley and Madelyn Dunham. The Obama's were not known to be living there at the time.

Now that Abercrombie has made this discovery, he has announced that he cannot release the President's birth records and has decided to abandon his search. In the meantime, criminal co-conspirators in Hawaii continue to stand by the long campaign to cover for Zero, who finally resolved the question of his site of birth, date of birth, and the identity of his mother and father with the release of a made-up birth certificate done on a White House laptop.

For instance, back on October 31, 2008, Dr. Chiyome Fukino, the Director of the Hawaii Department of Health released the following statement:

There have been numerous requests for Sen. Barack Hussein Obama's official birth certificate. State law (Hawai'i Revised Statutes §338-18) prohibits the release of a certified birth certificate to persons who do not have a tangible interest in the vital record. Therefore, I as Director of Health for the State of Hawai'i, along with the Registrar of Vital Statistics who has statutory authority to oversee and maintain these type of vital records, have personally seen and verified that the Hawai'i State Department of Health has Sen. Obama's original birth certificate on record in accordance with state policies and procedures.

Well, I guess this begs the question as to exactly what you are calling an "original birth certificate." Co-conspirators Chris Matthews and Bill O'Reilly have both called a print-out of a forged Photoshop internet image purporting to be a Certification of Live Birth (not a Birth Certificate) to be an original birth certificate, even though the certificate number had been blacked out, and the seal at the bottom of the COLB declared the alteration to render the Certificate invalid. If those two idiots could call that piece of toilet paper a birth certificate, it is a certainty that Fukino could have called the affidavit of the Grandparents as to the birth "an original birth certificate."

Of course, Fukino believes that she hedged her language by saying that it was an original birth certificate "in accordance with state policies and procedures. Given the corruption of the State of Hawaii, a hundred dollar bill could meet this requirement. However, here is a summary of Hawaii's "state policies and procedures" in 1961. At that time in the State of Hawaii, there were four different ways to get a so-called "original birth certificate" on record. Some are actually sufficient to establish a birth site as a matter of law; some are not.

First: If the birth was attended by a physician or mid wife, the attending medical professional was required to certify to the Department of Health the facts of the birth date, location, parents' identities and other information.[250] This information is common to most birth certificates issued worldwide, and yes, it was a requirement even back in the 1960s. (Yes, Virginia, we even had automobiles back in the 60s). It seems that facts sought by people who are responsible to determine the bona fide birth records of people in the documentation of the populous are the same all over the world. Most jurisdictions provide for the disclosure of the birth hospital, the doctor doing the delivery, and two witnesses, including the signature of both the mother and the father. Hawaii has this form of birth certificate.

Below is a true and accurate facsimile of a "long form" birth certificate used by the State of Hawaii in 1961, carefully denoted as a "Certificate of Live Birth." This language is extremely important, when compared with the fraudulent document released by Soetoro, the Daily Kos and fightthesmears.org., and is apparently the pro forma later layered over at the White House using Adobe Illustrator to create the new multi-layered long form birth certificate. What the heck? It is possible to pass off any piece of garbage on the American public, and to do so without actually exposing the document to a forensic audit. We are all experts, aren't we?

---

[250] Section 57-8 & 9 of the Territorial Public Health Statistics Act in the 1955 Revised Laws of Hawaii which was in effect in 1961

Second: In 1961, if a person was born in Hawaii but not attended by a physician or midwife, then all that was required was that one of the parents send in a birth certificate to be filed. The birth certificate could be filed by mail. There appears to have been no requirement for the parent to actually physically appear before "the local registrar of the district." It would have been very easy for a relative to forge an absent parent's signature to a form and mail it in. The Dunhams didn't even do this.

In addition, if a claim was made that "neither parent of the newborn child whose birth is unattended as above provided is able to prepare a birth certificate, the local registrar shall secure the necessary information from any person having knowledge of the birth and prepare and file the certificate."[251]   The Hawaiian Department of Health currently (as of 2008) requires only proof of residency to back up a parent's claim that a child was born in Hawaii, such as a driver's license, although given the current climate, it is likely that illegal aliens can subvert this process with fake IDs or faked drivers' licenses.

Apparently, Ann Dunham had a driver's license in the summer of 1961 at the age of 17. The state of Hawaii would also accept a telephone bill, a pre-natal (statement or report that a woman was pregnant) and a post-natal (statement or report that a new-born baby has been examined) certification by a physician, although pre-natal and post-natal certifications had probably not been in force in the 1960s. There is and was no requirement for a physician or midwife to witness, state or report that the baby was born in Hawaii. However, none of this appears on the record.

Third: In 1961, if a person was born in Hawaii but not attended by a physician or midwife, then, up to the first birthday of the child, a "Delayed Certificate" could be filed, which required that "a summary statement of the evidence submitted in support of the acceptance for delayed filing or the alteration [of a file] shall be endorsed on the certificates", which "evidence shall be kept in a special permanent file." This means you could write a letter, and the state would file the letter in the permanent file. The statute provided that "the probative value of a 'delayed' or 'altered' certificate shall be determined by the judicial or administrative body or official before whom the certificate is offered as evidence."[252]   Any bureaucrat with a rubber

---

[251] Section 57-8&9 of the Territorial Public Health Statistics Act in the 1955 Revised Laws of Hawaii which was in effect in 1961

[252] Section 57- 9, 18, 19 & 20 of the Territorial Public Health Statistics Act in the 1955 Revised Laws of Hawaii which was in effect in 1961

stamp could approve of the letter, and bingo! the child has a Hawaiian birth certificate. This may be what is on file, although given the recent discovery of Governor Abercrombie, the evidence on file "in accordance with state policies and procedures" is even less certified than this. Ann Dunham did not have to be present for this statement or even in the country.

In the fourth instance: If a child is born in Hawaii, for whom no physician or mid-wife filed a certificate of live birth, and for whom no Delayed Certificate was filed before the first birthday, then a Certificate of Hawaiian Birth could be issued upon testimony of an adult (including the subject person [i.e. the birth child as an adult) if the Office of the Lieutenant Governor was satisfied that a person was born in Hawaii, provided that the person had attained the age of one year.[253] In 1955 the "secretary of the Territory" was in charge of this procedure. In 1960 it was transferred to the Office of the Lieutenant Governor ("the lieutenant governor, or his secretary, or such other person as he may designate or appoint from his office" §338-41 [in 1961]). Let's see if we can understand this: the child himself can put together some piecemeal evidence (maybe a hundred dollar bill or the equivalent in fully inflated terms), together with his sworn statement pursuant to the laws of perjury in Hawaii (which means absolutely nothing), even forty-five years after the fact, and obtain a birth certificate from Hawaii. It is even possible under this scenario that Hawaii may have considered the fraudulent COLB produced by the Daily Kos to be sufficient to satisfy the partisan and corrupted Office of the Lieutenant Governor of Hawaii in determining whether Zero was actually born there.

---

[253] Section 57-40 of the Territorial Public Health Statistics Act in the 1955 Revised Laws of Hawaii which was in effect in 1961

In 1982, the vital records law was amended to create a fifth kind of "original birth certificate." Under Act 182 H.B. NO. 3016-82, "Upon application of an adult or the legal parents of a minor child, the director of health shall issue a birth certificate for such adult or minor, provided that the proof has been submitted to the director of health that the legal parents of such individual while living without the Territory or State of Hawaii had declared the Territory or State of Hawaii as their legal residence for at least one year immediately preceding the birth or adoption of such child."

To summarize: Hawaii has a wide-open law that allows for the issuance of a document of some sort that shows an Hawaiian birth which can be obtained with much less evidence than the sworn statement of the delivering physician, the sworn statement of the parent, or the sworn statement of two witnesses. Once this procedure is married with the notoriously corrupt Hawaiian bureaucracy, anything less than an internationally recognized standard for a birth certificate is simply unacceptable.

Zero has admitted that he was a Kenyan citizen until 1982, and it is possible that he believes that he achieved citizenship when he secured a BC5 in 1982 under the assumed name Barack Hussein Obama II. It is noteworthy that this Certification of Live Birth (not a Certificate of Live Birth) has the conspicuous statement at the bottom: ANY ALTERATIONS INVALIDATES THIS CERTIFICATE, and that the Certification has been altered, as the number has been blacked out. This document, together with a newspaper clipping from 1961, were the only two pieces of evidence provided by Zero to buttress his claims of an American birth, prior to the release of another and yet another Certification of Live Birth that surfaced on the internet following Polarik's forensic audit which declared this particular certification to be a forgery.

Sections 57-8, 9, 18, 19, 20 & 40 of the Territorial Public Health Statistics Act may explain why Barack Obama has refused to release the original vault birth certificate. If the original certificate were the standard first model type of birth certificate, he would have allowed its release and brought the controversy to a quick end. But if the original certificate is of the other kinds, then Obama would have a very good reason not to release the vault birth certificate. For if he did, then the tape recording of Obama's Kenyan grandmother asserting that she was present at his birth in Kenya becomes far more important. As does the Kenyan ambassador's assertion that Barack Obama was born in Kenya, as well as the sealing of all government and hospital records relevant to Obama by the Kenyan government. And the fact that though there are many witnesses to Ann Dunham's presence on Oahu from Sept 1960 to Feb 1961, there are no witnesses to her being on Oahu from March 1961 to August 1962 when she returned from Seattle and the University of Washington. No Hawaiian physicians, nurses, or midwives have come forward with any recollection of Barack Obama's birth.

The fact that Obama has yet to release a true copy of the vault birth certificate indicates that the vault birth certificate is not a first model birth certificate. The actual certificate is probably housed in vital records in Washington under a name no one would recognize, and subsequent copies may have been created to reflect his adoption. There is also a chance he took on a third identity to cover his activity in Pakistan under the name Ubayd.

The third or fourth model birth certificate of the "Certification of Live Birth" posted on the Daily Kos blog and the fightthesmears.com website by the Obama campaign is a forgery. Ron Polarik has made the case that it is a forgery, and I accept his analysis as true.[254]

However, the likelihood that Obama lost his citizenship along the way, is, increased by the fact that Obama "either didn't register for the draft or did so belatedly and fraudulently. The documents indicate that it's one or the other."[255]

The forgery of Obama's selective service registration was necessary, because according to Federal law, "A man must be registered to be eligible for jobs in the Executive Branch of the Federal government and the U.S. Postal Service. This applies only to men born after December 31, 1959."[256]

Dr. Fukino's statements in no way attested to (or even addressed the issue of) the authenticity of the "Certification of Live Birth" (and the information that appears on it) that the Daily Kos blog and the Obama campaign posted on line. Dr Fukino merely stated that "I as Director of Health for the State of Hawai'i, along with the Registrar of Vital Statistics who has statutory authority to oversee and maintain these type of vital records, have personally seen and verified that the Hawai'i State Department of Health has Sen. Obama's original birth certificate on record in accordance with state policies and procedures."

When someone has a home birth or is not born in a hospital, this becomes a part of his family's lore and is now and again spoken of by his parents. He and his siblings

---

[254] See http://bogusbirthcertificate.blogspot.com/ and http://bogusbithcertificate.blogspot.com/

[255] http://www.debbieschlussel.com/archives/004431print.html

[256] http://usmilitary.about.com/cs/wars/a/draft2.htm

grow up knowing that he was born at home or his uncle's house, etc. The fact that someone in the campaign told a Washington Post reporter that he was born in Kapiolani hospital and his sister said he was born at Queens hospital indicates that there was not and is not any Obama/Dunham family memory of a home birth or non-hospital birth in Hawaii. And if there is no hospital record in the original vault birth certificate, then he was not born in a hospital in Hawaii.

Instead of the birth certificate on file at the Hawaii Dept of Health, the Obama campaign posted on the Daily Kos blog and the Fightthesmears website a "Certification of Live Birth". The Certification of Live Birth is not a copy of the original birth certificate. It is a computer-generated document that the state of Hawaii issues on request to indicate that a birth certificate of some type is "on record in accordance with state policies and procedures". And there is the problem. Given the statutes in force in 1961, the Certification of Live Birth proves nothing unless we know what is on the original birth certificate. There are several legal areas (involving ethnic quotas and subsidy) for which the state of Hawaii up until June 2009 did not accept its computer-generated Certification of Live Birth as sufficient proof of birth in Hawaii or parentage. Why should the citizens of the United States be content with lower standards for ascertaining the qualifications of their President?

If you combine an awareness of what the Certification of Live Birth posted on the internet really is with 1) a knowledge of the relevant statutes in 1961 and 2) Obama's stubborn refusal to permit the release of the real birth certificate and his determination to fight any legal actions that would compel him to do so, it becomes clear that there is no logical explanation for Obama's inability to produce a true long form birth certificate without taking into consideration the relevant statutes. Then his behavior becomes clear. The Territorial Public Health Statistics Act in the 1955 Revised Laws of Hawaii is the missing piece of the puzzle.

Most people think of a birth certificate as a statement by a hospital or midwife with a footprint, etc. (That may be why some main-stream journalists have straight out lied about this. Jonathan Alter, senior editor at Newsweek magazine, for example, told Keith Olbermann on MSNBC on Feb 20, 2009 that "They [the Republicans] are a party that is out of ideas so they have to resort to these lies about the fact that he's not a citizen. This came up during the campaign, Keith. The Obama campaign actually posted his birth certificate from a Hawaii hospital online." But it is Alter who resorted to lying to the American people on television. "The Obama campaign" never "actually posted his birth certificate from a Hawaii hospital online." On July 17, 2009 CNN's Kitty Pilgrim lied when she stated that the Obama campaign had produced "the original birth certificate" on the internet and that FactCheck.org had examined the original birth certificate; whether it was forged or not, the Certification of Live Birth that was posted by the campaign and FactCheck.org is not, and by definition, cannot be the original birth certificate or a copy of the original birth certificate. There were no computer generated Certifications of Live Birth in 1961, the year Obama was born. Obama's original birth certificate (whether it was filed in 1961 or later) was a very different document from the Certification of Live Birth on FactCheck.org. On the FactCheck.org web site, the claim is made that "FactCheck.org staffers have now seen, touched, examined and photographed the original birth certificate." So FactCheck.org is lying about this as well.

FactCheck.org gets its prestige from a reputation for objectivity. Why would those who run this site choose to tell so obvious a lie and so endanger the site's reputation? The answer is in the date of the posting, August 21, 2008. It was in mid-August that questions about the Certification of Live Birth began to reach a critical mass and threaten to enter the public discourse. The mostly pro-Obama television and newspaper/magazine media had to be given an excuse and cover for their collective decision to dismiss or ignore the substantial questions about whether Obama met the qualifications for the office set forth in Article II section I of the Constitution. And those reporters and editors who were not in the tank for Obama had to be deceived. After Labor Day the swing voters would begin to pay attention to the Presidential campaign. The truth had to be killed. And with its lie about "how it examined and photographed the original birth certificate", FactCheck.org killed it.

Most people would not consider a mailed-in form by one of his parents (who could have been out of the country or whose signature could have been forged by a grandparent) or a sworn statement by one of his grandparents or by his mother or even a sworn statement by himself many years later to be sufficient evidence (when set next to the statements by his paternal grandmother and the Kenyan ambassador that he was born in another country). Unless the American people are shown the original birth certificate, all of these are possibilities. And if Obama refuses to allow the state of Hawaii to release the original birth certificate, it begins to look like he was not born in a Hawaii hospital or at home with the assistance of a doctor or midwife. A reasonable person would acknowledge that there are serious reasons to doubt that Barack Obama was born in the United States. This would be especially true because, if Obama was born in a foreign country, his family had a compelling reason to lie about it.

In 1961 if a 17 year old American girl gave birth in a foreign country to a child whose father was not an American citizen, that child had no right to any American citizenship, let alone the "natural born" citizenship that qualifies someone for the Presidency under Article II, Section 1 of the Constitution.

In 1961, the year that Barack Obama was born, under Sec. 301 (a) of the Immigration and Nationality Act of 1952, Ann Dunham could not transmit citizenship of any kind to Barack Obama. "7 FAM 1133.2-2 Original Provisions and Amendments to Section 301 (CT:CON-204; 11-01-2007) "a. Section 301 as Effective on December 24, 1952: When enacted in 1952, section 301 required a U.S. citizen married to an alien to have been physically present in the United States for ten years, including five after reaching the age of fourteen, to transmit citizenship to foreign-born children. The ten-year transmission requirement remained in effect from 12:01 a.m. EDT December 24, 1952, through midnight November 13, 1986, and still is applicable to persons born during that period.

"As originally enacted, section 301(a)(7) stated: Section 301. (a) The following shall be nationals and citizens of the United States at birth: (7) a person born outside the geographical limits of the United States and its outlying possessions of parents one of whom is an alien, and the other a citizen of the United States who, prior to the birth of such person, was physically present in the United States or its outlying possessions for a period or periods totaling not less than ten years, at least five of which were after attaining the age of fourteen years: Provided, That any periods of honorable service in the Armed Forces of the United States by such citizen parent may be included in computing the physical presence requirements of this paragraph."

The Immigration and Nationality Corrections Act (Public Law 103-416) on October 25, 1994 revised this law to accommodate "a person born outside the geographical limits of the United States and its outlying possessions of parents one of whom is an alien, and the other a citizen of the United States who, prior to the birth of such person, was physically present in the United States or its outlying possessions for a period or periods totaling not less than five years, at least two of which were after attaining the age of fourteen years".

But in 1961, if Barack Obama had been born outside of the country, the Dunham family had no way of knowing that in 1994 Congress would pass a law that would retroactively make him a citizen. At that time, the only way to get citizenship for him would be to take advantage of one of the loopholes in the Territorial Public Health Statistics Act.

Chapter Sixteen

Fundamental Change

18 U.S.C. § 2385. Advocating overthrow of Government

Whoever knowingly or willfully advocates, abets, advises, or teaches the duty, necessity, desirability, or propriety of overthrowing or destroying the government of the United States or the government of any State, Territory, District or Possession thereof, or the government of any political subdivision therein, by force or violence, or by the assassination of any officer of any such government; or

<u>*Whoever, with intent to cause the overthrow or destruction of any such government, prints, publishes, edits, issues, circulates, sells, distributes, or publicly displays any written or printed matter advocating, advising, or teaching the duty, necessity, desirability, or propriety of overthrowing or destroying any government in the United States by force or violence, or attempts to do so*</u>*; or*

Whoever organizes or helps or attempts to organize any society, group, or assembly of persons who teach, advocate, or encourage the overthrow or destruction of any such government by force or violence; or becomes or is a member of, or affiliates with, any such society, group, or assembly of persons, knowing the purposes thereof—

Shall be fined under this title or imprisoned not more than twenty years, or both, and shall be ineligible for employment by the United States or any department or agency thereof, for the five years next following his conviction.

If two or more persons conspire to commit any offense named in this section, each shall be fined under this title or imprisoned not more than twenty years, or both, and shall be ineligible for employment by the United States or any department or agency thereof, for the five years next following his conviction.

As used in this section, the terms "organizes" and "organize", with respect to any society, group, or assembly of persons, include the recruiting of new members, the forming of new units, and the regrouping or expansion of existing clubs, classes, and other units of such society, group, or assembly of persons.

18 U.S.C. § 2386. Registration of certain organizations

(A) For the purposes of this section:

"Attorney General" means the Attorney General of the United States;

"Organization" means any group, club, league, society, committee, association, political party, or combination of individuals, whether incorporated or otherwise, but such term shall not include any corporation, association, community chest, fund, or foundation, organized and operated exclusively for religious, charitable, scientific, literary, or educational purposes;

*"Political activity" means any activity the purpose or aim of which, or one of the purposes or aims of which, **is the control by force or overthrow of the Government of the United States or a political subdivision thereof, or any State or political subdivision thereof;***

An organization is engaged in "civilian military activity" if:

(1) it gives instruction to, or prescribes instruction for, its members in the use of firearms or other weapons or any substitute therefor, or military or naval science; or

267

(2) it receives from any other organization or from any individual instruction in military or naval science; or

(3) it engages in any military or naval maneuvers or activities; or

(4) it engages, either with or without arms, in drills or parades of a military or naval character; or

(5) it engages in any other form of organized activity which in the opinion of the Attorney General constitutes preparation for military action;

An organization is "subject to foreign control" if:

(a) it solicits or accepts financial contributions, loans, or support of any kind, directly or indirectly, from, or is affiliated directly or indirectly with, a foreign government or a political subdivision thereof, or an agent, agency, or instrumentality of a foreign government or political subdivision thereof, or a political party in a foreign country, or an international political organization; or

(b) its policies, or any of them, are determined by or at the suggestion of, or in collaboration with, a foreign government or political subdivision thereof, or an agent, agency, or instrumentality of a foreign government or a political subdivision thereof, or a political party in a foreign country, or an international political organization.

(B)

(1) The following organizations shall be required to register with the Attorney General:

Every organization subject to foreign control which engages in political activity;

Every organization which engages both in civilian military activity and in political activity;

Every organization subject to foreign control which engages in civilian military activity; and

Every organization, the purpose or aim of which, or one of the purposes or aims of which, is the establishment, *control, conduct, seizure, or overthrow of a government or subdivision thereof by the use of force, violence, military measures, or threats of any one or more of the foregoing.*

Every such organization shall register by filing with the Attorney General, on such forms and in such detail as the Attorney General may by rules and regulations prescribe, a registration statement containing the information and documents prescribed in subsection (B)(3) and shall within thirty days after the expiration of each period of six months succeeding the filing of such registration statement, file with the Attorney General, on such forms and in such detail as the Attorney General may by rules and regulations prescribe, a supplemental statement containing such information and documents as may be necessary to make the information and documents previously filed under this section accurate and current with respect to such preceding six months' period. Every statement required to be filed by this section shall be subscribed, under oath, by all of the officers of the organization.

(2) This section shall not require registration or the filing of any statement with the Attorney General by:

(a) The armed forces of the United States; or

(b) The organized militia or National Guard of any State, Territory, District, or possession of the United States; or

(c) Any law-enforcement agency of the United States or of any Territory, District or possession thereof, or of any State or political subdivision of a State, or of any agency or instrumentality of one or more States; or

(d) Any duly established diplomatic mission or consular office of a foreign government which is so recognized by the Department of State; or

(e) Any nationally recognized organization of persons who are veterans of the armed forces of the United States, or affiliates of such organizations.

(3) Every registration statement required to be filed by any organization shall contain the following information and documents:

(a) The name and post-office address of the organization in the United States, and the names and addresses of all branches, chapters, and affiliates of such organization;

(b) The name, address, and nationality of each officer, and of each person who performs the functions of an officer, of the organization, and of each branch, chapter, and affiliate of the organization;

(c) The qualifications for membership in the organization;

(d) The existing and proposed aims and purposes of the organization, and all the means by which these aims or purposes are being attained or are to be attained;

(e) The address or addresses of meeting places of the organization, and of each branch, chapter, or affiliate of the organization, and the times of meetings;

(f) The name and address of each person who has contributed any money, dues, property, or other thing of value to the organization or to any branch, chapter, or affiliate of the organization;

(g) A detailed statement of the assets of the organization, and of each branch, chapter, and affiliate of the organization, the manner in which such assets were acquired, and a detailed statement of the liabilities and income of the organization and of each branch, chapter, and affiliate of the organization;

(h) A detailed description of the activities of the organization, and of each chapter, branch, and affiliate of the organization;

(i) A description of the uniforms, badges, insignia, or other means of identification prescribed by the organization, and worn or carried by its officers or members, or any of such officers or members;

270

(j) A copy of each book, pamphlet, leaflet, or other publication or item of written, printed, or graphic matter issued or distributed directly or indirectly by the organization, or by any chapter, branch, or affiliate of the organization, or by any of the members of the organization under its authority or within its knowledge, together with the name of its author or authors and the name and address of the publisher;

(k) A description of all firearms or other weapons owned by the organization, or by any chapter, branch, or affiliate of the organization, identified by the manufacturer's number thereon;

(l) In case the organization is subject to foreign control, the manner in which it is so subject;

(m) A copy of the charter, articles of association, constitution, bylaws, rules, regulations, agreements, resolutions, and all other instruments relating to the organization, powers, and purposes of the organization and to the powers of the officers of the organization and of each chapter, branch, and affiliate of the organization; and

(n) Such other information and documents pertinent to the purposes of this section as the Attorney General may from time to time require.

All statements filed under this section shall be public records and open to public examination and inspection at all reasonable hours under such rules and regulations as the Attorney General may prescribe.

(C) The Attorney General is authorized at any time to make, amend, and rescind such rules and regulations as may be necessary to carry out this section, including rules and regulations governing the statements required to be filed.

(D) *Whoever violates any of the provisions of this section shall be fined under this title or imprisoned not more than five years, or both.*

Whoever in a statement filed pursuant to this section willfully makes any false statement or willfully omits to state any fact which is required to be stated, or which is necessary to make the statements made not misleading, shall be fined under this title or imprisoned not more than five years, or both.

Obama has proposed fundamental change, which is nothing more than a complete overthrow of the constitutional republic as he ignores Congress, violates numerous federal criminal statutes, bribes members of Congress, and redirects American tax dollars to overthrow the free election process in the United States while funding a private army in violation of the principals of federalism and the applicable laws preventing such an overthrow.

Obama has created and funded a private army in direct competition with state and local law enforcement and ultimately the United States Armed Forces. The force is not the national guard, but a civilian one, and it is not sworn to uphold the Constitution.

On July 2, 2008 Barack Obama called for a police state in a speech in Colorado Springs, under his command, of course. This private army has now been made lawful and is funded. Under Subtitle C of the Health Care Bill - Increasing the Supply of the Health Care Workforce Sec. 5201. Federally supported student loan funds. Sec. 5202. Nursing student loan program. Sec. 5203. Health care workforce loan repayment programs. Sec. 5204. Public health workforce recruitment and retention programs. Sec. 5205. Allied health workforce recruitment and retention programs. Sec. 5206. Grants for State and local programs. Sec. 5207. Funding for National Health Service Corps. Sec.

5208. Nurse-managed health clinics. Sec. 5209. Elimination of cap on commissioned corps. Sec. 5210. Establishing a Ready Reserve Corps, and Subtitle D - Enhancing Health Care Workforce Education and Training. Also see the Patient Protection Affordable Care Act, page 1312: SEC. 5210. ESTABLISHING A READY RESERVE CORPS. Section 203 of the Public Health Service Act (42 U.S.C. 204) is amended to read as follows: SEC. 203. COMMISSIONED CORPS AND READY RESERVE CORPS. (a) ESTABLISHMENT (1) IN GENERAL "There shall be in the Service a commissioned Regular Corps and a Ready Reserve Corps for service in time of national emergency. (2) REQUIREMENT. All commissioned officers shall be citizens of the United States and shall be appointed *without regard* to the civil-service laws and compensated without regard to the Classification Act 2 of 1923, as amended. (3) APPOINTMENT. Commissioned officers of the **Ready Reserve Corps shall be appointed by the President** and commissioned officers of the Regular Corps shall be appointed by the President with the advice and consent of the Senate. (4) ACTIVE DUTY. Commissioned officers of the Ready Reserve Corps shall at all times be **subject to call to active duty by the Surgeon General**, including active duty for the purpose of training. (5) WARRANT OFFICERS. Warrant officers may be appointed to the Service for the purpose of providing support to the health and delivery systems maintained by the Service and any warrant officer appointed to the Service shall be considered for purposes of this Act and title 37, United States Code, to be a commissioned officer within the Commissioned Corps of the Service. (b) ASSIMILATING RESERVE CORP OFFICERS INTO THE REGULAR CORPS.—Effective on the date of enactment of the Affordable Health Choices Act, **all**

273

individuals classified as officers in the Reserve Corps under this section (as such section existed on the day before the date of enactment of such Act) and *serving on active duty shall be deemed to be commissioned officers of the Regular Corps*.

Those officers who are personally appointed by Obama -- without advice and consent of the Senate -- automatically become a part of the Regular Corps.

(c) PURPOSE AND USE OF READY RESERVE. (1) PURPOSE. The purpose of the Ready Reserve Corps is to fulfill the need to have additional Commissioned Corps personnel available on short notice (similar to the uniformed services reserve program) to assist regular Commissioned Corps personnel to meet both routine *public health and emergency response missions*. (2) USES. The Ready Reserve Corps shall (A) participate in routine training to meet the general and specific needs of the Commissioned Corps; (B) be a*vailable and ready for involuntary calls to active duty during national emergencies and public health crises*, similar to the uniformed service reserve personnel; (C) be available for backfilling critical positions left vacant during deployment of active duty Commissioned Corps members, as well as for *deployment to respond to public health emergencies, both foreign and domestic*; and (D) be available for *service assignment in isolated, hardship, and medically underserved communities* (as defined in section 399SS) to improve access to health services. (d) FUNDING.—For the purpose of carrying out the duties and responsibilities of the Commissioned Corps under this section, there are authorized to be appropriated such sums as may be necessary to the Office of the Surgeon General for each of fiscal years 2010 through 2014. *Funds appropriated under* *this subsection shall be used for recruitment and training of Commissioned Corps Officers*.

Obama has created an entirely new army, whose officers are appointed by him and who may be called up for "routine" purposes across with nation, and without regard for Posse Comitatus or other constitutional prohibitions on the quartering of soldiers in homes. Posse Comitatus is set forth in 18 U.S.C. § 1385:

The original provision was enacted as Section 15 of chapter 263, of the Acts of the 2nd session of the 45th Congress.

From and after the passage of this act it shall not be lawful to employ any part of the Army of the United States, as a posse comitatus, or otherwise, for the purpose of executing the laws, except in such cases and under such circumstances as such employment of said force may be expressly authorized by the Constitution or by act of Congress ; and no money appropriated by this act shall be used to pay any of the expenses incurred in the employment of any troops in violation of this section and any person willfully violating the provisions of this section shall be deemed guilty of a misdemeanor and on conviction thereof shall be punished by fine not exceeding ten thousand dollars or imprisonment not exceeding two years or by both such fine and imprisonment.

The text of the relevant legislation is as follows:

18 U.S.C. § 1385. Use of Army and Air Force as posse comitatus

Whoever, except in cases and under circumstances expressly authorized by the Constitution or Act of Congress, willfully uses any part of the Army or the Air Force as a posse

275

comitatus or otherwise to execute the laws shall be fined under this title or imprisoned not more than two years, or both.

Also notable is the following provision within Title 10 of the United States Code (which concerns generally the organization and regulation of the armed forces and Department of Defense):

10 U.S.C. § 375. Restriction on direct participation by military personnel

The Secretary of Defense shall prescribe such regulations as may be necessary to ensure that any activity (including the provision of any equipment or facility or the assignment or detail of any personnel) under this chapter does not include or permit direct participation by a member of the Army, Navy, Air Force, or Marine Corps in a search, seizure, arrest, or other similar activity unless participation in such activity by such member is otherwise authorized by law.

I will summarize without alarm. America has placed into its most powerful office a man whose has not established that he is an American citizen, has not demonstrated his legal name, is operating under a falsified social security number, who is federally prohibited from working within the Executive Branch of the federal government for his failure to properly register for the draft, who is an Ikhwan loyal to the jihadist overthrow of the United States in order to bring in a totalitarian Caliphate under Islam, who has funded the overthrow of all applicable elections by placing over $400 million with the corrupt ACORN and who has now funded

a private army directly under his own
no loyalty to the constitution.

This is his presidency. Now, y̲ ̲ ̲
see how such things manifest themselves into a force that brings death and destruction in its wake – first to the enemies of Ikhwan, and then to those who would strike back in the name of all things decent, to render the United States of America a wasteland – where the trillions of dollars spent in the development of its extraordinary infrastructure is bombed to rubble, burying in debris the millions of corpses not yet entombed in the hundreds of thousands of plastic coffins that currently sit waiting outside the hundreds of FEMA concentration camps deployed in the Obama *change* campaign.

When the dust on history settles, those who placed this man in power and kept him there will be *forever condemned* – first by humanity, and then by the eternal Father.

Chapter Seventeen

Treason in Africa

And I saw, and behold a white horse[257]: and he that sat on him had a bow; and a crown was given unto him: and he went forth conquering, and to conquer.

- Revelation 6:2

The year 2011 opened with a great deal of drama in the Islamic world. The very first day of the year opened with riots in Obama's old stomping grounds - Pakistan. Records indicate that Obama had lived in Pakistan well over a year during the term of the Sunni Muslim dictator Ul-Haq in the early eighties. As a presidential candidate, Obama promised substantial involvement in Pakistan (Pok'-ee-ston) during his 2008 election campaign. Obama began killing Pakistani civilians with unarmed drones very early into his presidency, and eventually, one of his covert agents got caught in a shoot-out with Pakistani ISI[258] when he was caught trying to smuggle information on Pakistan's nuclear weapons to the Taliban in Waziristan.[259] That's

---

[257] See *Behold! A White Horse!* http://www.amazon.com/Behold-White-Horse-Stephen-Pidgeon/dp/1453858458/ref=sr_1_3?ie=UTF8&s=books&qid=1301182556&sr=1-3

[258] Rob Crilly, *Raymond Davis 'was acting head of CIA in Pakistan',* the Telegraph, April 2, 2011 http://www.telegraph.co.uk/news/worldnews/asia/pakistan/8340999/Raymond-Davis-was-acting-head-of-CIA-in-Pakistan.html

[259] David Richards, *Arrest of CIA's Davis in Pakistan Confirms Illuminati Behind Terror,* PakAlertPress, March 4, 2011

correct; an American CIA agent was caught trying to destabilize Pakistan by allegedly aiding and abetting our enemies in Afghanistan. He killed two Pakistani intelligent agents who were supposedly trying to interrupt the transfer of information.[260]

Speaking of the ISI, there are those who are convinced that the hundreds of millions we spend on Pakistani intelligence are merged with the backroom bribes and corruption of the Karzai regime in Afghanistan to fund and train the Taliban[261] so our armed forces will actually have someone to fight in the region. This way the Opium Occupation otherwise known as the Afghan war may continue – without reason, without justification . . . and without end.

On the twelfth of January, the pressure placed on Lebanon by the International War Crimes Tribunal who sought to indict the upper leadership of Hezbollah for the assassination of the former prime minister of Lebanon, rose to a point of imminence that the Hezbollah faction within the government posted their resignation – which amounted

---

http://www.pakalertpress.com/2011/03/04/arrest-of-cias-davis-in-pakistan-confirms-illuminati-behind-terror/

[260] Washingtonblog.com, *CIA Agent Caught Red-Handed Aiding Pakistani Terrorism,* PakAlertPress.com, February 25, 2011. http://www.pakalertpress.com/2011/02/25/cia-agent-caught-red-handed-aiding-pakistani-terrorism/

[261] The World Affairs Blog Network, of Global Organized Crime WikiLeaks suggests that "US Officials believe Pakistan's ISI has been aiding the Taliban and al-Qaeda in Afghanistan for years, cooperating in suicide attacks, and maintaining bonds with Taliban leaders Pakistan knows will take back power when the US and NATO pulls out." Kathleen Miller, *WikiLEADS . . . Whose following up?,* Global Organized Crime, December 13, 2010http://globalorganizedcrime.foreignpolicyblogs.com/tag/isi/

to an abandonment of the political process in preparation for a civil war. The war crimes tribunal was in turn being pressured by the US State Department under the direction of Hillary Clinton, who in turn was under the direction of Obama. Hillary pushed, Hezbollah flexed, the government fell, and Hezbollah – the "army of Allah" and a military wing of Iran, came to control Lebanon.

Three days later, pressured by the Muslim Brotherhood who were exacerbating an economic crisis in Tunisia caused by unemployment, food shortages and price inflation, which itself was a direct result of the stimulus spending of Obama, encouraged by CIA assets in the United States, caused President Zine El Abidine Ben Ali to flee to Saudi Arabia following 30 days of sustained riots. Tunisia is now in turmoil, and refugees are spilling into neighboring countries.

It was just a few days later that the situation in Libya began to destabilize, as al-Qaeda operatives crossed from Tunisia into Libya, but it was not just Libya. The destabilization was moving through many Islamic nations in North Africa and the Middle East. Sunni Sudan set itself to either divide or continue in civil war. Sunni Morocco experienced riots on food and corruption following Tunisia's collapse into anarchy. Syria started on its road to destabilization, experiencing riots from Kurdish nationals and Muslim Brotherhood members in the south.

Obama has done absolutely nothing to assist those rioting in Iran, however; instead, the Voice of America broadcasting into Iran banned stories about the violent crackdown on protesters in Tehran, and discouraged VOA reporters and producers from inviting guests who were calling for an election boycott,[262] helping to legitimize the

---

[262] Ken Timmerman, Is the Voice of America Pro-Iran? Newsmax.com, February 11, 2010, http://www.newsmax.com/KenTimmerman/iran-

rigged election that reinstated Ahmadinejab as the President of Iran. Obama is using the VOA as the Farsi-speaking equivalent of a "no spin zone" in broadcasting - yet another American propaganda pie-hole working in concert with Obama's treasonous agenda.

On January 25, 2011, Egypt entered into its insurgency and riots. This affair was engineered through the direct involvement of Obama and his state department operatives in interface with the leadership of the Muslim Brotherhood – a group personally invited by Obama to his "apologize for America" speech given in Egypt early on in 2009. In the Islamic world, actions speak louder than words (primarily because of *Taqqiya* – the art of lying to infidels); the mere invitation to the Brotherhood without making special invitations to other members of the Egyptian leadership was an empowering gesture, and it was a gesture that would soon yield fruit.

On April Fool's day of 2011, Cal Thomas reached the conclusion, following the lead of the New York Times, that the Muslim Brotherhood was now the rising political force in Egypt; right on cue. Thomas reminds us of what was demonstrated in the early parts of this book; that the Muslim Brotherhood has an agenda: "Allah is our objective; the Prophet is our leader; the Quran is our law; dying in the way of Allah is our highest hope."[263] The Obama administration replied: *April Fool's!*

---

voa-coverage-protests/2010/02/11/id/349670

[263] Cal Thomas, *Middle East keeps burning, While Obama does his thing, enemy continues to gain ground in crucial region,* Bowling Green Daily News, April 1, 2011.
http://bgdailynews.com/articles/2011/04/01/opinion/commentary/comment1.txt

As Avi Lipkin has told the world: Obama disclosed to the Egyptian foreign minister that he was in fact a Muslim on his trip to Egypt, and this fact was widely broadcasted on Egyptian media. Avi's wife grew up in Egypt and speaks Arabic fluently. She regularly monitors Egyptian broadcasts in order to determine exactly what is being said in the Arab world. What is happening in the Middle East right now is Obama's demonstration to the Muslim Brotherhood worldwide what kind of a Muslim Obama truly is. The phrase *stealth jihadist* comes to mind – but what would I know.

Let's take a look and see how well our man's community organizing skills are doing, now that he is openly working with the Brotherhood in their own back yard. He has organized the community in Jordan, and they are now experiencing riots and demanding regime change. He has organized the community in Yemen, where the regime has shot protestors dead, and the population has grown more and more hysteric, demanding regime change. There are Cloward and Piven moves being made in Algeria to destabilize the regime there, and the government reshuffled its cabinet following food riots. It's almost like the whole thing was engineered.

But wait just a minute! Obama can't get away with organizing the community in Saudi Arabia – they paid for his degree at Columbia and his schooling at Harvard. He wouldn't kick a close friend like that under the bus, would he? Answer: yes we can! On January 30, 2011, Saudi Prince Turki bin Abdul Aziz Al Saud warned the country's royal family to step down and flee before a military coup or a popular uprising overthrows the kingdom.[264] There was some remark that referenced "getting out of Dodge."

[264] *Fears of Uprising in Saudi Arabia, Prince Warns Royals to Flee*, Pakalert, January 30, 2011

Unlike Libya, Saudi Arabia was *allowed* to kill its protestors, as was Iran. Libya, on the other hand, became a *humanitarian* issue. One has to be able to speak left-wing whacko to understand what the term *humanitarian* means. When used as an excuse to go to war, it means we have no national interest involved, and that we are going to bomb the place indiscriminately from 60,000 feet without ever placing an American soldier in harm's way on the ground. For example, see Clinton's war in the Balkans in the 1990s, when American forces under the leadership of NATO (an alias for *America*) bombed the Christian forces of Serbia, in alliance with al Qaeda and Osama bin Laden, to carve out an Islamic Republic in Kosovo, reversing the Christian hegemony staked out in the region since the defeat of the Ottomans in Croatia in the 18th century. Clinton remains an unindicted war criminal.

Not to be outdone by hubby, the New York Times reports that Secretary of State Hillary Clinton, Stephanie Power, and U.N. Ambassador Susan Rice ganged up on the reluctant defense and military leaders in the United States to pull Obama's lobster-drenched strings and to cause him to launch military operations against Col. Gadhafi's forces, under the guise of protecting "civilians" from those forces. Hillary expressed regret over not intervening even more in the Balkans in the 1990s.[265] It has since been discovered that the "civilians" have ties to al Qaeda. In fact, there is a

---

http://www.pakalertpress.com/2011/01/30/fears-of-uprising-in-saudi-arabia-prince-warns-royals-to-flee/

[265] Andy Thibault, *Anti-genocide advocate credits Obama for Libyan uprising,* Washington Times, March 28, 2011
http://www.washingtontimes.com/news/2011/mar/28/aide-credits-obama-for-libyans-uprising/

strong possibility that the "rebels" are the same 111 al Qaeda fighters that entered Iraq to join with Iraqi resistance against the US armed forces.[266] Col. Gadhafi has told the State Department that this is the case; which means Gadhafi is fighting on behalf of the US troops, and Obama is fighting on behalf of the enemies of armies of the US. Some might call that treason.

Obama however continues to push his agenda to bring life to the Neo-Ottoman Empire and to honor his temporarily not-yet-under-the-bus covenant with Erdoğan of Turkey. Turkey is not having riots; have you noticed? This pact with Turkey is why Turkey offered to invade Libya if the EU agreed to admit Turkey as a member.[267]-[268]-[269] Obama brokered the plan in a form of a demand to the leadership in the EU.[270] French President Sarkozy expressed his opposition in unprintable language.[271]

---

[266] Joseph Felter, Brian Fishman, *The Enemies of Our Enemy, Libya contributed hundreds of the fiercest foreign fighters to Iraq's al Qaeda-led insurgency. Should Washington be worried that it's now backing these guys against Qaddafi?* Foreign Policy. March 30. 2011 http://www.foreignpolicy.com/articles/2011/03/30/the_enemies_of_our _enemy

[267] http://www.menewsline.com/article-22151-Turkey-Offers-To-Invade-Libya.aspx

[268] http://www.network54.com/Forum/248068/thread/1299146272/last-1299165313/Turkey+Offers+To+Invade+Libya+(menewsline)

[269] http://www.shoebat.com/blog/archives/799

[270] http://csea-1.newsvine.com/_news/2011/03/02/6169604-obama-said-to-back-turkey-offer-to-invade-libya

[271] Barack Obama supported the Turkish proposal, believed to have also been endorsed by Saudi Arabia. Obama, regarded as *a close ally* of Erdogan, said Ankara deserves membership in the EU. But Brussels

Chapter 1 of the United Nations charter, Section 7 provides that "Nothing contained in the present Charter shall authorize the United Nations to intervene in matters which are essentially within the domestic jurisdiction of any state or shall require the Members to submit such matters to settlement under the present Charter; but this principle shall not prejudice the application of enforcement measures under Chapter Vll." This means that it is a violation of International law to arm rebels in the middle of a civil war ("intervene"), when the nation that you seek to invade has not engaged in acts of aggression against the nation seeking to "intervene."

Compare this law with the opinions of unindicted international war criminal Stephanie Powers, who has defended the policy called the "Responsibility to Protect." The "Responsibility to Protect" is code for "Opportunity to Intervene" based upon the capability of an aggressor nation to intervene (invade) at the discretion of the nation seeking to intervene. We now have our second code word among leftist whackos: "protect" means "invade." Compare with "humanitarian" which means "bomb indiscriminately."

The witches coven behind Obama consists of Clinton *protect*-more-in-the-Balkans, Powers *protect*-everyone, Rice *protect* Rwanda, and Medelson Forman, *protector* of Haiti.

---

appeared cold to the Turkish plan. French President Nicolas Sarkozy opposed the Erdogan proposal despite U.S. pressure. "What Sarkozy said is unprintable, but basically that the United States is not a member of the EU and cannot dictate who should be a member," the diplomat said.

Intelligence Briefing, *Obama said to back Turkey offer to invade Libya,* WorldTribune.com, March 1, 2011

http://www.worldtribune.com/worldtribune/WTARC/2011/me_turkey0214_03_01.asp

The UN Security Council adopted Resolution 1973 (2011) with Brazil, China, Germany, India and the Russian Federation abstaining, which authorized a no-fly zone over Libya, and provided that regional organizations (NATO) could "take all necessary measures to protect civilians, excluding a foreign occupation force of any form on any part of Libyan territory. The resolution also sought to ensure the rapid and unimpeded passage of *humanitarian* assistance, which means *bombing* was authorized; but *no ground troops*.

The Security Council further imposed an arms embargo. Unindicted international war criminals Clinton, Powers, Rice and Obama nonetheless considered arming the al Qaeda personnel in Benghazi. This decision was either patently stupid, or simply criminal, or both.

"I think it's fair to say that if we wanted to get weapons into Libya, we probably could," Obama told ABC. "We're looking at all our options at this point."[272]

Obama's operatives, the Muslim Brotherhood, are now bringing about Obama's ultimate agenda: the rise of the new Caliphate. The spiritual leader of the Brotherhood, Shaykh al-Qaradawi (the *dajjal*) tells us of the new rule of law we can expect under this system: "Islam is by its nature comprehensive in all aspects of life: material and spiritual, individual and society." Under Islam, there is no separation of church and state.

---

[272] CNN Wire Staff, *Obama signals willingness to arm Libyan rebels,* CNN, March 29, 2011
http://articles.cnn.com/2011-03-29/politics/obama.libya.interviews_1_libyan-leader-moammar-gadhafi-libyan-people-libyan-mission?_s=PM:POLITICS

Chapter Eighteen

Impeachment – the constitutional standard

The call for impeachment goes out once again, but this time with a vengeance. We have seen many things in this country in our quest to form a more perfect union, but this time we have come up way short. Never has there been a person holding the office of the President who has been more incompetent, more inept, more ineligible, more unqualified, and most importantly, more criminal than this fellow, who for the time being, calls himself Barack Hussein Obama.

Impeach we must, and impeach we will; not merely for the reason that the law commands it; but also for the very sake of the Constitution and the constitutional republic, which the Constitution creates. This nation can no longer afford to maintain the constitutional crisis that is the presidency of Barack Hussein Obama, nor will we survive his malevolence, his racism, his narcissism, his Mugabean Economics, his Marxist policies, and his totalitarian propensity. The man who would be Messiah must soon find himself in an iron mask.

The process of impeachment, simply put, originates in the House of Representatives, who impeach the President by means of Articles of Impeachment, ratified by a simple majority. Once these Articles have been ratified, the President has been impeached. Thereafter, the House presents the Articles of Impeachment to the Senate, who then decides whether or not they will move ahead to try the President on the charges by a simple majority vote. Following the vote to try the President, the President stands trial in the Senate, and if convicted, the President is then removed from office. Following his removal, the President can be charged by other authorities, tried in a common court, convicted and jailed in accordance with the laws in place at that time.

Article I, Section 4 of the U.S. Constitution provides that "the President, Vice President and all civil Officers of the United States, shall be removed from Office on Impeachment for, and Conviction of, Treason, Bribery, or other high Crimes and Misdemeanors." The argument will be made here that Obama has in fact committed treason, committed bribery, committed high crimes and committed misdemeanors worthy not only of impeachment, but conviction, removal, and subsequent charges.[273]

The actual process of impeachment is set forth throughout the Constitution. For instance, Article I, Section 2, clause 5, gives to the House of Representatives "the sole power of impeachment." The actual act of impeaching takes place in the House of Representatives, a house of Congress that has now gone through a political revolution otherwise unseen in the nation, as Americans have discovered that Barack Obama obtained the office of President by means of an enormous fraud; a fraud that rises to a criminal level as we shall see.

Article I, Section 3, clause 6[274] gives to the Senate "the sole power to try all impeachments." This could be

---

[273] Judgment in Cases of Impeachment shall not extend further than to removal from Office, and disqualification to hold and enjoy any Office of honor, Trust or Profit under the United States: but the Party convicted shall nevertheless be liable and subject to Indictment, Trial, Judgment and Punishment, according to Law.

[274] The Senate shall have the sole Power to try all Impeachments. When sitting for that Purpose, they shall be on Oath or Affirmation. When the President of the United States is tried, the Chief Justice shall preside:

difficult for the Senate, because the Article requires that Senators be under oath or affirmation when sitting for that purpose. Some of these Senators may be required to tell the truth in Senate chambers for the very first time! There is no other jury, and the Sixth Amendment is therefore not applicable.

Article I, Section 3, clause 6 also provides that the Chief Justice of the United States is to preside when the President of the United States is tried. Again, we have a problem, given that Chief Justice John Roberts administered the several oaths of office to Obama following during and following the inauguration, while cases challenging his eligibility to hold the office were before the Supreme Court. Roberts had a conflict then, and his complicity in installing a fellow whose eligibility was at issue at the time may warrant his recusal on the part of the Senate.

Article I, Section 3, clause 6 provides that a conviction may be had only on the vote of two–thirds of the members present. Article I, Section 3, clause 7, limits the judgment after impeachment to removal from office and disqualification from future federal office holding, but it allows criminal trial and conviction following impeachment. This is something that most certainly will be advocated herein. It is not simply enough to impeach – a conviction for the crimes is warranted.

Article II, Section 2, clause 1, deprives the President of the power to grant pardons or reprieves in cases of impeachment. Nixon was able to circumvent this provision, using Leslie Lynch King Jr. to ascend through

And no Person shall be convicted without the Concurrence of two thirds of the Members present.

the office long enough to provide a Presidential pardon to a President who was facing Articles of Impeachment.

Article III, Section 2, clause 3, excepts impeachment cases from the jury trial requirement, because the jury is the Senate.

The word "impeachment" may be used to mean several different things. Any member of the House may "impeach" an officer of the United States by presenting a petition or memorial, which is generally referred to a committee for investigation and report. The House votes to "impeach," the meaning used in Sec. 4, when it adopts articles of impeachment. The Senate then conducts a trial on these articles and if the accused is convicted, he has been "impeached." See 3 A. Hinds' Precedents of the House of Representatives of the United States (Washington: 1907), 2469–2485, for the range of forms.

Few provisions of the Constitution were adopted from English practice to the degree as was the section on impeachment. In England, impeachment was a device to remove from office one who abused his office or misbehaved but who was protected by the Crown.[275] It was a device that figured in the plans proposed to the Convention from the first, and the arguments went to such questions as what body was to try impeachments and what grounds were to be stated as warranting impeachment.[276]

The chapter has been preceded by evidence demonstrating that Barack Hussein Obama has in fact committed numerous high crimes, and is engaged in the

---

[275] 1 W. Holdsworth, *History of English Law* (London: 7th ed. 1956), 379–385; Clarke, *The Origin of Impeachment,* in Oxford Essays in Medieval History, Presented to Herbert Salter (Oxford: 1934), 164.

[276] Simpson, Federal Impeachments, 64 U. Pa. L. Rev. 651, 653– 667 (1916).

perpetration of additional high crimes as we speak. For instance, his insistence that men, women and children be photographed in the nude in order to board an airplane is the Class A felony of Voyeurism – at least here in the State of Washington. Every person who is "scanned" is a felony that has been committed by Obama, Napolitano, and the TSA agent enforcing the scanning. He is committing hundreds of felonies every day. We haven't spoken about the sexual molestation that is going on should you elect to avoid the radioactive invasion.

Some people argue that we cannot argue impeach a person who is not rightfully in office. To this I say "hogwash." Any trial for this fellow who has held the reins of power now for two years must be commenced, and must be commenced in the Senate pursuant to Articles of Impeachment.

However, there is another alternative that is something other than revolution in the streets. Before we get to that option, allow me to address the concept of violent revolution against the dark forces of the unconstitutional regime of the Muslim usurper. I do not favor armed revolution, primarily because I don't trust people with weapons that have not been vetted under some lawful regime. Consider the choice between the totalitarian you know, versus the untrained militia man you don't know. Who knows what you will get? The chances are very good that you will end up with random slaughter until the most vicious and violent murderer ascends to power, followed by the mass murder of all his enemies or perceived enemies.

Those who know me will tell you that I favor a change of the heart of the average American. My agenda is radical, for I believe (in fact, I am certain) that the Torah will come out of Zion, and the Word of Yehovah from

Yerushaliym.   This – the Ten Commandments and its progeny – is a radical doctrine indeed.   Just keep in mind that the meek shall inherit the earth.   Here is my advice: know the Torah and follow it.

Now, let us consider the 25th Amendment:

Section 1.

In case of the removal of the President from office or of his death or resignation, the Vice President shall become President.

Section 2.

Whenever there is a vacancy in the office of the Vice President, the President shall nominate a Vice President who shall take office upon confirmation by a majority vote of both Houses of Congress.

Section 3.

Whenever the President transmits to the President pro tempore of the Senate and the Speaker of the House of Representatives his written declaration that he is unable to discharge the powers and duties of his office, and until he transmits to them a written declaration to the contrary, such powers and duties shall be discharged by the Vice President as Acting President.

Section 4.

*Whenever the Vice President and a majority of either the principal officers of the executive departments or of such other body as Congress may by law provide, transmit to the President pro tempore of the Senate and the Speaker of the House of Representatives their written declaration that **the President is unable to discharge the powers and duties of his office**, the Vice President shall immediately assume the powers and duties of the office as Acting President.*

Thereafter, when the President transmits to the President pro tempore of the Senate and the Speaker of the

House of Representatives his written declaration that no inability exists, he shall resume the powers and duties of his office unless the Vice President and a majority of either the principal officers of the executive department or of such other body as Congress may by law provide, transmit within four days to the President pro tempore of the Senate and the Speaker of the House of Representatives their written declaration that the President is unable to discharge the powers and duties of his office. Thereupon Congress shall decide the issue, assembling within forty-eight hours for that purpose if not in session. If the Congress, within twenty-one days after receipt of the latter written declaration, or, if Congress is not in session, within twenty-one days after Congress is required to assemble, determines by two-thirds vote of both Houses that the President is unable to discharge the powers and duties of his office, the Vice President shall continue to discharge the same as Acting President; otherwise, the President shall resume the powers and duties of his office.

The Twenty-Fifth Amendment was being openly threatened when Obama was being boldly disobedient to the representatives of the New World Order. See Ulsterman's diatribe at the front of this book. Unfortunately, the Trilateral Group, the CFR, the *Bildebergers* and so forth, are running short of imagination and willpower.

If you ever wonder how Adolf Hitler or Napoleon Bonaparte came to power, you can now see the model. President Kennedy said "success builds success," but in Obama's case, "corruption builds corruption" and eventually, the nation expends all of its effort trying to keep the rotten oak tree from falling, while like a rising tumor, that last king rises to a dictatorship, bringing a totalitarian regime to bear over a series of contrived crises that the public is willing to accept, because they no longer love the truth.

Make no mistake about it: if we do not restore the rule of law in this country as it applies to first the President and then members of Congress, we will not long have a nation of any substance. Obama believes that he can ascend to dictatorial powers ignoring a fundamental truth about which he knows nothing: even dictatorships require wealth, and his Mugabean economic policies are not only killing off the American economy, they are killing off the fiat currencies of the entire world, which will ultimate drive the whole planet into an economic spiral of doom to a new dark age. He thinks he will control – but he will control only what is left, after our enemies take this piece of flesh from the dying corpse that was once called "the land of the free and the home of the brave."

You have seen the facts and the law; now, let us see what you do about it.

* * * * * *

About the author

Stephen Pidgeon is an author of both fiction and non-fiction works, the founder of several companies in high technology, an inventor, a student of theology and philosophy, and a pianist, guitarist, vocalist and composer of music. He is also the founder and director of the human rights organization DecaLogos  International, the world's foremost human rights organization advocating the Ten Commandments as the source of all human rights, and he has written numerous treatises on the *Midrash Halakha* and what he calls the Torah Redeemed. Stephen has been a practicing lawyer since 1996, and has engaged in advocacy on behalf of clients from municipal courts to the United States Supreme Court.

Get other titles from this author:

____   **Behold! A White Horse!**

____   **Behold! A Pale Green Horse!**

____   **Behold! A Red Horse!**

____   **Behold! A Black Horse!**

____   **Overthrown!**

DecaLogos International
www.decalogosintl.org
3002 Colby Avenue, Suite 306
Everett, Washington 98201

10796823R1

Made in the USA
Lexington, KY
20 August 2011